The Politics of
Twin Peaks

Politics, Literature, and Film

Series Editor: Lee Trepanier, Saginaw Valley State University

The Politics, Literature, & Film series is an interdisciplinary examination of the intersection of politics with literature and/or film. The series is receptive to works that use a variety of methodological approaches, focus on any period from antiquity to the present, and situate their analysis in national, comparative, or global contexts. Politics, Literature, & Film seeks to be truly interdisciplinary by including authors from all the social sciences and humanities, such as political science, sociology, psychology, literature, philosophy, history, religious studies, and law. The series is open to both American and non-American literature and film. By putting forth bold and innovative ideas that appeal to a broad range of interests, the series aims to enrich our conversations about literature, film, and their relationship to politics.

Advisory Board

Richard Avaramenko, University of Wisconsin-Madison
Linda Beail, Point Loma Nazarene University
Claudia Franziska Brühwiler, University of St. Gallen
Timothy Burns, Baylor University
Paul A Cantor, University of Virginia
Joshua Foa Dienstag, University of California at Los Angeles
Lilly Goren, Carroll University
Natalie Taylor, Skidmore College
Ann Ward, University of Regina
Catherine Heldt Zuckert, University of Notre Dame

Recent Titles

Milton's Socratic Rationalism: The Conversations of Adam and Eve in Paradise Lost by David Oliver Davies

Walker Percy and the Politics of the Wayfarer by Brian A. Smith

Romanticism and Civilization: Love, Marriage and Family in Rousseau's Julie by Mark Kremer

Aldous Huxley: The Political Thought of a Man of Letters by Alessandro Maurini

Sinclair Lewis and American Democracy by Steven Michels

Liberty, Individuality, and Democracy in Jorge Luis Borges by Alejandra M. Salinas

Philip Roth and American Liberalism: Historical Content and Literary Form in the Later Works by Andy Connolly

Seeing through the Screen: Interpreting American Political Film by Bruce E. Altschuler

Cowboy Politics: Myths and Discourses in Popular Westerns from The Virginian *to* Unforgiven *and* Deadwood, by John S. Nelson

Beyond Free Speech and Propaganda: The Political Development of Hollywood, 1907–1927, by John D. Steinmetz

Politics, Hollywood Style: American Politics in Film from Mr. Smith *to* Selma, by John Heyrman

Civil Servants on the Silver Screen: Hollywood's Depiction of Government and Bureaucrats, by Michelle C. Pautz

The Pursuit of Happiness and the American Regime: Political Theory in Literature, by Elizabeth Amato

Imagination and Environmental Political Thought: The Aftermath of Thoreau, by Joshua J. Bowman

The American Road Trip and American Political Thought, by Susan McWilliams Barndt

Flattering the Demos: Fiction and Democratic Education, by Travis Smith and Marlene Sokolon

Soul of Statesmanship: Shakespeare on Nature, Virtue, and Political Wisdom, by Khalil M. Habib and L. Joseph Hebert Jr.

Part of Our National Culture: Part of Our National Culture, by Eric Kasper and Quentin Vieregge

Short Stories and Political Philosophy: Power, Prose, and Persuasion by Erin A. Dolgoy, Kimberly Hurd Hale, and Bruce Peabody

Human Nature and Politics in Utopian and Anti-Utopian Fiction by Nivedita Bagchi

Wonder and Cruelty: Ontological War in It's a Wonderful Life by Steven Johnston

Rabelais's Contempt for Fortune: Pantagruelism, Politics, and Philosophy by Timothy Haglund

The Coen Brothers and the Comedy of Democracy by Barry Craig and Sara MacDonald

Popular Culture and the Political Values of Neoliberalism by George A. Gonzalez

The Final Frontier: International Relations and Politics through Star Trek *and* Star Wars by Joel R. Campbell and Gigi Gokcek

We Govern by Tenderness: Flannery O'Connor and the Perils of Modern Political Thought in America by Jerome C. Foss

The Politics of Twin Peaks edited by Amanda DiPaolo and Jamie Gillies

The Politics of *Twin Peaks*

Edited by Amanda DiPaolo
and Jamie Gillies

LEXINGTON BOOKS
Lanham • Boulder • New York • London

Published by Lexington Books
An imprint of The Rowman & Littlefield Publishing Group, Inc.
4501 Forbes Boulevard, Suite 200, Lanham, Maryland 20706
www.rowman.com

6 Tinworth Street, London SE11 5AL

Copyright © 2019 by Lexington Books

All rights reserved. No part of this book may be reproduced in any form or by any electronic or mechanical means, including information storage and retrieval systems, without written permission from the publisher, except by a reviewer who may quote passages in a review.

British Library Cataloguing in Publication Information Available

Library of Congress Cataloging-in-Publication Data Available
ISBN 978-1-4985-7837-0 (cloth)
ISBN 978-1-4985-7839-4 (pbk)
ISBN 978-1-4985-7838-7 (electronic)

Contents

List of Photographs	ix
Acknowledgments	xi
Introduction *Amanda DiPaolo and Jamie Gillies*	1

PART I: INNOCENCE, NOSTALGIA, AND THE POLITICAL

Chapter One	The Nuclear Anxiety of *Twin Peaks: The Return* *Ashlee Joyce*	13
Chapter Two	Is It Future or Is It Past?: The Politics and Use of Nostalgia in *Twin Peaks* *Amanda DiPaolo*	35

PART II: AMERICA AND THE POLITICAL

Chapter Three	Rural and Suburban Lynch: Characterizations of Hard Times in Reagan's and Trump's America *Jamie Gillies*	55
Chapter Four	"Dirty Bearded Men in a Room!": *Twin Peaks: The Return* and the Politics of Lynchian Comedy *Martin Fradley and John A. Riley*	69

PART III: IDENTITY, REPRESENTATION, AND THE POLITICAL

Chapter Five	Violence, Representation, and Girl Power: *Twin Peaks'* Female Characters and Third Wave Feminism *Stacy Rusnak*	95

| Chapter Six | The Owls Are Not What They Seem: Retaking Queer Meaning in *Twin Peaks*
Benjamin Kruger-Robbins | 117 |

PART IV: THE POLITICAL AS IT RELATES TO PHILOSOPHICAL, THEORETICAL, AND SPIRITUAL WAYS OF KNOWING

Chapter Seven	Zen, or the Art of Being Agent Cooper Darci Doll	145
Chapter Eight	The Transmigration of Cooper: Echoes of Plato's Recollection in *Twin Peaks* Jean-Philippe Ranger	161
Chapter Nine	Life in the Black Lodge: The Twin Challenge of Watching *Twin Peaks* Shai Biderman, Ronen Gil, and Ido Lewit	177

| Index | 193 |
| About the Contributors | 197 |

List of Photographs

Fig. 0.1.	Episode 1.1 "Northwest Passage"	3
Fig. 1.1.	Episode 3.7 "There's a Body All Right"	16
Fig. 2.1.	Episode 2.11 "Masked Ball"	42
Fig. 3.1.	Episode 3.5 "Case Files"	63
Fig. 4.1.	Episode 3.13 "What Story Is That, Charlie?"	70
Fig. 5.1.	Episode 2.9 "Arbitrary Law"	100
Fig. 6.1.	Episode 2.3 "The Man behind the Glass"	130
Fig. 7.1.	Episode 1.3 "Zen, or the Skill to Catch a Killer"	146
Fig. 8.1.	Episode 3.15 "There's Some Fear in Letting Go"	163
Fig. 9.1.	Episode 1.2 "Traces to Nowhere"	181

Acknowledgments

Amanda DiPaolo would first and foremost like to thank her husband, James, who has endured her talking about *Twin Peaks* for years. He is always willing to read proofs of her work and allows her to bounce ideas off him. Thanks to Jamie Gillies whose discussions regarding both *Twin Peaks* and politics made pursuing this edited collection an easy decision. She also wants to express genuine gratitude to her research assistant, Abbie LeBlanc. Abbie's focus and work ethic allowed us to meet our manuscript deadline, and her expertise in Chicago style and formatting were also greatly appreciated. She is also very thankful for the support from her colleagues Christina Szurlej, Andrew Moore, and Matt Dinan. Finally, she would like to thank her wonderful parents, Jim and Judy DiPaolo, for allowing her to watch *Twin Peaks* at an age far too young than was appropriate.

Jamie Gillies is very thankful to his co-editor Amanda DiPaolo whose passion and excitement for *Twin Peaks* inspired a mutual interest in developing this project. He appreciated the guidance, suggestions, and help from colleagues Tom Bateman, Lissa Beauchamp, Michael Camp, Brad Cross, Mike Dawson, Dennis Desroches, Philip Lee, Patrick Malcolmson, Shaun Narine, Roger Saul, and Alan Sears. Lastly, he is very thankful for all the support and genuine interest in his work from his parents, Jim and Liz Gillies, and last but not least from his amazing partner Amanda and their wonderful daughter Hannah for allowing him hours and hours of time to revisit Agent Cooper's world.

We are both extremely grateful to Lee Trapanier, editor of the Lexington Books series Politics, Literature, & Film, for his support for this book. All at Lexington, especially Joseph Parry, Madhu Koduvalli, Ashleigh Cooke, and Bryndee Ryan, were so supportive and helpful. And finally, we are grateful for the administrative support provided by our departmental assistants, Penny Granter and Lehanne Knowlton.

Introduction
Amanda DiPaolo and Jamie Gillies

In the pilot of *Twin Peaks*, Special Agent Dale Cooper leaves no room for misunderstanding regarding who oversees the investigation of who killed Laura Palmer. After meeting Sheriff Harry S. Truman at the hospital to examine the body of Ronette Pulaski, the FBI agent raises his hand and stops Truman mid-sentence. "There's a few things that we gotta get straight right off the bat," Cooper says authoritatively, and in a tone that would not be heard from him many times throughout the original run of the series. "I've learned about this the hard way; it's best to talk about it up front. When the Bureau gets called in, the Bureau's in charge. Now, you're going to be working for me. Sometimes local law enforcement has a problem with that. I hope you understand," he explains (1.Pilot). While Harry has no problem with the FBI's presence in Twin Peaks, the scene sets the stage for how power dynamics and politics are involved within the narratives and relationships explored in *Twin Peaks*. The political doesn't stop with the exploration of law enforcement tropes. From female representation (both regarding their abuse and empowerment) to the economics and representations of small-town America, there is something inherently political about *Twin Peaks*. The series invites its audience to think critically about these representations and what they signify in American culture.

With a plot of investigating the murder of a teenage girl, the series is equal parts murder mystery and soap opera. In 1990, David Lynch and Mark Frost created a land that embodies American society where patriotism, pie, and secrets run rampant. Artful, surreal, and at times mythological, political is one adjective that often has eluded the academic work conducted on Lynch's film and television projects. Commentators have indicated that Lynch stays away from the political, declining to enter the realm of social commentary.[1] Lynch himself seems to back this position, claiming to know nothing about politics and by noting that he doesn't think about his work politically.² There are signs to the contrary, however. Lynch is a noted fan of Ronald Reagan, drawn to the 40th president because of his "cowboy image." He is an avid proponent of individual freedom, believing that liberty has been limited by societal constructs with its "rules and regulations."³ But there are contradictions here as well; Lynch may be a believer in the rhetoric of individual freedom but he also, sometimes inadvertently, points to the hypocrisy of the Reagan and subsequent political era policies and the effects they would have on a community like Twin Peaks. These, and other, political ideals are avidly expressed throughout the narrative of *Twin Peaks*.

As an example, consider the character of Audrey Horne. The audience sees Audrey as someone pigeonholed into something she does not want to be, where small acts of rebellion are the only way for her to regain her individuality and freedom that have been stifled by her father specifically, but also society at large. From her introductory scenes in the pilot where she performs a school-locker wardrobe change from the 1950s saddle shoes to red high heels to telling a group of would-be investors about the murder of Laura to ruin a business deal for her father, Audrey's acts of rebellion, both big and small, illustrate a yearning for freedom that elludes her (1.Pilot). While Audrey can certainly be read as a victim of patriarchal conventions with the male gaze and the damsel in need of rescuing, Lynch and Frost paint a portrait of someone who is more complex. Audrey is often in control. She breaks away from being just the object of the male gaze through her attempts to place herself in the action to assert her individuality and freedom. In the second episode of season 2, Audrey, masquerading as an escort at One-Eyed Jack's, forces Emory Battis to tell her everything he knows about Laura and Ronette. "I'm Audrey Horne, and I get what I want," she says to Battis, store manager of Horne's Department Store, as she strangles him waiting for the answers she seeks (2.2). Just as Audrey gains the relevant information, she is caught and in need of help. She has been restrained, bringing her back to the conventional trope as the princess who awaits her prince, Agent Cooper. Despite the obvious attraction between the two, Agent Cooper denies Audrey because of her age. Societal rules and regulations hold her back. The liberty and control Audrey sought, in the end, would elude her. From the bank vault she had chained herself to in protest of her father in the original series finale, to awakening in part 16 of *The Return* in what appeared to be some sort of health-care facility, Audrey's attempts at gaining freedom and liberty failed. In looking at Audrey through an ideologically conservative lens, Lynch's *Twin Peaks* offers a commentary on the futility of yearning for individuality. Audrey's character narrative prompts the audience to consider how the societal rules and regulations Lynch is so suspicious of constrain freedom and individuality in the

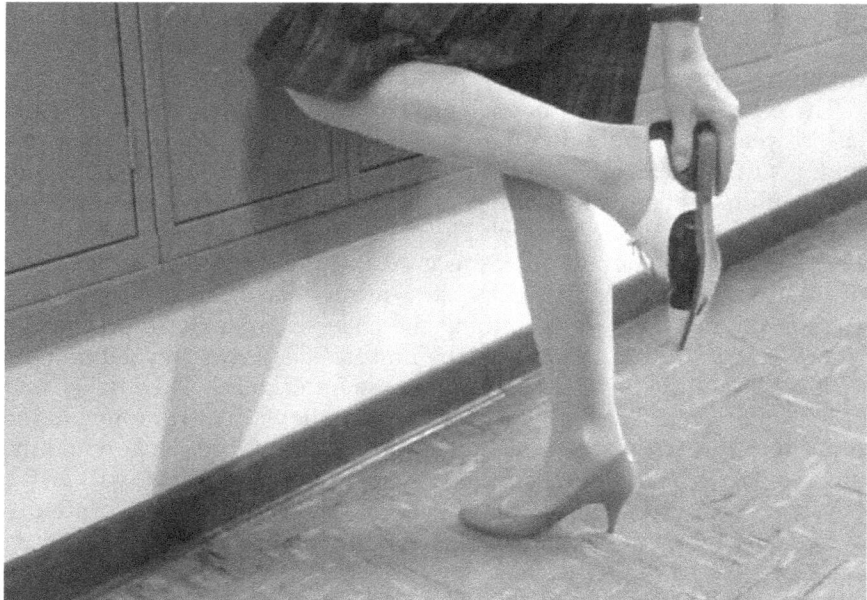

Fig. 0.1. Episode 1.1 "Northwest Passage"
Twin Peaks

context of the time. What effect has the generational change between the airing of the series in 1990 and again in 2017 had on individuality and freedom of choice? What kind of individuality and choice? And freedom for who? Considering the conclusion of Audrey's story arc, for Lynch, the passage of time has not amounted to greater freedom, but rather more societal constraints.

At its very core, *Twin Peaks* is about the politics of American culture. With its focus on small-town politics and life outside urban centers, rural and suburban values play a big part in the overall *Twin Peaks* narrative. Showcasing the anxiety of both the end of the Cold War and the uncertainty of today, the series becomes a metaphor for the political years in which it is set. Moreover, subtle aspects of what Lynch and Frost are trying to do with their work can illustrate how identity politics permeate the political landscape, allowing scholars to explore *Twin Peaks* through different lenses, looking at the show from female and queer perspectives. As Theresa Geller notes, *Twin Peaks* "offers a rich postmodern critique of the metanarratives of race, gender, history, psychology, law, science, realism, patriarchy and the mastery of the centered subject implied in each."[4] This illustrates one of the reasons why *Twin Peaks* continues to resonate with viewers. Lynch and Frost have woven a mythology of *Twin Peaks* that is so rich and open to analysis, it leaves a lot to interpretation. As such, reading the political subtlety can be interpreted in a variety of ways and through a variety of disciplinary lenses.

There have been many books and articles about *Twin Peaks* over the last 28 years, and more no doubt will be on their way. With their focus on the surreal, cultural, sociological, and literary impact of the program, these volumes all add something valuable to the scholarly discussion of *Twin Peaks*. From David Lavery's *Full of Secrets: Critical Approaches to* Twin Peaks examining the various aspects of the show through a multitude of interdisciplinary lenses[5] to Jeffrey Andrew and Catherine Spooner's edited volume of essays examining the cultural impact of the show, its legacy, and its future,[6] analyzing the impact *Twin Peaks* has had on television and culture has been a popular take for scholars. These texts, and many others,[7] offer rich perspectives on the show. This volume adds to this ongoing discussion by examining the politics of *Twin Peaks* with nine new essays focusing on a different element of the political within the landscape that the series has to offer. By doing so, this volume continues the already broad discussion of the series and opens it up by considering areas of focus through a political lens previously unexplored. By examining both the original run of *Twin Peaks* as well as *Twin Peaks: The Return*, this edited collection of essays seeks to draw out some common elements with respect to two broad themes: American politics and identity politics. With a close relationship between the two, we conclude that *Twin Peaks* is the rare cultural landmark in both film and television whose timelessness is defined by the fact that it can constantly be reinterpreted. Yes, even using a political lens. That quality has made *Twin Peaks* a cultural standard.

CHAPTER OUTLINE

This edited collection of essays seeks to draw out political themes that, when examined closely, can be expressed through Lynch's longing for a version of 1950s America that appears safe and welcoming, but that is corrupt. With that as the starting point, the authors of the following essays interpret the political within the episodes, drawing out themes, patterns, and in some cases subtle or vaguely implied contexts that either Lynch and Frost consciously included or less consciously kept in the final cut but purposely left unfocused or unclear.

We divide the collection into four parts with each part featuring essays devoted to a broad political theme highlighted throughout the series. The four parts attempt to weave together an image of *Twin Peaks* that is inherently political in nature. What becomes apparent in the analysis and interpretation is that Lynch is political without being political, using supernatural and even horror and science fiction genre tropes as lenses through which he shows America as it really is. In other words, by being purposefully non-political, Lynch accentuates the political because he does not use it as a blunt object or as an ideological or philosophical device. He is not an Aaron Sorkin but he is also not an Ayn Rand. Like other film auteurs, especially French New Wave directors, he challenges audiences to interpret his films for themselves. And that of course leads to a lot of interpretation, which in many respects is his overall point.

Innocence, Nostalgia and the Political

There is something about the past that attracts us to it. Nostalgia and innocence are used in narrative as plot devices in fiction, film, and television to create a sense of longing for characters that find themselves in predicaments later in life. But it is also a useful political tool used frequently in elections, in asking an electorate to evaluate life based on past interpretations. For every generation, that longing for innocence and nostalgic retrospective interpretation of the past can be used to bring out people's resentment and anger at modern life. Lynch and Frost are intuitively aware of how powerful these forces are in *Twin Peaks*.

In "The Nuclear Anxiety of *Twin Peaks: The Return*" Ashlee Joyce looks at *Twin Peaks: The Return* as an expression of nuclear anxieties that persist far beyond the end of the Cold War as well as the perceived loss of an American "age of innocence." Joyce examines part 8 of *The Return* using nuclear criticism and literary trauma theory to suggest that Lynch's focus on the nuclear bomb connects the Cold War with our present era, marking a sharp break with seasons one and two of *Twin Peaks* by dropping its nostalgic 1950s feel, but maintaining all the nuclear anxiety of the time. The imagery and symbolism of the bomb in part 8, Joyce posits, allows *The Return* to become a mediation on the evils of WWII that ushered in the modern era.

In "Is It Future or Is It Past: Nostalgia in *Twin Peaks*," Amanda DiPaolo complements chapter one by examining the use of nostalgia in both *Twin Peaks* and in American culture more broadly. DiPaolo argues that nostalgia is both a political tool to maintain a cultural identity when the present is perceived to be in crisis and a coping mechanism used in response to pain or distress. Using Leland Palmer and Benjamin Horne as examples, she points out that it is the villains of the original series that truly highlight the uses of nostalgia. In *The Return*, nostalgia is rejected with most original cast members of *Twin Peaks* being stagnant, repeating past mistakes, and irrelevant to moving the plot. As such, *The Return* shows the dangers of remaining in the past.

America and the Political

The original series that aired in 1990 depicted a rural part of Washington state showcasing the differences and disconnections of rural America to more urban places. In *Twin Peaks: The Return*, suburban Las Vegas is depicted rather strikingly after the 2007 and 2008 subprime mortgage crisis, and the details of life in suburbs where home values declined dramatically offer a vivid take on life after the Obama years. The set of essays in this section look at the more obvious political elements in *Twin Peaks*, aspects of the show that are a metaphor for the political years in which they are set, showcasing the anxiety and uncertainty of today.

In "Rural and Suburban Lynch: Characterizations of Hard Times in Reagan's and Trump's America," Jamie Gillies considers the American economic disparities of two different eras that subtly interact with the characters in the show. Gillies considers the first two seasons as depictions of Reagan-era economic and class politics. Often without explicit dialogue, the greed decade and the forces that would consume the American economy following the 1980s play themselves out, from milltown narratives and the lines between the wealthy and townspeople who work for them. In *The Return*, Lynch adds the suburban experience into the narrative as well, with a suburban subdivision in Las Vegas acting as a backdrop to the other existential challenges rooted in the concept of the American community on the precipice of the Trump era. That anxiety, showcased especially in the insurance office in *The Return*, parallels the undercurrents in American politics where nationalism and populism became an organizational tool and rallying cry.

In "'Dirty Bearded Men in a Room!' *Twin Peaks: The Return* and the Politics of Lynchian Comedy," Martin Fradley and John A. Riley do what other Lynchian scholars have yet to do—focus specifically on the comedy of *Twin Peaks* and its greater meaning. They suggest that *The Return* is the most political of Lynch's work, using laughter to say something meaningful about the socio-economic realities of the time. Fradley and Riley argue the grotesque, the ironic, the absurd, the uncanny, and the repetitious are carefully employed by Lynch to shine a light on the state of society today.

Identity, Representation and the Political

Twin Peaks has been criticized for its portrayal of women in both *Twin Peaks* and its return in 2017. Similarly, the series is not known for its diversity in casting. In *The Return*, the one indigenous character, Hawk, has been elevated from deputy to deputy chief. But his role in *The Return*, while at times touching and emotional, is mostly used as a pawn to help show the white protagonists the way—the magical negro trope. So *Twin*

Peaks can be interpreted by critically considering Lynch's and Frost's heteronormative and predominantly white perspectives. At the same time, the conventionality *Twin Peaks* presents is in many respects Lynch's point; that the town and characters themselves are inherently white, racist, sexist, homophobic, or at the very least ignorant, gendered, and unequal; a reflection of what a town like that might have been in the 1980s and how many rural towns still are in the second decade of the twenty-first century. These two essays consider identity politics as the show is explored through female and queer perspectives.

In "Violence, Representation, and Girl Power: *Twin Peaks'* Female Characters and Third Wave Feminism," Stacy Rusnak situates the women of *Twin Peaks* in third wave feminist theory. More than victims, Rusnak demonstrates the agency of Laura, Maddy, and Shelly, the women who suffer excessive violence at the hand of their male oppressors. Rusnak argues that these memorable roles mark the beginning of third wave feminism challenging patriarchal authority as well as traditionalist values. Additionally, by looking at Lucy, Nadine, and Norma, Rusnak shows how those who would be held back by society's patriarchal institutions also challenge the traditional view of femininity through sexual freedom, economic independence, entrepreneurial aspirations, and physical strength.

In "The Owls Are Not What They Seem: Retaking Queer Meaning in *Twin Peaks*," Benjamin Kruger-Robbins offers reconstructions of queerly coded relationships in *Twin Peaks*, interpreted through fan fiction entries. Kruger-Robbins argues that these fan fiction entries act as corrective measures to how the show was framed by the media as a masculine-oriented precursor to the current golden age of television. Kruger-Robbins largely places focus on the second season, arguing that erasure and limitation of queerness are in fact a defining attribute of the second season of *Twin Peaks* both in its narrative as well as the critical response to it.

The Political as It Relates to Philosophical, Theoretical, and Spiritual Ways of Knowing

This final section of the volume looks more closely at the theoretical political, and the not so inherent philosophical theories at play in both the writing and plot.

In chapter 7, Darci Doll approaches *Twin Peaks* from the spiritual and political especially regarding Agent Cooper's fascination with Tibetan Buddhism, mysticism, and Daoist belief systems. Doll points to how Cooper's deductive method is guided by Eastern philosophies and religion in both his relentless focus on figuring out the identity of Laura Palmer's killer and in how Cooper's doppelgangers and tulpas play out in *The Re-*

turn, where part of the real Agent Dale Cooper is still part of both other Cooper spirits, Mr. C and Dougie Jones.

In the penultimate chapter, Jean-Philippe Ranger considers *Twin Peaks* from a political philosophy perspective, considering Plato's myths of reincarnation and theory of recollection as it relates to Cooper's return from being trapped in the Red Room of the Black Lodge and his reincarnation as Douglas Jones, and metamorphosis back into Special Agent Cooper. Ranger links Plato and the philosophical concept of Meno's paradox to clues sprinkled throughout the show, from the Log Lady to Laura Palmer's diary.

In the ninth and final chapter, Shai Biderman, Ronen Gil, and Ido Lewit explore *Twin Peaks* in terms of how viewership and generational audiences have shifted, suggesting that the ways in which we watch television have shifted fundamentally. *Twin Peaks* in its original inception really was ahead of its time but in the era of television's golden age, it is now more the norm. In considering a media viewership as generational politics motif, the authors incorporate long-standing media theories to provide an important linkage to the politics of television programming. In connecting *Twin Peaks* to the technological changes that have occurred since its first airing, they provide key insights into how and why the show was such cutting edge and avant garde television.

NOTES

1. Jonathan Rosenbaum, "Bad Ideas: The Art and Politics of *Twin Peaks*," in *Full of Secrets: Critical Approaches to* Twin Peaks, ed. David Lavery (Detroit: Wayne State University Press, 1995), 25.

2. Dennis Lim, "Donald Trump's America and the Visions of David Lynch," *The New Yorker*, last modified June 29, 2018, https://www.newyorker.com/culture/culture-desk/donald-trumps-america-and-the-visions-of-david-lynch.

3. John Powers, "Getting Lost is Beautiful," *LAWeekly*, last modified October 17, 2001, https://www.laweekly.com/news/getting-lost-is-beautiful-2133916.

4. Laura Geller, "Deconstructing Postmodern Television in *Twin Peaks*," *Spectator* 12, no. 2 (Spring 1992): 65.

5. David Lavery, *Full of Secrets: Critical Approaches to* Twin Peaks (Detroit: Wayne State University Press, 2009).

6. Jeffrey Andrew Weinstock and Catherine Spooner, *Return to* Twin Peaks: *New Approaches to Materiality, Theory, and Genre on Television* (Basingstoke, U.K.: Palgrave MacMillan, 2006).

7. This list is by no means exhaustive. See Andreas Halskov, *TV Peaks:* Twin Peaks *and Modern Television Drama* (Odense: University Press of Southern Denmark, 2015); Andy Burns, *Wrapped in Plastic:* Twin Peaks (Toronto: ECW Press, 2015); Eric Hoffman and Dominick Grace, eds., *Approaching* Twin Peaks: *Critical*

Essays on the Original Series (North Carolina: McFarland & Company, Inc., 2017); John Thorne, *The Essential Wrapped in Plastic: Pathways to* Twin Peaks (Dallas, Texas: John Thorne, 2016).

WORKS CITED

Burns, Andy. *Wrapped in Plastic:* Twin Peaks. Toronto: ECW Press, 2015.

Geller, Laura. "Deconstructing Postmodern Television in *Twin Peaks*," *Spectator*, 12, no. 2 (Spring 1992): 64–71.

Halskov, Andreas. *TV Peaks:* Twin Peaks *and Modern Television Drama*. Odense: University Press of Southern Denmark, 2015.

Hoffman, Eric, and Dominick Grace, eds. *Approaching* Twin Peaks: *Critical Essays on the Original Series*. North Carolina: McFarland & Company, Inc., 2017.

Lavery, David, ed. *Full of Secrets: Critical Approaches to* Twin Peaks. Detroit: Wayne State University Press, 2009.

Lim, Dennis. "Donald Trump's America and the Visions of David Lynch." *The New Yorker*. Last modified June 29, 2018. https://www.newyorker.com/culture/culture-desk/donald-trumps-america-and-the-visions-of-david-lynch.

Powers, John. "Getting Lost is Beautiful." *LAWeekly*. Last modified October 17, 2001. https://www.laweekly.com/news/getting-lost-is-beautiful-2133916.

Rosenbaum, Jonathan. "Bad Ideas: The Art and Politics of *Twin Peaks*." In *Full of Secrets: Critical Approaches to* Twin Peaks, edited by David Lavery, 22–29. Detroit: Wayne State University Press, 1995.

Thorne, John. *The Essential Wrapped in Plastic: Pathways to* Twin Peaks. Dallas, Texas: John Thorne, 2016.

Weinstock, Jeffrey Andrew, and Catherine Spooner. *Return to* Twin Peaks: *New Approaches to Materiality, Theory, and Genre on Television*. Basingstoke, U.K.: Palgrave MacMillan, 2006.

I

INNOCENCE, NOSTALGIA, AND THE POLITICAL

ONE

The Nuclear Anxiety of *Twin Peaks: The Return*

Ashlee Joyce

Perhaps no episode in 2017's *Twin Peaks: The Return* has garnered as much critical attention as Part 8, titled "Gotta Light?"—not just for its compelling depiction of the first detonation of a nuclear bomb, but also for the way in which these visuals offer a key to the entire *Twin Peaks* mythology (or at least as close to a key as fans of David Lynch can ever hope to expect). For audiences of Lynch's work, this is what we crave, and Lynch has given us just enough, it seems, to produce a rabbit hole's worth of fan- and critic-driven rumination to which this chapter hopes to offer a valid contribution. Functioning almost as a stand-alone short film, Part 8's lack of continuity with the rest of the series primes viewers for answers that are never delivered—at least not explicitly—and functions as a sort of trauma that remains unresolved. In this way, the episode re-enacts the trauma of the deployment of nuclear weaponry itself—a cataclysmic event that birthed anxieties that persist far beyond the end of the Cold War and that pose a crisis of representation for artists who wish to bear witness to it.

This chapter examines *Twin Peaks: The Return* as an expression of these nuclear anxieties. Critics have called the new season of *Twin Peaks* a culmination of David Lynch's life's work[1] and have pointed out several thematic elements that connect the series to past films in the Lynchian oeuvre. One that is arguably shared among all of Lynch's works is a would-be nostalgia for a version of 1950s America that inevitably reveals itself to be corrupt at its core. Lynch's dark yet nostalgic visions of American culture—represented in ways that purposely muddle attempts to locate them within a precise historical time frame—suggest an attempt to work through unresolved anxieties related to the Cold War and the perceived loss of an American "age of innocence."

Twin Peaks: The Return repeats many of these themes, but with differences in tone that throw the apparent nostalgia of seasons one and two of *Twin Peaks* into question (much to the chagrin of many fans who were expecting a return to the series' more soapy/campy elements). Whereas *Twin Peaks* seasons one and two may indulge in nostalgia, *The Return* eschews the comforts of 1950s small-town America but keeps all its nuclear anxiety. Through the symbolism of the bomb offered in Part 8, the series turns into a meditation on the evils wrought by nuclear technology that brings political and artistic anxieties latent since the Cold War into sudden and urgent dialogue with twenty-first-century neoliberal America—a dialogue that can be understood through the lenses of nuclear criticism and literary trauma theory.

Lynch is certainly not alone in continuing to grapple with themes of the nuclear age, both political and artistic—the awe and threat posed by nuclear technology, a Reaganite desire to name easily identifiable foes, and a concern for the crisis of representation posed by the threat of total nuclear annihilation, to name a few—well beyond the end of the Cold War and despite the quickness with which politicians abandoned the idea of nuclear annihilation as a potential threat with the fall of the Iron Curtain. In a 2006 article, critic Daniel Cordle re-examines the assumption that nuclear issues ceased to be pressing with the fall of the Berlin Wall, making a case for a new, contemporary "nuclear criticism" that suggests continuities between contemporary conceptions of "terror" and an earlier geopolitics of nuclear anxiety.[2] Cordle's call for a new nuclear criticism echoes David Lynch's own assertion, in interview with Chris Rodley, that "the Fifties are still here."[3] Of course, like seemingly everything Lynch has ever written, this is a statement loaded with potential interpretations. Does Lynch long for a return to an age of pre-Cold War American innocence? Or is he making a statement about the unresolved anxieties of the nuclear age that have never gone away, despite impressions that the defeat of the U.S.S.R. was so final as to usher in what Francis Fukuyama calls the End of History: an era in which all political conflict becomes nullified by the dismantling of trade barriers and global acceptance of Western-style capitalism.[4] By examining *Twin Peaks: The Return* (particularly Part 8) alongside earlier works like *Eraserhead*, I argue that Lynch's oeuvre indicates a desire by the nuclear generation to imagine the Cold War into an issue that continues to be pressing in the period that has succeeded it, in order to suggest continuities with our current historical moment and to take stock of nuclear armament's continued repercussions.

"NOT A POLITICAL PERSON"?
LOOKING BACK AT THE LYNCHIAN OEUVRE

Critics have persistently attempted to locate some cohesive meaning both within and among Lynch's works and to link this meaning up with some historical, political, or social context. However, to undertake a sustained analysis of the images and themes presented in *Twin Peaks: The Return*, like much of Lynch's art in general, sometimes feels like an exercise in free association as arbitrary as agents Chester Desmond and Sam Stanley's interpretation of Lil's blue rose and surreal dance in the series prequel, *Twin Peaks: Fire Walk with Me*. Often, trying even to identify the message Lynch intends to drive home (if intent can even be spoken of) feels like peddling a hard sell akin to Dr. Lawrence Jacoby/ Dr. Amp's golden shit-digging shovel. Any of these characters could be read as stand-ins for the critics who attempt in futility to pin down some consistent system of meaning in places where Lynch intends to invoke something highly personal, as attested by his tendency to throw questions of interpretation back onto anyone who asks.[5] But if one thing is clear about the *Twin Peaks* reboot, it is that the new season distills many of the themes and images that have appeared over the course of Lynch's long and storied career. As Jack Nicholls writes, "You could knock yourself out with a Lynchian drinking game involving slow zooms into tight spaces, waitresses in diners, or headlights on dark roads."[6] And if one thing is clear about Lynch's body of work, it is that it stems from a highly personal and often directly autobiographical place.

Citing Lynch's assertion that the grimly comic surrealism of his debut feature *Eraserhead* (1997) was significantly influenced by his time spent living in Philadelphia, Glenn Kenny writes that "images, textures and moods" of Lynch's work are "derived from his personal experience."[7] All of this within reason, of course. It is telling, however, that the framed photograph of the Trinity nuclear test that appears in *Eraserhead* over the nightstand in Henry Spencer's bachelor apartment is the same photograph that appears (significantly, in much larger scale) in *The Return*, hanging over the desk of FBI Deputy Director Gordon Cole, who is played by Lynch himself, linking the feature that launched David Lynch's film career with this most recent work through a vein of persistent, ever-present nuclear anxiety that crackles like an electrical current (3.7). And yet, like the volatile, often magical, and sometimes malevolent energy that zaps Agent Dale Cooper back into our world from the Black Lodge via Dougie Jones and seemingly permits him to travel interdimensionally, this energy is accepted and presented as

Figure 1.1. Episode 3.7 "There's a Body All Right"
Twin Peaks

an uncanny fixture of the domestic, of everyday life (think the Palmer house's portentous ceiling fan and *The Return*'s ominous, buzzing telephone wires and electrical sockets).

The anxiety embedded within the domestic and the everyday has been a feature of arguably every work in the Lynchian oeuvre, contributing to its uncanny quality. Nicholls—writing particularly about *Twin Peaks* in relation to *Mulholland Drive, Wild at Heart,* and *Blue Velvet*[8]—links this uncanniness to "the darkness hiding beneath the hypocritical comforts of America in the 1950s" and attributes its presence to Lynch's having been "conceived in Eden and born After the Fall"[9]—that is, in January 1946, just seven months before the dropping of Little Boy by U.S. forces on Hiroshima. Nicholls slots Lynch, along with Stephen King and Steven Spielberg, into a trio of pop-culture icons all of whom were born within two years of each other and all of whose work, he argues, grapples with the cognitive dissonance arising from having to balance their memories of an idyllic childhood growing up in 1950s America with the knowledge of the true horrors of the Holocaust and the nuclear age.

For Nicholls, it needn't be argued that for Lynch and his contemporaries, the idea of the dropping of the atomic bomb is a threshold event that put an end to an earlier "age of innocence" (not just within America, but globally) and ushered in an age of modern evil: "It's clear that for a whole lot of people now in their 70s, The War, The Holocaust, and The Bomb were the crucibles that formed the modern world." And with *The Return*'s distillation of the themes and images that repeat across Lynch's body of work, the series appears to represent the culmination not only of Lynch's artistic career (or, as Tom Huddleston goes as far as to suggest, his "Long, perfect goodbye"), but also of his political attitudes, namely his ongoing critique of the insidious horrors of the nuclear age.

One cannot take this stance on *Twin Peaks: The Return*, however, without acknowledging the vast caveat that comes with assuming any work of art to reflect authorial intent, especially given the ambivalent tone of both the *Twin Peaks* reboot and its original counterpart. This is especially true of Lynch, whose politics are, as *Guardian* writer Rory Carroll notes, "all over the map." In the most recent federal election, he first endorsed Bernie Sanders in his bid for the Democratic nomination, later voted for Libertarian candidate Gary Johnson, and most recently suggested that Donald Trump might go down as "one of the greatest presidents in history"[10] due to his having exposed the ineptitude of American political leaders and, indeed, of the whole system. It should come as no surprise that the politics of *Twin Peaks*, like those of its creator, should be difficult to pin down. Though the implications of Lynch's comments to *The Guardian* were furiously overblown, pulled and used as headlines by online media outlets in search of clicks—Lynch has since clarified, in an open letter to the president posted to Facebook, that he believes Trump to be "causing suffering and division" and advises him to "treat all the people as you would like to be treated."[11] The sentiment behind it is nonetheless telling: Lynch prefaces his comment with "I'm not a political person," a classically privileged viewpoint to hold, and it is clear from his silver-linings outlook that he is not likely to ever be personally affected by any of the Trump administration's policies (barring nuclear cataclysm, that is).

Despite the way Lynch's comment was taken out of context, for fans it may still come as a painful realization that he might be more conservative than audiences would like to believe. Lynch's outsider-artist persona may tempt audiences to brand him as left leaning, but the politics expressed in *Twin Peaks*—in both its 1990–91 and 2017 iterations—are, like the political stance of the man himself, not so straightforward. Critics have noted the series' oscillation between a critique of the hypocrisy of 1950s America—of the falseness of the apparent innocence of the 1950s masking the potential horrors of nuclear weaponry—and a nostalgia for this state of innocence, however false (symptomatic, perhaps, of the general yearning for the 1950s evident during the Reagan administration). M. K. Booker writes that although the original series was highly subversive in terms of its formal qualities, these subversions "were accompanied by little in the way of subversive political statements" and argues that the series, if anything, conveys "a nostalgic call for a return to the values of an idyllic past, when life wasn't so weird."[12] It seems puzzling, at first, that

Booker would see the original series as a window onto a "not-so-weird" past, given the uncanniness that permeates every aspect of the town of Twin Peaks, but what Booker identifies is the series' appropriation of the conventions of familiar genres like, in addition to the soap opera, the detective story, the film noir, and the Gothic tale, which it then subverts in order to convey a longing for the kind of predictability these modes of writing offer (particularly the stable binary oppositions—the sort of "Us vs. Them" conflicts—that often characterize the conflict in these genres), alongside a sense that this predictability can no longer be sustained in the postmodern world. This pattern of appropriation and subversion projects an overall ambivalent attitude toward American culture at the time of the series' original run.

Linnie Blake goes even further than Booker in her critique of the veiled ambivalence of seasons one and two. She suggests that *Twin Peaks* is far from subversive but is, in fact, a neoliberal, postmodern artifact that united viewers in "a form of disorganized capitalism" in its disavowal of coherent meaning in favor of "contingent and eminently revisable representations of the individual and the world."[13] Of course, this sort of reading could be made of almost any piece in Lynch's body of work. Nonetheless, it is interesting to note Blake's impressions of having been, as an undergrad, among the first viewers of the series, an experience she describes as a process of seduction "by the ethical relativism of Lynch's dark illogicality."[14] But writing almost twenty-five years later, Blake points out how the series "publicly champions the institutions of family, hard work, and moral rectitude [and] displays attitudes toward women, the learning disabled, and those who are not white that would not have been out of place during the Cold War," arguing that the series was "at best politically conservative and replete with dangerous representations of already marginalized groups."[15] Blake places Lynch's work squarely within a Baudrillardian framework that sees differences in political ideologies homogenized and subsumed under the spectacle of mass media itself, in which entertainment replaces ideology and viewers become mere consumers of ambiguous images and messages offered up for their own sake.[16] But there is more to *Twin Peaks* than mere reveling in ethical and interpretive ambiguity, especially in light of *The Return*, which, though even more confounding, is far less comforting than the original.

ANXIETY OR NOSTALGIA?
THE SHIFTING POLITICS OF *TWIN PEAKS*

It is not as though *The Return* doesn't itself engage in conservative processes of gender- and class-based "othering." The series seems to revel, for example, in the objectification of women as perpetual victims of sexual violence. Scenes like that in which Richard Horne grabs a woman at the Roadhouse and threatens her with rape work at best as devices to develop *Twin Peaks'* male antagonists, but characters like Candie, Mandie, and Sandie, the three "casino girls," while packaged as lighter fare, are more insidious. Given Part 10's scene in which Candie must beg for forgiveness for smacking her boss, Rodney, upside the head with a remote control while trying to kill a fly, not to mention the trio's perpetual silence, it is difficult to view them, if not devices for the development of the series' male villains, as simply fodder for the male gaze.

On top of its theme of the abuse of women, the series seems to long for some lost masculine archetype. Consider the inept Dougie who stares with a sort of confused and transfixed longing at the bronze statue of a man dressed in Western garb wielding a pistol outside of Lucky 7 Insurance's corporate office, an image complemented by the Old West wallpaper that covers Sonny Jim's bedroom. The series is also rife with easily identifiable working-class criminal "others," like the drug-addled Becky and Steven (daughter and son-in-law of Shelly Briggs) and the heroin-abusing mother of Part 15, who seems to appear purely for viewers to gawk at her while she yells "1–1–9!" repeatedly for one agonizingly long scene. Alongside the presence of these conservative depictions of gender and class, blends of old and new technologies—like the wood-framed computer that rises out of sheriff Frank Truman's desk and the flip phone Mr. C uses to make the alarm system in the Las Vegas police station go haywire—make the series difficult to locate in time. While the Man from Another Place asks, "Is it future, or is it past?," and later, Dale Cooper asks in *The Return*'s finale, "What year is this?," the conservative vein that runs through the series seems to echo Lynch's sentiment that "the Fifties are still here."[17]

What might this vein of conservatism have to do with nuclear anxiety in *The Return*? The series' conservative depictions of gender and class, while not explicitly linked to the Cold War, are nonetheless indicative of a longing for a sort of Cold War era social order in which binaries like male/female, rich/poor, and good/evil are easily identifiable. And yet, as easily as we can identify the conservative gender and class politics of the reboot, we can identify the ways in which the series subverts this very conservatism, exemplified in the series' depiction of Las Vegas as a seat of evil, corruption, and excess, which enacts a well-worn critique of corporate American greed. It is important, then, to recognize that the politics of *Twin Peaks*—both the original series and *The Return*—are, if at all reflective of Lynch's own politics, necessarily fraught with contradictions. Lynch is unlikely to give viewers any help in arriving at a conclusion to the question of whether the politics of *Twin Peaks* fall on either side of the conservative/liberal binary. The series seems to grapple with a general sense of malaise brought about by having lived through the Cold War era, an era which gave rise to the notion of a triumph of Western liberalism that would bring an end to political revolution only to see the threat of nuclear warfare renewed with "fire and fury" in the time of Trump.[18] So the oscillation between an apparently liberal subversiveness and a conservative longing for stability reflects the cognitive dissonance that the revival of the threat of nuclear war engenders, and which defies easy comprehension. It is this very incomprehensibility—the same incomprehensibility that causes Lynch to throw up his hands and declare himself an apolitical person—that *Twin Peaks: The Return* captures.

The Return makes seasons one and two of *Twin Peaks* look downright nostalgic by comparison. Booker writes that the town of Twin Peaks "would be a virtual embodiment of 1950s-style small-town American values were it not for the fact that it is threatened by numerous evil forces (many of them supernatural) from both within and without."[19] But despite these evil forces, the world of the original run of *Twin Peaks* is one viewers want to immerse themselves in because of the way it invokes a lost past. Booker points out how the names of two of the series' most lovable characters, Deputy Andy Brennan and Lucy Moran, "evok[e] two of the greatest stars of the television sitcom, Andy Griffith and Lucille Ball," and their comedic timing offers a comforting relief from some of the series' darker tensions.[20] Booker argues that the town's oddball characters generate a self-referential element to the series, so as "to produce thrills (as if viewers were getting away with something by being able to see such strange programming on commercial television) more than chills."[21] The series' many throwbacks to 1950s America are delivered to viewers in tongue-and-cheek fashion, creating for audiences of the original *Twin Peaks* the sense that they were in on a private joke. Viewers could rest in the knowledge that this would-be idyllic vision of 1950s Americana never existed, as the numerous forces of evil that corrupt the town of Twin Peaks to its very core make obvious. The America of seasons one and two was the America of these viewers' parents, and with its diners, jukeboxes, high school quarterbacks and homecoming queens, seasons one and two proffered a vision of a past that was, if a simulacrum, at least a comforting and familiar one—one that the cynical, neoliberal, postmodern 1990s viewer could either pine for or scoff at (or, perhaps, both), but always from a comfortably and confidently knowing position.

The nostalgic tone of seasons one and two is, if not entirely lost, far more complicated in *The Return*, which is likely to blame for the series' mixed critical reception. Carroll, in his interview with Lynch for *The Guardian*, accurately notes that it is "still debated as either the best or worst television of 2017."[22] The series spends relatively little time in the town of Twin Peaks, swapping it out for various locales in which viewers have far less of an emotional stake: the Nevada desert housing development known as Rancho Rosa; Las Vegas; Buckhorn, South Dakota; the Fat Trout Trailer Park in Deer Meadow, Washington (also used in *Fire Walk With Me*); and the strange Manhattan studio in which the entity known as the "Experiment" tears the faces off one ill-fated couple (3.2). Instead of the dreamy, soap-opera quality of the original, the reboot participates in the genres of the forensic thriller and crime drama, with the occasional foray into Tarantinoesque shootouts. In "Gotta Light?" it seemed the series reached new heights of surrealism and appeared poised to offer answers to questions left unresolved by either the original series run or *Fire Walk with Me*, but the intense, generative energy of Part 8 is not sustained, and viewers are soon returned to witnessing the torturous fumblings of Dougie, who seems almost universally loathed as the doppelganger of the beloved Agent Cooper, whose return audiences so desperately crave. Some of the original series' most beloved characters, like Lucy and Andy, have a smaller role to play than in the original (although the spirit of Marlon Brando does make an appearance in the form of their son, Wally, who shares Brando's birthday and mannerisms [3.4]). And despite Angelo Badalamenti's having composed the music for *The Return*, his original lilting score, which contributed so much to the drama, romance, and dread of seasons one and two, is conspicuously absent—as critic Benjamin Porter notes, the original score is used sparingly and "with 'weaponized' precision to maximize the emotional impact on the viewer," that is, to generate maximum nostalgia for the original series.[23] *The Return* is *Twin Peaks* with all the evil and corruption and seemingly none of the comforting Cold War era signifiers. The consequences of drug use are far more explicit in *The Return*, with the cocaine-smuggling ring led by the cartoonish One-Eyed Jack's swapped out for a more serious depiction of the American opioid crisis, personified in Becky, Steven, and the 1–1–9 woman. Even the R&R Diner is not spared from the forces of modernization, as would-be investor Walter is hell-bent on converting the mom-and-pop restaurant into a global franchise, at the expense of the quality of Norma's cherry pie (3.15). If the original run of *Twin Peaks* approaches the dawn of globalization with a detached cynicism that pokes fun at the Cold War era with a kind of gallows humor or postmodern snobbishness, *The Return* has dropped the joke.

WITNESSING THE BOMB:
THE RETURN'S NUCLEAR SUBLIME

Instead, the series, departing from the nostalgia of the original, revisits the connection between our neoliberal present and the nuclear past by way of the image of the detonation of the first atomic bomb—depicting it as an exceptional event that constitutes nothing less than the birth of contemporary evil. Daniel Cordle, writing about the exceptional nature of the threat of total nuclear annihilation, argues that this exceptionality produces a crisis of representation: fictions seeking to represent the prospect of total nuclear war are "caught in a bind because they have to postulate a perspective on the end of culture, from within culture."[24] Much in the same way that Theodor Adorno famously stated, about the Holocaust, that "to write poetry after Auschwitz is barbaric,"[25] Cordle is suggesting that the threat of nuclear war demands modes of representation that capture the exceptional strangeness of the event in ways that conventional modes of representation (i.e., realism) alone cannot. Cordle's "nuclear criticism" can provide a key to understanding the mythology of *Twin Peaks*, suggesting that in order to represent such an unprecedented historical event as nuclear holocaust, modes of representation of nuclear warfare and its related traumatic tensions must be found that both meet this "challenge [to] the capacity of the mind to imagine its own non-existence" and capture it in ways that realism may be insufficient in doing.[26]

One mode of representation that is suited to representing the crisis of witnessing posed by nuclear war is the sublime, which has its origins in Gothic literature. The idea of a "nuclear sublime," a concept first coined to describe the particular mixture of fear and awe that characterized the development of the atomic bomb, has already been theorized by several critics. In "Techno-Euphoria and the Discourse of the American Sublime," Rob Wilson calls the development of the atom bomb a "history-shattering event."[27] Similarly, in "A Terrible Beauty: the Nuclear Sublime in Philip Ridley's *The Reflecting Skin* (1991)," Deborah Lovatt describes the "alarming discrepancy between the power of the Bomb and the descriptive powers of language" as felt by the first witnesses to the Trinity test.[28] Witnesses "reported nuclear explosions in terms of a crisis of the imagination, of speechlessness."[29] The original concept of the sublime, an aesthetic theory developed in the eighteenth century by Edmund Burke,[30] describes the feeling of overwhelming awe and, often, terror at objects that are immeasurably vast and that break the viewer's frame of reference with regard to scale (in other words, which lead the viewer to a newfound sense of their own relative puniness). Wilson and Lovatt both argue that this concept is apt for representing nuclear technology in literature from both the Cold War era and beyond and, along with Cordle, call for a new nuclear criticism capable of grappling with the enduring legacy of nuclear war. Since *Twin Peaks* spans the period just after the fall of the Berlin Wall to the renewed threat of nuclear war under the current Republican administration,[31] Cordle's nuclear sublime is an apt conceptual tool for understanding *The Return*'s nuclear episode, Part 8's "Gotta Light?"

The Trinity detonation scene follows a nuclear-sublime aesthetic. The scene opens over the Jornada del muerto desert with the title card reading "July 16, 1945 / White Sands, New Mexico / 5:29 AM (MWT)," locating viewers at the exact time and place of the detonation of the first atomic weapon (3.8). The scene is shot from overhead and pans toward the detonation at an agonizingly slow pace, prompting viewers to soak in the sheer scale of the event. Krzysztof Penderecki's original composition, "Threnody to the Victims of Hiroshima," with its screaming violins overlaid over the discordant notes of a horn section that evokes the sound of a nuclear air-raid siren, suggests the screaming of victims and contributes both to the elegiac tone and to the overall anxiety and tension that permeates the scene. Nostalgia for the 1950s this is not. The shooting of the episode in black and white further locates viewers in the Cold War era, evoking original footage of early nuclear tests. Lynch films the detonation scene on a sublime scale; from the sweeping aerial shots of the detonation, the camera moves into the mushroom cloud itself, seeming to travel through a sort of quantum wormhole (or birth canal) into another dimension: the world of the Fireman and Senorita Dido, who survey events on-screen from a sort of bunker perched on a cliff in the middle of a flat, featureless ocean. And it is through this wormhole that the series' most terrifying entities are unleashed: we witness the Experiment, who in Part 1 gored a young couple to death in a New York City studio, the woodsmen,[32] who whisper the incantatory "Gotta light?" and crackle with noise reminiscent of a Geiger counter picking up radiation from nuclear fallout, and of course, BOB, whose face appears within a bubble, seemingly prompting Senorita Dido to send Laura Palmer within a glowing orb of her own to earth in order to counteract BOB's evil. Nine Inch Nails' performance of "She's Gone Away" in the preceding scene, in which they sing the lyrics "Spread the infection where you spill your seed," leaves no question as to the significance of the nuclear detonation scene, and indeed of the entire episode: that the development of the atomic bomb birthed a new kind of evil force that, as the rest of the series (and especially the final episode) suggests, cannot be destroyed, and from which we as viewers are unable to look away.

The episode's only moment of nostalgia, the scene immediately following Laura Palmer's transfer via space orb to Earth and the hatching of the strange frog-wasp creature—a mutant apparently born from Trinity—is one in which two young teens walk home together (presumably after a date) as The Platters' "My Prayer" plays on the radio, although it is soon undercut by the appearance of the bizarre frog-wasp hybrid entering the young girl's bedroom via her open window and seemingly compelling her to hitch her jaw unnaturally wide, open her mouth, and allow it to crawl down her throat. The scene plays out, we are told, in 1956 New

Mexico and at first offers a moment of innocent 1950s romance, opening with two virginal teens strolling chastely together through town and making banal conversation about lucky pennies. Shot, like the Trinity detonation, in black and white, the scene evokes the romance of vintage film (a contrast with the found nuclear testing footage evoked by the same black and white in the Trinity scene). But as critic Alci Rengifo points out, "like the cinema of Luis Bunuel, elegant images of domestic bliss are mere portents for subconscious specters to come."[33] Are we witnessing a birth of evil similar to the one invoked by the bomb, only this time on a much smaller, indeed, private, personal scale? It certainly seems that way; Sarah Palmer's narrative, which is given particular attention in prior episodes, is already on our minds, and fan theories suggest that this is the young Sarah Palmer,[34] whose swallowing of the frog-wasp constitutes the beginning of her descent into neurosis, madness, and alcoholism that will culminate in Part 14's revelation, shortly after she rips the throat out of one well-deserving misogynist, that her body is acting as a host for what appears to be the Experiment. Here nostalgia only amplifies the episode's theme of innocence corrupted: this smaller-scale domestic scene, with the frog-wasp akin to a forbidden fruit swallowed by the otherwise pure female, offers an image of Edenic corruption that reinforces the event of the Trinity test as a moment of original sin for contemporary humanity—the manifestation of a forbidden knowledge we cannot unlearn.

The scenes following the birth of BOB and transmigration of Laura Palmer, which presumably reflects the balancing of the forces of evil with the forces of good, are among the most nostalgic and most conspicuously "Cold War" in the entire reboot, and not just because of the young couple who so quintessentially embody 1950s innocence and wholesomeness, but also because of the way this wholesomeness is co-opted and reconfigured by the woodsmen. We have the mechanic at the neighbourhood garage, the waitress wiping the counter at the local diner, and the disc jockey spinning records during the golden age of radio—all symbols of 1950s small-town America—who are either mesmerized or have their heads brutally crushed by the woodsman, another Black Lodge entity seemingly unleashed by the atomic bomb, who has arrived to destroy these fixtures of 1950s America one by one. The death of the radio DJ is particularly significant, as it leads to the cutting out of the song that plays as a background to the scene and its replacement with the portentous words of the woodsman: "This is the water and this is the well. Drink full and descend. The horse is the white of the eyes and dark within" (3.8). Repeated over and over, it is these words that seemingly compel the young girl to allow the frog-wasp to crawl into her mouth. Any nostalgia produced by the 1950s rock 'n' roll that forms the background of this scene is destroyed and replaced by a refrain that defies comprehension but suggests something ominous, elemental, and primal: water, well, horse, white, eyes, dark. A descent into darkness and chaos that is to ensue in the following decades, perhaps. If, as Booker suggests, the first two seasons of *Twin Peaks* aimed to produce "thrills ... more than chills,"[35] *The Return*'s critique of 1950s nostalgia in Part 8 is as chilling as it is possible to get, offering a bleak view of a humanity charged with Black Lodge entities released by the atomic bomb and suggesting that these entities manifest the "dark within"—acting as forces of suffering that apparently cannot be destroyed but rather, as the final episode's alternate realities and doubling of Laura indicate, only deferred.

THE BLACK LODGE ENTITIES: EMBODYING AN UNASSIMILABLE TRAUMA

If the detonation of Trinity represents the birth of evil in the world and the loss of American innocence, then BOB, as the issue of the bomb, is this evil personified. Of course, BOB has links to something much older than the atomic bomb. As we are told by FBI Special Agent Tammy Preston, the Black Lodge entities are manifestations of an age-old demon that possesses two forms—a male, called Ba'al, and a female, called Jouday—who have been in existence since 3000 BC. As per *Twin Peaks: The Final Dossier*, Jouday is a member of a species of wandering Sumerian demons called the *utukku* who "feas[t] on human flesh" and thrive "on human suffering."[36] As Brien Allen points out, these demonic behaviors parallel those of BOB, who "feed[s] on garmonbozia and rip[s] the soul out of Windom Earl in the Season 2 finale."[37] This has led many fans to conclude that "Ba'al became known as Bob, in the same manner, that Jouday became known as Judy."[38] If we accept this theory, then what does this mean for the apparently conservative politics driving the idea of the bomb as the birth of evil? It would seem to suggest otherwise: that nuclear war might *not* in fact be a starting point for evil but, instead, merely its latest iteration. However, the idea of BOB/Judy as ancient entities that connect the evil of the bomb to something much older nonetheless reinforces the dubious "apolitical" posture that Lynch expresses in his *Guardian* interview. By linking the evil that BOB/Ba'al and Judy/Jouday wreak in Twin Peaks and beyond to the bomb, the bomb itself, conversely, becomes a manifestation of a force of evil thousands of years old, a move that downplays the specific politics of nuclear armament. The linking of Judy and BOB to the bomb and vice versa typifies the posture of "apolitical" detachment toward destructive politics that Lynch takes in conversation with interviewers—a posture that (even if Lynch doesn't know it) depends on a certain level of conservatism.

Audience fascination with BOB as a villain depends on the same "detached aesthetic fascination" that Dennis Lim, writing for *The New Yorker*, identifies in Lynch's work. BOB embodies the political climate in which *Twin Peaks: The Return* aired.[39] In other words, he is the perfect villain of the Trump era; we love to hate him, but we are also captivated by his origin story. Lim writes that Lynch's views on the current administration "are irksome not because they endorse Trump—as numerous headlines falsely declared—but because they represent the privileged position of distance. Lynch, needless to say, is insulated from, and perhaps oblivious to, the most cruel and backward of Trump's policies."[40] But Lim does not recognize that we, as viewers, are mesmerized by this same detached aesthetic fascination. Our appreciation of BOB depends on our distance from the evil he perpetrates. The same, of course, is true of our appreciation of the series' depiction of the bomb itself. Part 8 is known as the most beautifully shot episode of the entire series (it has been nominated for an Emmy for outstanding cinematography for a limited series or movie), and the views we get of Trinity are sweeping, panned out, detached. The musical score accompanying the Trinity test scene renders the experience of the bomb as sensuous, aesthetic, beautiful, and terrifying—in other words, as sublime. The camera's slow procession into the cloud offers to viewers an impossible perspective on nuclear war: what it would be like if the viewer were impervious to the bomb's destruction. Even if *The Return* was, as Lim states, "a summer-long fever dream of dread and dissociation, seemingly tailor-made for our real-life waking nightmare of crisis and collapse," it nonetheless, at least in this episode, indulges in the sublime aesthetic experience of the bomb and in the captivating origins of its age-old villain, if only to convey the sheer incomprehensibility of the development of the evils of nuclear armament: a sort of "how did we get here?" sentiment that is not unexpected coming from one so chronically closemouthed, solitary, and obtusely "apolitical" as Lynch. What is key, though, to understanding BOB's place in Lynch's politics is navigating the role of disruption in Lynch's work. As Lim points out, Lynch calls Trump "great" only because of his ability to disrupt, and Lynch's work also thrives on disruption, which Lim calls "generative."[41] Like it or not, BOB is effective as a villain because of his disruptive energy, released with the detonation of the bomb. And everything about the way BOB's birth is portrayed conveys the generative potential of the destruction wrought by nuclear weaponry. This ambivalent portrayal of BOB signals Lynch's own political detachment, which his privileged position as an affluent, white, elite member of Hollywood affords him.

The position of ostensibly apolitical detachment that Lynch displays and that *Twin Peaks: The Return* adopts informs the series' focus on the ineffable quality of nuclear warfare—the way in which it overwhelms any attempt to comprehend or to represent its repercussions. It addresses the crisis of representation posed by nuclear war, which may be understood further by way of Cathy Caruth's theory of trauma fiction. In her seminal work, *Unclaimed Experience: Trauma, Narrative, and History*, Caruth, drawing on the Freudian model of trauma as an event that overwhelms the victim's psyche so that it is experienced via belated, fragmented, intrusive memories of the event, argues that since the traumatic event lies "lodged" in the victim's psyche like an "unassimilated" foreign object, attempts by traumatized victims to represent it will inevitably be tainted, with the results being correspondingly marked by fragmentation, aphasia, repression, repetition—in other words, the symptoms of trauma.[42] Trauma fiction, for Caruth, captures "not only the reality of the violent event but also the reality of the way that its violence has not yet been fully known."[43] In conveying the experience of the victim of trauma, then, trauma fiction cannot help but convey the limits of the trauma's very capacity to be represented, and this is the posture—that of bewildered witness to the trauma of a potentially cataclysmic nuclear event—that *Twin Peaks: The Return* reflects back to viewers.

Caruth's test case for her theory of "literary" trauma, one that has parallels with Lynch's work, is another film about nuclear holocaust—Alain Resnais's *Hiroshima, mon amour*, a film that indirectly retells the story of the Hiroshima nuclear bombing, using the event as a backdrop to the love story that it develops between its two protagonists, referred to only as "Her" and "Him." Caruth argues that the film treats as its subject the difficulties of communicating trauma and the connections that can occur between individuals across these difficulties. This connection allows Caruth, for example, to interpret the faithfulness of "Her," the protagonist of *Hiroshima, mon amour*, to her dead German lover, along with her subsequent refusal to see and understand his death, through the image of Her's "body's fragmentation."[44] This fragmentation is the result, according to Caruth, of an "unbridgeable abyss" between the "when" of seeing her lover die and the "when" of his actual death. This "missing of the 'when' within the shock of sight" is "experienced as a confusion of the body; for in missing the moment of his death, the woman is also unable to recognize the continuation of her life . . . Her bodily life, that is, has become the endless attempt to witness her lover's death."[45] While Caruth's manner of elaborating her analysis is highly theoretical, its core message is that the experience of trauma involves a temporal disconnect between the event and the victim's understanding. Trauma fiction like *Hiroshima, mon amour* is often about how the body can bear witness to aspects of trauma that cannot otherwise be put into words.

The idea of trauma as an inability or unwillingness to testify may redeem *Twin Peaks: The Return*'s apparently ambivalent politics. In *The*

Return, Lynch conveys the resistance of global nuclear cataclysm to representation via an inability to see or speak via the character of Naido, a woman who has only scars where her eyes should be and who cannot communicate except by desperate chattering and grasping at thin air. Naido (whose similarity in name to NATO bears mentioning) has the frantic mannerisms of a distressed victim of trauma but also embodies the trauma victim in her inability to either see or to speak—the two vehicles of testimony. Without these abilities, Naido cannot testify to the trauma she has suffered (as indeed none of the casualties of nuclear war can), but despite Naido's inability to testify, her body, by way of its limitations, nonetheless bears witness to the truth of trauma's inherent resistance to representation, both personal and artistic. And in addition to her significance as symbolic of nuclear trauma, she carries an added layer of significance that comes with her status as a doppelganger (or perhaps a "tulpa") of Diane, who, having been raped by Mr. C, is another victim of trauma in her own right. In this character, then, are collapsed two visions of trauma: one large scale and collective (Hiroshima), the other individual and personal (sexual assault). Thus, despite the privileged position that allows for the detached position from which *Twin Peaks: The Return* regards nuclear war, this perspective should not necessarily be interpreted as blasé (even if we might read the detachment of the original as such), but instead should be read as a sympathetic acknowledgment of the way in which the experience of (the threat of) nuclear cataclysm, as well as other forms of trauma, in many ways defies adequate representation.

CONCLUSION

What, then, can we ultimately glean from *Twin Peaks: The Return*'s political ambivalences? The nuclear sublime evident in the series' sensuous, aesthetic treatment of the development of the atomic bomb creates a sense of awe alongside the terror of the prospect of nuclear technologies, which contradicts the rhetoric that surrounded the end of the Cold War that suggested that the fall of the Iron Curtain meant an end to global conflict and the triumph of capitalism. For Lynch, "the Fifties are still here," along with the ambivalences that nuclear technologies generated for the American public.[46] Cold War anxieties, for Lynch, have persisted long after the fall of the Berlin Wall. But have Lynch's politics changed since season one of *Twin Peaks*? Both the original and the reboot are unmistakably postmodern. The conservatism of seasons one and two is buried beneath a superficial layer of aesthetic subversion that is offered up to an audience whose identity as consumers subsumes their politics. *The Return* is ultimately more political than the original, wearing its nuclear anxieties on its sleeve, although it cannot escape conservative elements of its own. The idea of the bomb as the source of evil and a corrupting force marking the destruction of innocence is a conservative, ethnocentric idea, ignoring such large-scale global atrocities as slavery, genocide, and colonialism. Such a viewpoint depends on a certain degree of naiveté, if not willful blindness, and is not unexpected given Lynch's tendency to avoid implicating himself in political debate and the privilege that affords him the luxury of doing so. Part of privilege, after all, involves the privilege of not knowing. In this way, *The Return* displays some of the same conservatism evident in the original series. But at the same time, the series' departure from the nostalgia of the original marks a shift in politics from the typical cynical posture of the postmodernism of the 1990s toward a more destabilized, anxious, uncertain perspective on the nuclear age. We must not discount the profound impact the Cold War had on Lynch's generation, for better or for worse. To them, it must have seemed as though the world was on the verge of ending, much as it feels within *The Return*'s universe. The Twin Peaks of *The Return* is no longer an escape—it has been corrupted and is under threat by numerous contemporary anxieties, including neoliberalism, corporate greed, and the opioid crisis that ravages the Burnetts and others. Despite what the series' title may suggest, there is no returning to Twin Peaks, with the familiar terrors that we know and love. Far from the answers viewers might have expected from the series reboot, we are left, at the end of Part 18, more confused than ever. This confusion is a reflection, perhaps, of the confusion of the nuclear generation, twenty-six years removed from the end of the Cold War—a confusion generated by the prospect of nuclear war as an event that, as Herman Kahn argues, seems "immoral to think and even more immoral to write in detail about."[47] And it is a reflection, perhaps, of Lynch's own sense that we are less certain now about the fate of the world in our current, "new nuclear age"[48] than ever, despite the assurances of Fukuyama and others who believed that with the end of the Cold War and the dissolution of trade barriers came an end to political conflict—an end, in other words, to history. The ambivalence and anxieties of *Twin Peaks: The Return* indicate that the nuclear age continues to elude the full grasp of we who bear witness to it, and, with the current revival of the threat of thermonuclear war, may cause us to ask, "What year is this?"

NOTES

1. Tom Huddleston, "*Twin Peaks*: Was This the Long, Perfect Goodbye from David Lynch?" last modified 6 September 2017.
2. Daniel Cordle, "Cultures of Terror: Nuclear Criticism During and Since the Cold War." *Literature Compass* 3, no. 6 (2006): 1186.
3. David Lynch, *Lynch on Lynch*, ed. Chris Rodley (London: Faber & Faber, 2005), 4.

4. Francis Fukuyama appropriates the concept of an "End of History" from Karl Marx, who believed that the forces of history would cease only after the victory of the working class and the ushering in of a capitalist utopia. Fukuyama refers, of course, not to the triumph of Marxism, but the "ultimate triumph of Western liberal democracy." Francis Fukuyama, "The End of History?" in *The Geopolitics Reader*, ed. Simon Dalby et al., 113–24 (Abingdon, UK: Routledge, 2003), 114.

5. As Lynch states in interview, "It makes me uncomfortable to talk about meanings and things. It's better not to know so much about what things mean. Because the meaning, it's a very personal thing and the meaning for me is different than the meaning for somebody else." Jason Rogers, *My Love Affair with David Lynch and Peachy Like Nietzsche: Dark Clown Porn Snuff for Terrorists and Gorefiends* (Lulu Press, 2005), 7.

6. Jack Nicholls, "How David Lynch Never Learned to Stop Worrying and Love the Bomb," *Medium*, last modified 26 June 2017.

7. Glenn Kenny, "David Lynch Weaves Film History into *Twin Peaks: The Return*," *The New York Times*, last modified 13 July 2017.

8. Nichols identifies *Mulholland Drive*'s "bouncy pink ingenue singing 'Every Little Star,'" *Wild at Heart*'s Elvis imagery, and *Twin Peaks*'s original teenage cast as being "straight out of the 50s." But "beneath the bobby-socks," Nichols writes, "is always violence and horror, literalised in the unforgettable opening of *Blue Velvet* where insects writhe beneath suburban lawns"—another image of the domestic, the familiar, and the everyday corrupted by hidden horrors. Nichols, "How David Lynch Never Learned to Stop Worrying and Love the Bomb," *Medium*.

9. Nichols, "How David Lynch Never Learned to Stop Worrying and Love the Bomb," *Medium*.

10. Rory Carroll, "David Lynch: 'You Gotta Be Selfish. It's a Terrible Thing,'" *The Guardian*, last modified 23 June 2018.

11. David Lynch, "Dear Mr. President," *Facebook*, 26 June 2018 (3:08 p.m.).

12. M. K. Booker, *Strange TV: Innovative Television Series from the* Twilight Zone *to the* X-Files (Westport, CT: Greenwood Press, 2002), 98–99.

13. Linnie Blake, "Trapped in the Hysterical Sublime: *Twin Peaks*, Postmodernism, and the Neoliberal Now," in *Return to* Twin Peaks: *New Approaches to Materiality, Theory, and Genre on Television*, ed. Jeffery Andrews Weinstock and Catherine Spooner (New York, NY: Palgrave Macmillan, 2015), 232.

14. Blake, "Trapped in the Hysterical Sublime," 233.

15. Blake, "Trapped in the Hysterical Sublime," 235; 233.

16. Writing in 1994, Jean Baudrillard locates a trend in television media toward surface spectacle that produces an unimplicated, voyeuristic relationship between viewer and viewed. By arguing that "the media are producers not of socialization, but of exactly the opposite, of the implosion of the social in the masses," Baudrillard echoes Fukuyama's prediction within late twentieth-century culture of a dampening of political revolution, with the "dissuasive action of information, the media, and the mass media" promoting viewership without critical thought and without social responsibility. Jean Baudrillard, *Simulacra and Simulation*, trans. Sheila Faria Glaser (Ann Arbor: University of Michigan Press, 1994), 81, 79.

17. Lynch, *Lynch on Lynch*, 4.

18. According to the American Psychological Association, 75 percent of Americans now view North Korea's nuclear program as a "top threat," with clinicians reporting unprecedented "'frequency and intensity of fear and clinically significant anxiety,' even among clients who haven't previously experienced such symptoms." Jeremy Lybarger, "The Threat of Nuclear War." *American Psychological Association* 49, no. 3 (March 2018): 20.
19. Booker, *Strange TV*, 99.
20. Booker, *Strange TV*, 99.
21. Booker, *Strange TV*, 120.
22. Rory Carroll, "David Lynch: 'You Gotta Be Selfish. It's a Terrible Thing,'" *The Guardian*, last modified 23 June 2018.
23. Benjamin Porter, "The Subtle Yet Sharp Politics of *Twin Peaks: The Return*," *The Aggie*, last modified 10 June 2018.
24. Cordle, "Cultures of Terror,"1188.
25. Theodor W. Adorno, *Prisms* (Cambridge, MA: MIT Press, 1967), 34.
26. Cordle, "Cultures of Terror," 1188.
27. Rob Wilson, "Techno-Euphoria and the Discourse of the American Sublime," *Boundary* 2 19, no. 1 (1992): 204.
28. Deborah Lovatt, "A Terrible Beauty: The Nuclear Sublime in Philip Ridley's *The Reflecting Skin* (1991)." *European Journal of American Culture* 21, no. 3 (2002): 135.
29. Lovatt, "A Terrible Beauty," 135.
30. In his 1796 treatise, Burke defines the sublime as "whatever is fitted in any sort to excite the ideas of pain, and danger, that is to say, whatever is in any sort terrible, or is conversant about terrible objects, or operates in a manner analogous to terror." Edmund Burke, *A Philosophical Enquiry into the Origin of Our Ideas of the Sublime and Beautiful*, ed. Adam Phillips (Oxford: Oxford University Press [1796] 2008), 33.
31. The United States' decision in early 2018 to pull out of the Iran nuclear deal "could remove constraints on the Iranian regime and impel it to restart a uranium enrichment program that it had agreed to curtail through the 2020s," and recent nuclear "sabre-rattling" from major powers (often, for Trump, via Twitter), which includes the promise from both the United States and Russia to expand their nuclear arsenals, has the *New York Times* reporting "a spike in sales of potassium iodide, a drug that can block the thyroid gland from absorbing radioactive iodine released in a nuclear attack." Clyde Haberman, "'This is Not a Drill': The Threat of Nuclear Annihilation," *The New York Times*, last modified 13 May 2018.
32. Fans posit a link between the woodsmen and six loggers who died in a 1902 sawmill fire detailed in *The Secret History of Twin Peaks* called "The Night of the Burning River." When asked about the connection, Mark Frost answered cryptically that "If there's a link for you, there's a link. Something in between. Like life." Mark Frost, *The Secret History of Twin Peaks* (New York, NY: Flatiron Books, 2016), 68; Mark Frost, "I'm Mark Frost," *Reddit* Twin Peaks, 8 November 2017 (2:06 p.m.).
33. Alci Rengifo, "David Lynch's Dadaist Apocalypse via *Twin Peaks*," *Riot Material: Art. Word. Thought*, last modified 29 September 2017.
34. *Cf.* Gisela Fleischer, "Do You Really Want to Fuck with This? The Alternative Timeline of Sarah Palmer," *25 Years Later*, last modified 15 December 2017; Dylan Gilbert, "One & the Same: Judy/Mother/Experiment/Sarah Palmer," *Wel-*

come Back to Twin Peaks, last modified 9 July 2017; and u/dbz9. "[S3E14] Freeze Frame on Sarah May Reveal Something Familiar." *Reddit* Twin Peaks, 14 August 2017 (2:37 p.m.).

35. Booker, *Strange TV*, 120.
36. Mark Frost, *Twin Peaks: The Final Dossier* (New York, NY: Flatiron Books, 2017), 122.
37. Brien Allen, "The White of the Eyes: Revisiting Judy as Metaphor," *25 Years Later*, last modified 26 November 2017.
38. Ibid.
39. Dennis Lim, "Donald Trump's America and the Visions of David Lynch," *The New Yorker*, last modified 29 June 2018.
40. Lim, "Donald Trump's America."
41. Lim, "Donald Trump's America."
42. Cathy Caruth, *Unclaimed Experience: Trauma, Narrative, and History* (Baltimore, MD: Johns Hopkins University Press, 1996), 4.
43. Caruth, *Unclaimed Experience*, 6.
44. Caruth, *Unclaimed Experience*, 31
45. Caruth, *Unclaimed Experience*, 39
46. David Lynch, *Lynch on Lynch*, 4.
47. Herman Kahn, *Thinking about the Unthinkable* (New York, NY: Horizon Press, 1962),19.
48. Ian Morris, "The New Nuclear Age: a Journey Into the Unknown," *Forbes*, last modified 25 January 2018.

WORKS CITED

Adorno, Theodor W. *Prisms*. Cambridge, MA: MIT Press, 1967.

Allen, Brien. "The White of the Eyes: Revisiting Judy as Metaphor." *25 Years Later*. Last modified 26 November 2017. 25yearslatersite.com/2017/11/26/the-white-of-the-eyes-revisiting-judy-as-a-metaphor/.

Baudrillard, Jean. *Simulacra and Simulation*. Translated by Sheila Faria Glaser. Ann Arbor: University of Michigan Press, 1994.

Blake, Linnie. "Trapped in the Hysterical Sublime: *Twin Peaks*, Postmodernism, and the Neoliberal Now." In *Return to* Twin Peaks: *New Approaches to Materiality, Theory, and Genre on Television*, edited by Jeffery Andrews Weinstock and Catherine Spooner, 229–245. New York, NY: Palgrave Macmillan, 2015.

Booker, M. K. *Strange TV: Innovative Television Series from the* Twilight Zone *to the* X-Files. Westport, CT: Greenwood Press, 2002.

Burke, Edmund. *A Philosophical Enquiry into the Origin of Our Ideas of the Sublime and Beautiful*. Edited by Adam Phillips, Oxford: Oxford University Press, [1796] 2008.

Carroll, Rory. "David Lynch: 'You Gotta Be Selfish. It's a Terrible Thing.'" *The Guardian*. Last modified 23 June 2018. https://www.theguardian.com/film/2018/jun/23/david-lynch-gotta-be-selfish-twin-peaks.

Caruth, Cathy. *Unclaimed Experience: Trauma, Narrative, and History*. Baltimore, MD: Johns Hopkins University press, 1996.

Cordle, Daniel. "Cultures of Terror: Nuclear Criticism During and Since the Cold War." *Literature Compass* 3, no. 6 (2006): 1186–99.

Fleischer, Gisela. "Do You Really Want to Fuck with This? The Alternative Timeline of Sarah Palmer." *25 Years Later*. Last modified 15 December 2017. 25yearslatersite.com/2017/12/15/do-you-really-want-to-fuck-with-this-the-alternative-timeline-of-sarah-palmer/.

Frost, Mark. "I'm Mark Frost, co-creator of *Twin Peaks* and author." *Reddit* Twin Peaks, 8 November 2017 (2:06 p.m.). reddit.com/r/twinpeaks/comments/7bn45h/im_mark_frost_cocreator_of_twin_peaks_and_author/.

———. *The Secret History of Twin Peaks*. New York, NY: Flatiron Books, 2016.

———. *Twin Peaks: The Final Dossier*. New York, NY: Flatiron Books, 2017.

———, and David Lynch, creators. *Twin Peaks*. 1990–91. Lynch/Frost Productions, Propaganda Films, Spelling Television. DVD.

Fukuyama, Francis. "The End of History?" In *The Geopolitics Reader*, edited by Simon Dalby et al., 113–24. Abingdon, UK: Routledge, 2003.

Gilbert, Dylan. "One & the Same: Judy/Mother/Experiment/Sarah Palmer." *Welcome Back to* Twin Peaks. Last modified 09 July 2017. welcometotwinpeaks.com/discuss/twin-peaks-part-17–part-18/one-the-same-judymotherexperimentsarah-palmer/.

Haberman, Clyde. "'This is Not a Drill': The Threat of Nuclear Annihilation." *The New York Times*. Last modified 13 May 2018. nytimes.com/2018/05/13/us/nuclear-threat-retro-report.html.

Huddleston, Tom. "*Twin Peaks*: Was This the Long, Perfect Goodbye from David Lynch?" *The Guardian*. Last modified 6 September 2017. theguardian.com/tv-and-radio/2017/sep/06/twin-peaks-was-this-the-long-perfect-goodbye-from-david-lynch.

Kahn, Herman. *Thinking about the Unthinkable*. New York, NY: Horizon Press, 1962.

Kenny, Glenn. "David Lynch Weaves Film History into *Twin Peaks: The Return*." *The New York Times*. Last modified 13 July 2017. nytimes.com/2017/07/13/arts/television/david-lynch-weaves-film-history-into-twin-peaks-the-return.html.

Lim, Dennis. "Donald Trump's America and the Visions of David Lynch." *The New Yorker*. Last modified 29 June 2018. newyorker.com/culture/culture-desk/donald-trumps-america-and-the-visions-of-david-lynch.

Lovatt, Deborah. "A Terrible Beauty: The Nuclear Sublime in Philip Ridley's *The Reflecting Skin* (1991)." *European Journal of American Culture* 21, no. 3 (2002): 133–44.

Lybarger, Jeremy. "The Threat of Nuclear War." *American Psychological Association* 49, no. 3 (March 2018): 20. apa.org/monitor/2018/03/nuclear-war.aspx.

Lynch, David. "Dear Mr. President." *Facebook*. 26 June 2018 (3:08 p.m.), facebook.com/davidlynchofficial/posts/1800909923291220.

———, dir. *Eraserhead*. 1997. American Film Institute. DVD.

———. *Lynch on Lynch*. Edited by Chris Rodley. Faber & Faber, 2005.

———, and Mark Frost, creators. *Twin Peaks: The Return*. 2017. Rancho Rosa Partnership, Lynch/Frost Productions. DVD.

Morris, Ian. "The New Nuclear Age: A Journey into the Unknown." *Forbes*. Last modified 25 January 2018. forbes.com/sites/stratfor/2018/01/25/the-new-nuclear-age-a-journey-into-the-unknown/#3960fce21a6d

Nicholls, Jack. "How David Lynch Never Learned to Stop Worrying and Love the Bomb." *Medium*. Last modified 26 June 2017. medium.com/@jacknicholls/

twin-peaks-or-how-david-lynch-never-learned-to-stop-worrying-and-love-the-bomb-10bbacc83b8e.

Nine Inch Nails. "She's Gone Away." Released December 2016. Track 3 on *Not the Actual Events*, The Null Corporation. Compact disc.

Penderecki, Krzysztof. "Threnody for the Victims of Hiroshima." Released September 2017. Track 10 on *Twin Peaks: Limited Event Series Original Soundtrack*. Rhino. Compact disc.

Porter, Benjamin. "The Subtle Yet Sharp Politics of *Twin Peaks: The Return*." *The Aggie*. Last modified 10 June 2018. theaggie.org/2018/06/10/the-subtle-yet-sharp-politics-of-twin-peaks-the-return/.

Rengifo, Alci. "David Lynch's Dadaist Apocalypse via *Twin Peaks*." *Riot Material: Art. Word. Thought*. Last modified 29 September 2017. riotmaterial.com/david-lynchs-dadaist-apocalypse-via-twin-peaks/.

Rogers, Jason. *My Love Affair with David Lynch and Peachy Like Nietzsche: Dark Clown Porn Snuff for Terrorists and Gorefiends*. Lulu Press, 2005.

u/dbz9. "[S3E14] Freeze Frame on Sarah May Reveal Something Familiar." *Reddit*, 14 August 2017 (2:37 p.m.). reddit.com/r/twinpeaks/comments/6to11i/s3e14_freeze_frame_on_sarah_may_reveal_something/.

United States, Office of the Press Secretary. "Remarks by President Trump before a Briefing on the Opioid Crisis." The White House. Last modified 8 August 2017. whitehouse.gov/briefings-statements/remarks-president-trump-briefing-opioid-crisis/.

Wilson, Rob. "Techno-Euphoria and the Discourse of the American Sublime." *Boundary 2* 19, no. 1 (1992): 205–29.

Two

Is It Future or Is It Past?

The Politics and Use of Nostalgia in Twin Peaks

Amanda DiPaolo

From the vintage looks of the Double R Diner, the clothes, the musical score, and the abundance of stay-at-home moms, *Twin Peaks* sometimes felt like a portal to the 1950s. In all its darkness and duality, the little town with a small population (51, 201) felt cozy, with its quirkiness and retro looks. Such an aesthetic may, in fact, explain the show's initial success.[1] If the original run of *Twin Peaks* was a celebration of nostalgia, *Twin Peaks: The Return* warned about such predilections. David Lynch's return to television, and the director's chair, cements the uncomfortable reality that you can never truly go back home.

Twenty-five years after Laura Palmer told Agent Dale Cooper that she would see him again in a quarter century, it was announced that *Twin Peaks* was being revived by Showtime in the most nostalgic of ways. On October 4, 2014 at 11:30 am, show creators David Lynch and Mark Frost simultaneously tweeted "Dear Twitter friends: That gum you like is going to come back in style. #damnfinecoffee."[2] You could forgive a long-suffering fan of the series for feeling not only excitement, but also nostalgia at seeing such an iconic phrase from the show's original run appear on their Twitter feeds. You could also forgive the viewer for wanting a return to the original *Twin Peaks* with its melodrama and campy feel. *The Return* begins as the original ended: Laura Palmer, or a doppelganger, telling Agent Cooper she'll meet him again in 25 years. The familiar shot of the screaming student running across the high school courtyard is repeated from April 8, 1990's premiere episode and Laura Palmer's high school photo is shown on screen as an updated rendition of the beloved theme by Angelo Badalamenti kicks in. But the tease of a return to 1990s *Twin Peaks* is just that: a tease. By only showing glimpses into the lives of the familiar characters, we learn that a return is not what we needed, nor could the show have worked as fan service alone.

The Return places focus on loss and change, reminding the viewer that one's understanding of the past falters as time goes on. It certainly felt as though "Lynch [had] weaponized our longing to come home to the Twin Peaks we remembered."[3] His refusal to merely placate fans, while at the same time making *The Return* arguably better than its predecessor,[4] puts a spotlight on the problem of both staying static and yearning for a past that never existed. The relevance of such a point can be felt beyond the television screen, as nostalgia has become deeply rooted in American politics with its ability to allow one to hold onto their perceived vision of a cultural identity when there is a lack of confidence in the present.[5] This chapter examines the nature of nostalgia in American politics and culture, and how it is showcased throughout *Twin Peaks* and *Twin Peaks: The Return*. First, I examine nostalgia's intimate connection to loss regarding both time and the individual's sense of community and social acceptance. Second, I explore how the original series exemplifies the use of nostalgia as a coping mechanism when distress becomes unbearable. Finally, I examine the refutation of nostalgia in *Twin Peaks: The Return*. Ultimately, it becomes clear that nostalgia is not something to be rejected, but rather employed in the right fashion for the right reasons.

THE NATURE OF NOSTALGIA

Nostalgia was originally conceptualized as a medical term described as a "painful yearning to return home" and was commonly suffered by deployed soldiers.[6] In recent decades, nostalgia has been considered equal parts "positively toned evocation of a lived past"[7] and "wistful mood that may be prompted by an object, scene, a smell, or a strain of music."[8] It is a feeling, an emotion prompted by "reflection on things (objects, persons, experiences, ideas) associated" with our memories of the past.[9] This is problematic. Memories we think we have may not be reflective of our lived reality. As we age, we tend to idealize the past and often misremember what once was, resulting in an erroneously positive picture of a time gone by.[10] To feel nostalgic is such a natural occurrence that it is not exclusively reserved for those away from home or individuals of a certain age, but rather even features youth yearning for decades they were either too young to vividly remember or have never lived through to begin with.[11] Holbrook and Schindler point to a range of objects often seen through a nostalgic lens, citing pop cultural phenomena such as music, fashion, and film stars.[12] Psychologists suggest that the phenomenon of nostalgia is both universal and pervasive, but Alastair Bonnett points out that it is often "presented as a product of modernity, a direct response to a historically specific condition … characterized by change and a far more intense and urgent relationship with loss."[13] Nostalgia in a politically charged setting is most commonly appealed to when there is a (perceived) sudden change in society.

Nostalgia in the American context is not new and has been deployed as a strategy in politics for some time.[14] It can, in fact, be a deeply political tool used by both conservative and liberal politicians.[15] When the present seems bleak, we reach to the past for perceived better days. Nostalgia can be seen embodied in small-town America and is used by populist politicians who appeal to a specific narrative of nostalgia. James E. Combs argues:

> The politics of nostalgia asks for historical unlearning, suggesting not a wiser but rather a childish innocence. The popular covenant of the Town is a pact with youth and not maturity. The Town was the epic journey's end of the American quest, a domestic epic of the establishment of perfect symmetry. But such a completion of the human popular order suggests that everything that comes after is burdened with the corruption of time.[16]

The Trump campaign appealed to this notion of American nostalgia to foster support. Prior to the 2016 election, the annual American Values Survey revealed that 51 percent of the population believed "the American way of life has changed for the worse since the 1950s. Further, seven in ten likely Donald Trump voters said American society has gotten worse since that romanticized decade."[17] The romanticization of the 1950s and small-town America should be considered an oddity given that rural living itself is out of step with population trends in the United States. By 2016, only 19.3 percent (60 million) of the U.S. population lives in rural communities, despite 97 percent of the land area being rural.[18] These numbers have not changed much since the original airing of *Twin Peaks* with just 25 percent of the country's population living in rural areas at the time.[19]

Lynch's work has long been influenced by the 1950s specifically, and his reverence for the decade is evident. In the introductory scenes of *The Art Life* documentary, Lynch states that "I think every time you do something like a painting, or whatever, you go with ideas—sometimes the past can conjure those ideas. And even if they are new ideas, the past colors them."[20] It is not surprising that he longs for the past considering the way he describes his childhood: "When I look back, I had tremendous freedom. Nobody was overbearing. It's as if there was just a foundation of love." Born in 1946, Lynch's first memories were likely the 1950s and his emphasis on that decade coincides with his perceived memories of his past. "It was a fantastic decade in a lot of ways," Lynch said in Chris Rodley's interview book *Lynch on Lynch*, before going into a monologue about cars being "made by the right people" with the right design, despite their poor gas mileage and lack of safety features.[21] That contradiction between memory of feeling and emotion with specific facts is largely the point with nostalgia. Lynch speaks as though he desires a return to the oft-admired decade, ignoring its obvious failings. "It was a really hopeful time, and things were going up instead of going down. You got the feeling you could do anything. The future was bright," Lynch continues. "Little did we know we were laying the groundwork for a disastrous future," he laments, acknowledging all the problems currently plaguing society were present at that supposedly hopeful time.[22] This unfortunate branding of nostalgia allows memory to erase the historical legacy of colonialism and slavery in American culture, ignoring "pressing issues like the growing education and wage gap, police violence, discrimination and other acts of violence."[23] The rise of Trump coincides with the preeminence of this particular view of a nostalgic American public that ignores the reality of the nation's history allowing for "the poor [to be] labeled as 'lazy' instead of victims of centuries of systemic discrimination, im/migrants [to] become 'rapists' and 'drug dealers' instead of parents desperate to give their families a fighting chance at educational and financial opportunities."[24]

A return to the way of life in the 1950s would be a nightmare for many. The original run of *Twin Peaks* reflects Lynch's dichotomy, as it calls attention to the horrors while basking in 1950s aesthetic. With the town's dark secrets and rampant crime, the shiny exterior captures the heart and imagination of character and viewer alike. Upon closer examination, however, the lives of the Twin Peaks townsfolk are filled with sorrow, garmonbozia if you will. It is from within this distress that nostalgia finds a home. Bankrupt of goodness, Twin Peaks leaves its residents void of hope for a decent future. *The Return* showcases the reality that this lack of a decent future for most has indeed played out by offering "both a revisionist interrogation of *Twin Peaks'* earlier incarnation" this time dropping the alluring appeal of the glamorized decade, "*and* a surreal refraction of the politically emaciated culture and bleak socio-economic conditions which led inexorably to Trump's election."[25]

THE NOSTALGIA OF *TWIN PEAKS*

Twin Peaks features the typical small-town clichés viewers expect, including the biker (James Hurley), the dumb, loveable deputy (Andy Brennan), the lack of current technology, beautiful scenery, and disrespect from the nearby big city official (Albert Rosenfield). But it was more than just the small-town feel that made *Twin Peaks* the perfect breeding ground for nostalgia, so much so that Agent Cooper himself noted it was "a way of living I thought had vanished from the earth" (1.3). Cooper took notice how each life seemed to have meaning and was important to the citizens of the town. There was also the placement of loss and sadness in nostalgia itself that was featured so prominently.[26] And, like *Blue Velvet* before it, in perhaps an internal acknowledgment that this dreamlike vision of the 1950s is not real, Lynchian small-town America is "frightening, bizarre, filled with secrets, engulfed in dread and desire."[27] The town, and in fact nostalgia itself, serves as a form of manipulation as is evident in how both our FBI protagonist as well as the viewers at home fell for the fictional small rural town in the Pacific Northwest. Despite the murders, the violence against women, and the general lack of progress, Twin Peaks is a place where we can see ourselves living, a sentiment shared even by Cooper who investigates buying property nearby (2.12), and this after the murderer of Laura is revealed to be her sexually abusive father Leland Palmer (2.7).

Not everyone overlooked the obvious horror of the time, and warnings were given. Judge Clinton Sternwood asks Cooper about his stay in Twin Peaks. Cooper replies "Heaven" to which Judge Sternwood reminds our hero FBI Agent that "this week heaven includes arson, multiple homicides, and an attempt on the life of a federal agent" (2:4). Lynch may feel an authentic reverence towards an idealized vision of the American past, but his characters betray him as Judge Sternwood is warning the viewer to be wary of our nostalgic feelings as they are as deceptive as the town itself. Cooper, like the rest of us, ignores the warning and carries on, even telling Sheriff Truman that he is "really going to miss this place," after hearing about the political squabbles between brothers, one the mayor and the other the publisher of the town's only newspaper (2.10). This delusion is also expressed by DEA agent Denise Bryson, sent to Twin Peaks to investigate allegations made against Cooper by the Canadian RCMP. She, too, finds it "hard to imagine" any crime being committed in Twin Peaks. "I picture you chasing lost dogs and locking up the town drunk," she admits (2.11).

In the original run of *Twin Peaks*, the use of nostalgia, however, is two-fold. For the viewer, our own sense of Americana and the perceived golden age portrayed by the town, sounds, and its residents made us want more of the same. Indeed, we craved all the town of Twin Peaks had to offer, ignoring the surrounding reality of the characters being portrayed in it. Yet, outside of Cooper and other federal law enforcement visitors, for those very residents of the town itself, nostalgia's best use is exemplified as a coping mechanism for people who have lived through various degrees of stress and trauma. Just as nostalgia can be used to warp reality and concoct a nonexistent reality, it is also a coping mechanism used in response to pain or distress, triggered by loneliness and a sense of meaninglessness.[28] When remembering the past, over time, people filter out negative and painful memories, and as a result, "our past is constantly shifting to accommodate our present."[29] The cognitive function can be used to help us maintain self-continuity, or a sense of one constant self, "a permanent, unchanging self underneath the random events and crises that transform our circumstances over the years," protecting the self from disjuncture.[30]

Interestingly, it is the program's villains that exemplify the use of nostalgia in this way. Tied to views of an American culture of the past as a coping mechanism, Leland and Benjamin Horne both employ the mechanisms of nostalgia to cope with the various losses, distresses, and self-blame in their lives. Leland, having fallen prey to the Black Lodge entity BOB and subsequently sexually assaulting and murdering his daughter, uses music from his childhood as a coping mechanism. After "learning" of Laura's murder, Leland dances to Glenn Miller's 1940 hit *Pennsylvania 6–5000* with a photo of Laura in hand. "We have to dance for Laura," Leland says to his wife Sarah, spinning while holding the framed photo until Sarah begins to struggle with him to wrestle the photo away (1.3). The picture ultimately shatters, becoming a representation of the fragility of Laura's life, as both were broken by her father. With the loss of his only child, and his perceived lack of culpability in her death, Leland clings to comfortable feelings from his own youth, allowing nostalgia to "serve as an existential function by bolstering a sense of meaning in life."[31] Additionally, according to terror management theory, "people turn to meaning-providing structures to cope with the knowledge of inevitable mortality."[32]

A similar scene plays out when Leland breaks down at the Great Northern Hotel, asking all the guests: "somebody dance with me" (1.4). And again, at a Ghostwood Development event, Leland interrupts Jerry Horne's speech to the Norwegian investors. As Jerry speaks, loud music begins to play. Leland seems to be dancing but is in fact mourning his daughter. Hands up to his head and swaying around, Catherine Martell steps in to mimic his moves of distress at the behest of Ben. Other guests of the event join in, unaware that they are witnessing a father breaking down over the loss of his daughter to songs of an era gone by—a time when Leland's life may have been simpler. Perhaps the old songs of the 1940s and 1950s remind Leland of a time before he succumbed to BOB on Pearl Lakes as a boy (2.7). The use of music as a coping mechanism for Leland again manifests itself after he kills Jacques Renault. Upon hearing from the sheriff's department that Renault had been arrested as a person of interest in the murder of Laura, Leland goes to the hospital where Jacques is recovering from a gunshot wound to smother him in his sleep. The following morning, Leland, hair now white, gleefully greets the day singing The Pied Piper's 1944 hit *Mairzy Doats*, with a sense of lightness and relief (2.1). The song, based on a nursery rhyme, could have been a song Leland was sung as a child, and the killing of Renault was like a rebirth for Leland after he erroneously thought he got revenge for the murder of his daughter. Maddy's death provides a contrast to examples of Leland's use of nostalgia. With Louis Armstrong's *What a Wonderful World* playing on the phonograph, Maddy (Laura's look-a-like cousin who had been staying with the Palmers since her cousin's murder), informs her aunt and uncle that it was time for her to return home to Missoula, Montana.

As the announcement is made, Leland has a forlorn look, putting his paper down. Leland understands, he says, but is in fact plotting her murder. Maddy will never leave Twin Peaks (2.7). Later that night, with each skip of a now silent phonograph—marking the end of the music as well as Maddy's life—the audience sees Leland look in the mirror, but it is BOB who looks back at us. Revealing for the first time who killed Laura Palmer, BOB waits for Maddy to come down the stairs. As she enters the room, BOB chases, strangles, and punches Maddy in the face. During this brutal scene of violence and implied sexual assault, Leland begins to moan for Laura as he holds Maddy in his arms while she cries for her life. As he spins around slowly, in this moment Leland does have agency over his own actions before BOB again takes over and states "Leland says you're going back to Missoula," before smashing her face against a framed picture on the wall. There is no music, no coping, and no nostalgia. There is just pure destruction as Leland sinks further into a state of distress and meaninglessness.

Benjamin Horne, too, employs the mechanisms of nostalgia to cope with his own stresses after falsely being arrested for the murder of Laura, losing the Ghostwood development project's land to Catherine in exchange for an alibi, and having lost control of his brothel, One-Eyed Jack's. Horne, also owner of the Great Northern Hotel and Horne's Department Store, fondly remembers his childhood as he slides further and further into a nervous breakdown. Watching black and white footage of the groundbreaking for building the Great Northern Hotel when he was a child, with his unshaven face, Ben longs for the feelings of joy from his childhood that are now missing from his life. Ben smiles and laughs at the images of himself as a happy child, as tears well in his eyes. He stands to get a closer look at the black and white film; Ben quotes Shakespeare stating, "Now is the winter of our discontent, made glorious summer by this sun of York," the opening words of *Richard III* (2.11). In *Richard III*, the king is a deeply unhappy individual surrounded by people who truly dislike him. This description also describes Ben. His self-awareness in this moment prompted his gradual break from reality.

Feelings of loneliness can emerge when there is a lack of social support through community.[33] Ben's turn to the past marks an attempt to rectify this problem by evoking a nostalgic false reality whereby living through an ordeal where community building and social support were essential to survival. Ben envisions himself as Confederate general Robert E. Lee, recreating not only the Battle of Gettysburg, but also the sense of community he lacks.

While a focal point for Americana and nostalgia, Ben's recreation of the Battle of Gettysburg is his way of dealing with his lack of community and social acceptance. Dressed in full Civil War regalia, sword in hand and fake Southern accent in tow, Ben plays out the Civil War battle with elaborate miniature soldiers. At one stage of his breakdown, Catherine enters the room and Ben asks if she has come to gloat. "You have defeated me," he concedes to his former mistress, adding "as I have defeated General Meade," thus reversing his fortune (2.13). After proclaiming the time had come to finish the war by marching on Washington, D.C., Ben stands, turns on a fan for dramatic effect, grabs his Confederate flag and joins in with Dr. Lawrence Jacoby who is already singing the de facto Confederate national anthem, "Dixie" (2.14). In Horne's case, his trip down this memory lane never existed for him.

Figure 2.1. Episode 2.11 "Masked Ball"
Twin Peaks

He was not a Confederate soldier and is not even from the South. But by grasping onto this part of Americana and a romanticized nostalgia, Ben connects to a past America, rewriting history in the worst of ways. This is his attempt to fix his own past wrongs, as observed by Jacoby when he tells Ben's daughter Audrey and Bobby Briggs that "by reversing the South's defeat in the Civil War, he in turn will reverse his own emotional setback" (2.14). In a report by Dr. Jacoby in *The Secret History of Twin Peaks*, the psychiatrist explains that "he's assumed the side with the untenable moral position—attempting to alter or erase his own personal, and questionable, recent behavior."[34]

Once the war is won and the rewriting of history is complete with a Confederacy victory, Ben returns and speaks about his breakdown as if it had been a dream, a misremembering of the past that just occurred. "It was incredible," Ben says. "There was a war, and I was General Robert E. Lee and somehow in spite of incredible odds, I won," he proclaims, acknowledging that he is now home and feeling terrific (2.15). By glorifying an era that was awful for those living through it, the audience rolls its eyes at the storyline as one of the more ridiculous of the second season, but Ben's fascination with the Confederacy and the Civil War showcases how reaching for the old in troubled times allows individuals to cope with their own feelings of hopelessness. There is a role for nostalgia in our lives. Despite the use of two villains to demonstrate the point, feelings of depression, loneliness, and despair can be therapeutically helped with a turn to a revered past. Having said that, however, when nostalgia is glorified and heralded as the gold standard to achieve an ideal society, the usefulness of nostalgia ends and its dangers begin.

The Civil War storyline also highlights a dangerous theme in American politics today. Modern Americans idealize times of war, and build irrational attachments to historical figures, many of whom have committed heinous acts. People protesting the removal of Civil War statues view the action as an attempt to erase history, rather than admonishing America's history as a slave-holding nation.[35] The United States is not alone in holding a romanticized view of past wrongs. In Canada, a decision to remove a statue of first prime minister Sir John A. MacDonald due to his role in establishing residential schools (which saw about 150,000 indigenous children taken away from their family and culture) has been met with a divided crowd, as though the removal of such statues would somehow erase his role in the founding of Canada.[36] These oft irrational and glorified attachments to historical figures and moments in time underline the hard truth that in our everyday lives, there is no returning to a past time. This reality is nicely showcased in *Twin Peaks: The Return*.

STARTING POSITIONS: RETURNING TO *TWIN PEAKS*

In one of the most memorable scenes from *The Return*, Mr. C, the evil version of Cooper that left the Black Lodge all those years ago, makes his way to "the farm" to confront his former associate Ray Monroe. A gang of men await Mr. C upon his arrival, where he is quickly challenged to an arm wrestling match by the leader of the group, Renzo. Winner keeps Ray, loser meets death. Outmatched in size and muscle, it seemed like an easy victory for Renzo, but Mr. C toyed with the muscular group leader. "It hurt my arm when you moved it down here," Mr. C said moving his arm down towards the table, "but it really hurt when you moved it down here," again moving his own arm ever so close to hitting the table (3.13). Mr. C then proclaims that his arm felt better at a "starting position," moving their locked arms back to an upright position. While toying with Renzo, the viewer is also toyed with wanting nothing more than the return of their hero, the quirky, fun-loving Agent Cooper. It feels good in starting position, indeed, but part of growing is knowing when to evolve or walk away.

If the original series run is a service to nostalgia for the viewer, *Twin Peaks: The Return* fights the appeal of that starting position. Beyond the way the town of Twin Peaks is portrayed itself, the show also refuses to stay there, expanding the show's universe to Las Vegas, South Dakota, and Texas. In the first episode of *The Return*, the viewer is greeted with a great deal of the town that was so essential to the program's original run, but it quickly becomes clear that the plot would not be advanced through observances of the everyday lives of our beloved characters. The rants of Dr. Jacoby, now Dr. Amp, serve no real purpose to the plot, other than offering a message on the state of the political world and the economy. Lucy Moran, now Brennan, the receptionist at the sheriff's office, is the same Lucy, married to Andy. Hawk is now second in command and is told by Margaret Lanterman, the Log Lady, that something is missing that pertains to his heritage, but this never materializes the way it could in terms of plot development as evidenced by the fact that Cooper finds his way back to *Twin Peaks* on his own. And brothers Ben and Jerry are reintroduced to the viewer. Ben is divorced, spends all his time in his office of the Great Northern Hotel, and is trying to be a better man, presumably after losing contact with his daughter Audrey, as outlined in Mark Frost's *Twin Peaks: The Final Dossier, A Novel*.[37] Jerry has invested in cannabis and goes on a solo adventure in the woods, sampling his products. None of these side plots truly advance the story told in *The Return*, but the viewer is given just enough of the original characters and the town itself to feel the nostalgia they were expecting.

Lynch offers up morsels of this nostalgia for the original *Twin Peaks* during the first few episodes, with characters being reintroduced one by one accumulating with the reintroduction of both Bobby, now a deputy, and "Laura's Theme," the beautifully written score by Badalamenti. Tears stroll down Bobby's face as he catches a glimpse of the original photo of Laura now made famous by the series, as it sat on the conference-room table where Sheriff Truman and Agent Cooper once interrogated him as a suspect in her murder. "Man, brings back some memories," Briggs says speaking not only for himself, but also the viewer patiently (3.4).

As the season progresses, it becomes evident that for the town of Twin Peaks itself, the more things change, the more they stay the same. With the passage of time, however, the viewer is slowly shown that things staying the same in no way has worked out for the residents of the tired town. Norma and Ed are, initially, still not together. High school lovebirds Shelly and Bobby had married but are now divorced. Shelly appears to be in a new relationship with Red, just another bad boy running drugs through town, not unlike Leo Johnson. Shelly and Bobby's daughter, Becky, seems to be repeating mistakes of her mother's past. Becky is married to an unfaithful abuser and drug addict, Steven Burnett. Unable to hold down a job, we see his job interview with Mike Nelson, the one-time high school best friend of Bobby. Now a businessman, he scolds the younger version of his past self by informing Steve that his job application was a mess.

Mike and Bobby seemed helpless in the first two seasons of *Twin Peaks*; their resiliency and adaptability serve a reminder that change can be good. The world of *Twin Peaks* appears to be one where time has weathered most residents, most lacking the self-awareness that is necessary to grow. The sad reality for many residents is that they remain at the exact starting position of the show's original run, exemplifying how our desire to return to this world and the idealized vision of small-town America was never the small-town America worth living in. The benefits of self-awareness play out on screen when Nadine, now owning the silent drape store she dreamed of, takes a long walk to freedom, confronting Ed at his gas farm proclaiming, "I want you to be free," and "run to her, enjoy the rest of your lives together" (3.15). By giving Ed his freedom to be with Norma, Nadine was in fact freeing herself of an idealized vision of a marriage that was mostly a mirage, something Ed and Norma both failed to do on their own.

THE RETURN OF COOPER

The reality of being nostalgic may best be played out on screen in *The Return* by Dougie Jones, the manufactured insurance underwriter created to catch Cooper upon his release from the Black Lodge, allowing Mr. C to continue to wreak havoc out of the Lodge. Dougie's portrayal of nostalgia is important for two reasons. First, Dougie confronts the audience's desire for the old *Twin Peaks* by not only withholding Cooper from the viewer for 16 hours, but also in the surreal interaction with the audience each time Dougie recognizes key elements that are associated with the original run such as coffee and cherry pie. We are repeatedly teased by Lynch and Frost as Dougie would recognize law enforcement characteristics such as shiny badges, case files, and the American flag.

Second, Dougie Jones is reminiscent of something much bigger than a frustration for the return of Cooper, and everything that his character once represented. Jones exemplifies loss, and his actions are like those of someone who time has escaped. Dougie is said to have good days and bad days and is treated with kindness by everyone who encounters him, from co-workers to complete strangers. One of the more stunning examples is the care in which Dougie is treated by a cop who picks him up for loitering by a statue at night, returning him to his residence reminiscent of an individual suffering from memory loss who has wandered away from home and unable to return. The frustrations with futile attempts to re-create a longed for past bubbles over when Dougie is being driven to work by his wife, Janey-E. Looking at his son, tears well in his eyes. His heartbreak in that moment echoes the heartbreak of anyone lingering upon cherished memories. And yet, Janey-E. may be speaking on behalf of all viewers, longing for their hero's return, when she says, "You're acting weird as shit" (3:4). She does not have the same memory as Cooper or the viewer of what used to be, so Janey-E sees his behavior as bizarre. It is as though Janey-E is a first-time viewer of *Twin Peaks*, but began with *The Return*, thus not having the institutional memory that made the Dougie Jones story so frustrating to watch in the first place.

Lynch's refusal to bring Cooper out of his fugue-like state of Dougie until episode 16 is a message regarding the dangers of nostalgia. It has been 25 years since Dale Cooper entered the Black Lodge. Why did we expect the same Dale Cooper to emerge all these years later? As viewer discontent with the Dougie storyline continued, reminders of Cooper played out in frustrating fashion. But returning to starting position with Cooper doesn't work out. Despite a great return to the screen proclaiming "I am the FBI," and immediately taking control of the situation with decisiveness, again, the expected payoff never truly materializes. By time *The Return* concludes, it is evident that the program was presented to us the only way Lynch knew how, by pointing out that what works for *Twin Peaks* in 1990 could not work today.

The final two hours of *The Return* illustrate the futility of nostalgia in terms of wanting to re-create a past. In episode 17, Cooper in fact goes back to a time that took place during *Fire Walk with Me*, to the night before Laura was murdered. With Laura in the woods speaking to James regarding her fears that her father would kill him, too, Laura sees Cooper lurking in the woods and screams. After telling Cooper she has seen him in her dream, he reaches out for Laura and she tentatively takes his hand. She asks where they are going and Cooper replies, "We're going home" (3.17). The first scenes of the original run of *Twin Peaks* is played, and Pete Martell does not find Palmer wrapped in plastic on the water shore. He goes fishing. As the penultimate episode of *The Return* concludes, we return to the Roadhouse, like so many episodes before. Foreshadowing Cooper's pending failures, Julee Cruise is singing *The World Spins*, as she had done before Maddy was murdered. This home Cooper speaks of is not to the Palmer residence or the White Lodge. Laura ends up being in Odessa, Texas, where she lives as Carrie Page: All traces of Laura Palmer are gone. Cooper has no reason to go to the town of Twin Peaks at all. There is no murder to investigate. Remarkably, Lynch erases our beloved series with a few small tweaks.

As the final episode progresses, we see Cooper travel to Odessa, Texas to where he believes he can find Laura, but instead finds Carrie. Carrie looks exactly like Laura. After convincing her to travel to Twin Peaks with him, Cooper and Carrie knock on the door of the Palmer house, but an unknown woman answers. Her last name is Tremond. The previous owners were Chalfonts. (These surnames are familiar because Tremond appears in the original run of the series as an elderly neighbor of Harold Smith, and Mrs. Chalfont is the same elderly woman who gives Laura a painting of the room above the convenience store in *Fire Walk with Me*.) The one-armed man and the evolution of the arm asking, "Is it future or is it past?" comes to mind here, as it must have for Cooper, too, because he asks "What year is this?" (3.18) Carrie screams and the screen turns to black. The question is never quite answered, but one thing becomes clear; if our desires include holding onto the past and to return to it, this will affect both our present and future.

Cooper failed to free Laura. Traveling in time didn't work. We are surprised Cooper failed after the journey Lynch and Frost take us through during *The Return*, but perhaps we shouldn't be. Maybe he wasn't a great FBI agent to begin with, despite our misplaced allegiance to the lawman. After all, he fails to question Leland in the disappearance of his daughter, ultimately allowing BOB to kill again. "It is happening ... again," the Giant tells Cooper, interrupting Julee Cruise's *The World Spins* and seemingly stopping time itself. As Cruise resumes singing, the elderly waiter slowly walks over to Cooper and empathetically says "I am so sorry," as he pats him on the shoulder (2.7). The waiter is looking at Cooper as someone might look at a friend or family member who has lost a loved one. The profound sense of loss and dread in this scene is both palpable and indicative of Cooper's inability to stop BOB from taking the life of another teenage girl. Cooper knows it. And yet, 25 years later we expect a different result. He is not the FBI agent we (mis)remembered him to be. Such a sensation feels like ... well, nostalgia, doesn't it?

CONCLUSION

We tend to misremember (or idealize) the good and forget the bad. Lynch shows the dangers of nostalgia by shining a light on the citizens of Twin Peaks, exposing that an actual return to the past is not as ideal as it may seem. In many ways, Lynch denies the viewer what they originally tuned in to *The Return* to see. Instead, we see glimpses of the original cast in a way that does not truly advance the overall plot of the story. In doing this, Lynch shows that what was old was not worth returning to. He reinforces that notion by getting the audience invested in the new storylines, the feel, and overall presentation of *Twin Peaks'* revival. By going on the journey with Lynch and Frost, the viewer soon sees that the investment was worth it. Building off the original in context of the modern did a better service to the show that any return to *Twin Peaks* in its original format could have achieved. The point is not to avoid being nostalgic; such feelings may be unavoidable. However, we can learn to be nostalgic for the right things, at the right time, and in the right way, or in other words, be prudent about how we are nostalgic.[38] Yet it may be more prudent to forget because instead of "setting us free to face our situation, accurate recollection can trap us in the bitterness and conflict of the past."[39] Before exiting the red room, Cooper asks, "When can I leave?" (3:2) As Laura whispers a reply in his ear, Cooper offers a slight gasp that is shown again during the closing credits after the final episode of *The Return*, once we know that Cooper's efforts have been in vain. What did she whisper? Could it be that she informs him he has left "time and time again," only to fail and return to his starting position? "Time and time again," was this phrase, stated by the evolution of the arm as Cooper prepares to leave the Red Room for what seemed to be the first time in 25 years, a warning? One thing is clear: Cooper is trapped in the bitterness of the past with no way out, or in other words, no way to forget.

NOTES

1. Peter Hoskin, "*Twin Peaks*: The Ultimate Study in Nostalgia," *The Spectator*, last modified May 13, 2017, https://www.spectator.co.uk/2017/05/twin-peaks-the-ultimate-study-in-nostalgia/.

2. David Lynch, Twitter post, October 4, 2014, 10:30 am, https://twitter.com/david_lynch/status/518060411690569730?lang=en; and Mark Frost, Twitter Post, October 4, 2014, 10:30 am, https://twitter.com/mfrost11/status/518060486156230656?lang=en.

3. Laura Bogart, "How the *Twin Peaks* Revival Weaponized Our Longing for Homecoming," *The Week*, last modified September 1, 2017, http://theweek.com/articles/715796/how-twin-peaks-revival-weaponized-longing-homecoming.

4. Stewart Heritage, "Why the New *Twin Peaks* Is Way Better than the Original," *The Guardian*, last modified June 21, 2017, https://www.theguardian.com/tv-and-radio/2017/jun/21/why-the-new-twin-peaks-is-way-better-than-the-original

5. Griselda Pollock, *Conceptual Odysseys: Passages to Cultural Analysis* (London: I.B. Tauris, 2007), 120.

6. See Fred Davis, *Yearning for Yesterday: A Sociology of Nostalgia* (New York: The Free Press, 1979), 35; and Samuel Goldman, "The Legitimacy of Nostalgia," *Perspectives on Political Science* 45, no. 4 (2006): 211.

7. Russell W. Belk, "The Role of Possessions in Constructing and Maintaining a Sense of the Past," *Advances in Consumer Research* 17, (1990): 670.

8. Morris Holbrook and Robert Schnidler, "Echoes of the Dear Departed Past: Some Work in Progress on Nostalgia," *Advances in Consumer Research* 18 (1991): 330.

9. Goldman, "The Legitimacy of Nostalgia," 211.

10. Goldman, "The Legitimacy of Nostalgia," 212.

11. Sean Gammon, "Fantasy, Nostalgia and the Pursuit of What Never Was," in *Sport Tourism: Principles and Practice*, ed. Sean Gammon and Joseph Kurtzman (Eastbourne: Leisure Studies Association, 2002), 61.

12. Holbrook and Schnidler, "Echoes of the Dear Departed Past," 330.

13. Alistair Bonnett, *Left in the Past: Radicalism and the Politics of Nostalgia* (New York: Continuum, 2010), 19–20.

14. The United States had its first outbreak of nostalgia during the Civil War, with the cure being considered the battlefield (Goldman, 211). How fitting, then, that when Benjamin Horne in season 2 of *Twin Peaks* suffers a breakdown that he turns to the battlefield of the Civil War as his playground to cope with the trauma of his losses.

15. Nostalgia as a criticism of conservative movements has existed for a considerable time. Franklin Delano Roosevelt saw nostalgia as "an obstacle to the reorganization of society along rational lines (Goldman, 211)." As early as 1955, the new conservatism was being labeled as merely the "politics of nostalgia" (Goldman, 212, citing Arthur Schlesinger Jr. "The New Conservatism: Politics of Nostalgia," *The Reporter*, 1955, 9–12, reprinted in *The Politics of Hope*, Boston: Houghton Mifflin, 1963). Appeals to nostalgia led to the election of Ronald Reagan by "[appealing] to the side of Americans that want to feel good about their history, regardless of the unsettling facts" (Goldman, 211, citing Rick Perlstein, *The Invisible Bridge: The Fall of Nixon and the Rise of Reagan*, New York: Simon & Schuster, 2014, 166).

16. James E. Combs, *The Reagan Range: The Nostalgic Myth in American Politics*. (Bowling Green, OH: Bowling Green State University Popular Press, 1993), 38.

17. Mike Mariani, "How Nostalgia Made America Great Again: When the Present Looks Bleak, We Reach for a Rose-Tinted Past," *Nautilus*, last modified April 20, 2017, http://nautil.us/issue/47/consciousness/how-nostalgia-made-america-great-again.

18. United States Census Bureau, "New Census Data Show Differences between Urban and Rural Populations," last modified December 8, 2016, https://www.census.gov/newsroom/press-releases/2016/cb16-210.html.

19. United States Census Bureau, "Table 4. Population: 1790 to 1990—Census." Accessed September 15, 2018. https://www.census.gov/publication/census data/table-4.pdf.

20. *David Lynch: The Art Life*. Directed by Rick Barnes, Jon Nguyen, and Olivia Neergaard-Holm, (USA/Denmark: Criteria Collection, 2017).

21. David Lynch and Chris Rodley, *Lynch on Lynch*, rev. ed. (London: Faber, 2005), 4.

22. Lynch, *Lynch on Lynch*, 4.

23. Esther Suh, "The Racist Nostalgia behind 'Mak[ing] America Great Again,'" *Huffpost* (blog), last modified September 16, 2016 (3:15 p.m.), https://www.huffingtonpost.com/esther-suh/the-racist-nostalgia-behind-make-america-trump_b_8145962.html.

24. Suh, "The Racist Nostalgia behind 'Mak[ing] America Great Again.'"

25. Martin Fradley and John A. Riley, "'It is happening . . . again': Trumpism, Uncanny Repetition and *Twin Peaks: The Return*," in *Make America Hate Again: Trump-Era Horror and the Politics of Fear*, ed. Victoria McCollum (Routledge: Forthcoming).

26. Fradley and Riley, "'It is happening . . . again.'"

27. Greg Olsen, *David Lynch: Beautiful Dark* (Harpenden: Oldcastle Books, 2007), 281.

28. Mariani, "How Nostalgia Made America Great Again."

29. Mariani, "How Nostalgia Made America Great Again."

30. Mariani, "How Nostalgia Made America Great Again."

31. Clay Routledge, Jamie Arndt, Tim Wildschut, Constantine Sedekides, Claire M. Hart, Jacob Juhl, J. J. M. Vingerhoets, and Wolff Scholtz, "The Past Makes the Present Meaningful: Nostalgia as an Existential Source," *Journal of Personality and Social Psychology*, 101, no. 3 (2011): 638.

32. Clay Routledge, Jamie Arndt, Constantine Sedekides, and Tim Wildschut, "A Blast from the Past: The Terror Management Function of Nostalgia," *Journal of Experimental Social Psychology*, Vol. 44, No. 1, (2008): 132.

33. J.T. Cacioppo et. al., "Loneliness within a Nomological Net: An Evolutionary Perspective," *Journal of Research in Personality*, 40 (2006): 1054.

34. Mark Frost, *Secret History of Twin Peaks*, (New York: Flatiron Books, 2016), 232.

35. Martin Fradley and John A. Riley point out that "just as The Return was entering its latter stages, events in Charlottesville, Virginia, retrospectively imbued the much-maligned sub-plot with a depressing contemporaneity. On August 11–12, 2017, the now-notorious Unite the Right ... ended with a violent but unmistakable sense of uncanny repetition, with angry clashes between white nationalists and counter protestors resulting in one death and numerous injuries,"

followed by President Trump unwilling to condemn the neo-Nazis but instead suggesting there were "some very fine people on both sides." (Fradley and Riley, "'It is happening . . . again,'" n. 15.)

36. Nicole Crescenzi, "Removal of John A. Macdonald Statue at B.C. City Hall Met with Divided Crowd," *Surrey Now-Leader*, last modified August 11, 2018, https://www.surreynowleader.com/news/crowd-flocked-to-a-b-c-city-hall-to-see-macdonald-statue-removed/.

37. Mark Frost, *Twin Peaks: The Final Dossier, A Novel* (New York: Flatiron Books, 2017), 31–34.

38. Goldman, "The Legitimacy of Nostalgia," 214.

39. Hoskin, "Twin Peaks."

WORKS CITED

Belk, Russell W. "The Role of Possessions in Constructing and Maintaining a Sense of the Past." *Advances in Consumer Research* 17 (1990): 669–676.

Bogart, Laura. "How the *Twin Peaks* Revival Weaponized Our Longing for Homecoming." *The Week*. Last modified September 1, 2017. http://theweek.com/articles/715796/how-twin-peaks-revival-weaponized-longing-homecoming.

Bonnett, Alistair. *Left in the Past: Radicalism and the Politics of Nostalgia*. New York: Continuum, 2010.

Cacioppo, J.T. et. al. "Loneliness with a Nomological Net: An Evolutionary Perspective," *Journal of Research in Personality* 40 (2006): 1054–1085.

Combs, James E. *The Reagan Range: The Nostalgic Myth in American Politics*. Bowling Green, OH: Bowling Green State University Popular Press, 1993.

Crescenzi, Nicole. "Removal of John A. Macdonald Statue at B.C. City Hall Met with Divided Crowd." *Surrey Now-Leader*. Last modified August 11, 2018. https://www.surreynowleader.com/news/crowd-flocked-to-a-b-c-city-hall to-see-macdonald-statue-removed/.

Davis, Fred. *Yearning for Yesterday: A Sociology of Nostalgia*. New York: The Free Press, 1979.

Fradley, Martin, and John A. Riley. "'It is happening . . . again': Trumpism, Uncanny Repetition and *Twin Peaks: The Return*." In *Make America Hate Again: Trump-Era Horror and the Politics of Fear*. Edited by Victoria McCollum. Routledge: Forthcoming.

Frost, Mark. *Secret History of Twin Peaks*. New York: Flatiron Books, 2016.

———. *Twin Peaks: The Final Dossier, A Novel*. New York: Flatiron Books, 2017.

Gammon, Sean. "Fantasy, Nostalgia and the Pursuit of What Never Was." In *Sport Tourism: Principles and Practice*. Edited by Sean Gammon and Joseph Kurtzman, 61–72. Eastbourne: Leisure Studies Association, 2002.

Goldman, Samuel. "The Legitimacy of Nostalgia." *Perspectives on Political Science* 45, no. 4 (2006): 211–214.

Heritage, Stewart. "Why the New *Twin Peaks* Is Way Better than the Original." *The Guardian*. Last modified June 21, 2017. https://www.theguardian.com/tv-and radio/2017/jun/21/why-the-new-twin-peaks-is-way-better-than-the-original.

Holbrook, Morris, and Robert Schnidler, "Echoes of the Dear Departed Past: Some Work in Progress on Nostalgia." *Advances in Consumer Research* 18 (1991): 330–335.

Hoskin, Peter. "Twin Peaks: The Ultimate Study in Nostalgia." *The Spectator*. Last modified May 13, 2017. https://www.spectator.co.uk/2017/05/twin-peaks-the-ultimate-study-in-nostalgia/.

Lynch, David, and Chris Rodley. *Lynch on Lynch*. Revised edition. London: Faber, 2005.

Mariani, Mike. "How Nostalgia Made America Great Again: When the Present Looks Bleak, We Reach for a Rose-Tinted Past." *Nautilus*. Last modified April 20, 2017. http://nautil.us/issue/47/consciousness/how-nostalgia-made-america-great-again.

Olsen, Greg. *David Lynch: Beautiful Dark*. Harpenden: Oldcastle Books, 2007.

Pollock, Griselda. *Conceptual Odysseys: Passages to Cultural Analysis*. London: I.B. Tauris, 2007.

Routledge, Clay, Jamie Arndt, Tim Wildschut, Constantine Sedekides, Claire M. Hart, Jacob Juhl, J.J.M. Vingerhoets, and Wolff Scholtz. "The Past Makes the Present Meaningful: Nostalgia as an Existential Source." *Journal of Personality and Social Psychology* 101, no. 3 (2011): 638–652.

Routledge Clay, Jamie Arndt, Constantine Sedekides, and Tim Wildschut. "A Blast from the Past: The Terror Management Function of Nostalgia." *Journal of Experimental Social Psychology* 44, no. 1 (2008): 132–140.

Suh, Esther. "The Racist Nostalgia Behind 'Mak[ing] America Great Again.'" *Huffpost* (blog). Last modified September 16, 2016 (3:15 p.m.). https://www.huffingtonpost.com/esther-suh/the-racist-nostalgia-behind-make-america-trump_b_8145962.html.

United States Census Bureau, "New Census Data Show Differences between Urban and Rural Populations." Last modified December 08 2016, https://www.census.gov/newsroom/press-releases/2016/cb16-210.html.

II

AMERICA AND THE POLITICAL

Three

Rural and Suburban Lynch

Characterizations of Hard Times in Reagan's and Trump's America

Jamie Gillies

To understand David Lynch, not just in helming *Twin Peaks* but also in most of his film work, one needs to recognize his connection to location and space. In *Blue Velvet*, the lingering suburban landscape was almost a central character. In *The Straight Story*, the sides of the highway play as important a role as the riding lawnmower. In *Mulholland Dr.* and *Lost Highway*, the actual road surfaces are connected to the plot and the musical score. But nowhere is it more central than in both *Twin Peaks* and *Twin Peaks: The Return*. That sense of small town life, lingering on houses, on offices, on the furnishings and on what is displayed on tables and sideboards, is a key element to how Lynch and Mark Frost situate the storylines in late-1980s small town Washington State and especially in mid-2010s suburban Nevada. While overt political statements are not apparent, the subtle focus on the aesthetics of suburban and small-town life highlight the hard times in the United States. These characterizations, while tangential to key plot points, provide the context for what brought the FBI to Twin Peaks, had undercurrents in what happened to Laura Palmer, and were key in how the characters met again in *The Return*. It is also well understood that David Lynch is not a linear storyteller.[1] *Mulholland Dr.* for example contains no chapters in the DVD and Blu-Ray releases, demanding viewers to watch the film start to finish as it was intended. Lynch's vision in many of his more esoteric efforts require viewers to both consider a narrative operating on parallel planes and then consider what Lynch is driving at in each of those narrative lines. Almost dreamlike in terms of narrative, Lynch's films and television demand close attention and repeated viewings. In *Twin Peaks*, within those competing narratives, we can see a vision of America that is not benign.

It plays with the viewer throughout both series, ready to nod to the seething underbellies of American society and plainly and sometimes subtly show racial, class and economically unequal tensions at play. Whether it is the allegorical winks at Indigenous spirits through Native American characters interacting with white, small-town people, whether it is mortgage and insurance underlings casually dismissing burst housing bubbles and screwing over claimants, whether it is wrong side of the tracks versus debutante tensions, and whether it is rural living versus city slicker and government mentalities, Lynch weaves in American class consciousness throughout *Twin Peaks*. It is argued here that this class consciousness is in fact a central character to the plot and narrative in both series.

This chapter explores first the initial *Twin Peaks* episodes, looking at these characterizations of the Reagan and George H. W. Bush era. It then considers the reboot, with the post-2007 economic crisis and Trump's America displayed in two demographic and geographic areas, a rural mill town in a predominantly Democratic state like Washington, and a subdivision in what looks like an outer suburb in a purple state like Nevada, both of which would be considered Republican strongholds circa 2016. It considers a key question about both *Twin Peaks* and Lynch's films generally; how does the auteur consider class, politics and political space in a filmography that is resolutely non-political? Or is Lynch, ever the director as trickster, intending his films to be political but allowing the viewer to find that subtlety within the narrative. As Howard Hampton argues, "[a]cutely stylized and self-referential, [Lynch's] work is a disjunctive mixture of demented banality and stark unreality ... but it is not too far removed from the coded euphemisms that brought Reagan to power."[2] The key difference however might be that Ronald Reagan, and those who supported the Reagan revolution, actually believed in those euphemisms, as much as Donald Trump believes in his own success and making America great. Lynch, however, plays with the viewer in the sense that while he does not doubt that his characters believe in those same euphemisms, he lets the viewers decide for themselves if this is all a ruse. In fact, by not being overtly political about it, he actually presents a fairly accurate albeit fictional take on the Reagan years.

SEASON ONE OF THE ORIGINAL SERIES

Twin Peaks was filmed in 1989 and aired in 1990. The Reagan/Bush era anxieties Lynch brought to the screen depicted an America in which rural parts of the country, particularly the rural Pacific Northwest, had almost been frozen in time. Limited employment opportunities and the embrace of the Republican Party, social conservatism and evangelical Christianity had created a powerful voting bloc outside of urban areas. Often split down labor and class lines, union households and non-union households, the bulk of rural America abandoned the urban labor coalition within the Democratic Party and voted for the laissez faire capitalism of the Reagan era.[3] That economic philosophy did not bring the jobs back. Far from it, in many cases it sped up the rust belt's deindustrialization as globalized forces, especially multinational corporations not necessarily based in the United States, took manufacturing and resource extraction jobs to where labor was cheap. That was not Washington State. The economic anxiety plays a big role in the series, from keeping the Great Northern Hotel in Twin Peaks profitable to the strain on local resources.

In the original eight episodes, Lynch and Frost lay out a complex local economy in Twin Peaks, stratified along class and gender lines as well as the early anxiety over globalization. The meeting with investors from Norway in the very first episode is juxtaposed with millworkers barely getting by in a boom or bust mentality highly dependent on mill jobs and the price of lumber. Within those groups of people, we see the tensions in *Twin Peaks* play out, between Laura Palmer's family and the people who knew and were close to Laura, between the wealthy who own the hotel and the mill and the townspeople who work there, between local law enforcement and the FBI.

The Reagan-era "morning again in America" optimism is clearly winked at by those with means but the broken promises of rust belt jobs and hinterland prosperity all play out within Twin Peaks' class divide. In many ways, it perfectly captures the dichotomy of the wealth distribution problems in the Reagan era. American voters turned away from the idea of a social democratic state and embraced a version of unfettered capitalism, low regulation, and an "economic freedom" orthodoxy.[4] In the early episodes, the class dynamics are most represented in the relationships depicted, between teenagers and between husbands and wives. Almost all are dysfunctional, full of resentment and male hostility, gendered, loveless marriages and soul-deadening criticism. Big Ed and Nadine Hurley's marriage is more the norm in terms of outright hostility and anger. That dysfunction extends to the wealthy families and the poorer ones too. The turning away from a sense of community too, as part of an individualistic wealth and prosperity ethos, pits families against families. That rise in tension in the community might be why so many of these relationships are dysfunctional.

The town council scene in the first episode also outlines all the class tensions as the sheriff, Harry S. Truman, informs Agent Dale Cooper about the town's economic dramas. Sheriff Truman acts as Cooper's guide to the town. In his estimation the sheriff points out that Twin Peaks has a lot of good qualities, but there are lingering bad elements. As the plot in Season 1 unfolds, those bad elements are intertwined with the murder.

Even in the pilot episode, Benjamin Horne, who owns half the town, and the Packards, widow Josie and sister-in-law Catherine Martell, who own the mill and a large quantity of land, are dangling Twin Peaks as a product to be sold on the open market, from country club and development investment to selling the mill outright. And the townsfolk all know their fortunes and livelihoods are out of their control. Whether Lynch intended it, those small-town observations paint a not very rosy picture of America. If you look at most American community depictions in American film and television, they are often nostalgic and full of optimism. Whether the suburbs of Steven Spielberg in *E.T.* or the magical realism of Iowa baseball diamonds and cornfields in *Field of Dreams*, depictions of community are hopeful. In 1980s television shows like *Cheers, The Golden Girls, Family Ties,* and *The Wonder Years*, each presents a 1980s optimism and sense of community. David Lynch's vision, especially in *Blue Velvet* and *Twin Peaks*, is dread, betrayal and backstabbing; the thin veneer of suburban and small town nice hides a dark and ominous human nature.

Small town optimism exists in *Twin Peaks*, but it is very much stratified on "company town" lines. Those who control the town's politics and economic future run the Great Northern Hotel and the mill. The townspeople are resentful and angry not just at the wealthy but that they are being ignored and forgotten in the decisions of the area. The looks on the millworkers' faces and the resentment of some of the staff at the Great Northern Hotel throughout the series showcase this. That contrast plays out with the Norwegian and Icelandic "investors" being courted behind the scenes. There is no sense that the mayor and town council would have any say in this or that the public's opinion would matter.

Special Agent Dale Cooper presents an interesting contrast to the rest of the cast of characters from *Twin Peaks*.[5] Cooper is our way of seeing the town of Twin Peaks for what it truly is: a microcosm of a rural town in the Reagan/Bush era. Cooper wants to embrace this kind of living, from the coffee to the bacon to the cherry pie and his voice memos to his executive assistant convey his love and hope for the possibility that he would consider buying some land after the Palmer case is over and settling down in Twin Peaks. This is contrasted with Albert Rosenfield's observation that Twin Peaks is a dreadful place. "I have seen some slip-shod backwater burgs, but this place takes the cake," Albert says (1.3). Perhaps Albert knows from experience that places like Twin Peaks are not to be idealized, that they are a dime a dozen and what abhors him—the speed of life, the unbureaucratic nature of the town's institutions, and the unease that the locals have with people from the big city—are the very things Cooper likes. His fondness for the rural way of life underscores the mythologies around small town, "clean" living, and the getting away from it all mentality of rural versus urban life. As Scott Pollard has suggested,

[i]n Twin Peaks, Dale Cooper has his epiphany. In this "wide" world, he finds home. A fantasy mirror, an idyllic American utopia. Beyond the city and the suburbs, where family, community and morality decay at an ever-increasing pace, there is the small town at the edge of nature, beyond the corrupting influence of civilization ... [t]he forest and frontier shine with idealism.[6]

This also is part of the base of Reagan Republican support manifesting itself in the non-cosmopolitan identity politics that coalesced around the GOP platform. Whether Lynch and Frost are aware of these political trends in their creation of *Twin Peaks* is unclear. But they do capture an image of America that Garry Wills, Sean Wilentz and others identified when understanding and historically evaluating the 1980s.[7] Rural communities gravitated towards Reagan because he inspired a generation that optimism and good times were just around the corner. His *Morning Again in America* sloganeering in the 1984 election highlighted that optimism and the messaging particularly to the types of people who would live in a community like Twin Peaks, and it led to one of the largest landslides in U.S. political history.[8] A generation later, Donald Trump did a similar thing, in convincing rural America that good times could be brought back. Lynch seems intuitively aware of the false dichotomy here: economic changes, especially globalization, impact communities like Twin Peaks in profound ways. But politicians' promises for a better future often ring hollow because they, too, do not have the ability to change those circumstances.

At the heart of *Twin Peaks* is a familiar film and television narrative device. A town is preyed upon by dark forces. In American westerns, this has been a device used to tell the story of the lone sheriff holding out against outlaws. In film noir, the characters are often having to hole up in a house in a small town terrorized by a killer. In early science fiction television, like *The Twilight Zone*, episodes often revolved around a town where forces beyond its control get acted upon. Three more recent science fiction series, *The X-Files* of the 1990s and the subsequent return to finish the plot, the Netflix show *Stranger Things*, set in 1983 and 1984 America, and *Castle Rock*, a recent Hulu series based on the novels of Stephen King, also attempt to capture small-town life. While optimism is apparent in each of the shows, it is mostly about the foreboding that surrounds rural communities. It is interesting that each of these series consider the class divides in town in similar and very particular ways. All of them are not overtly political, apart from *The X-Files* trying to get resources from the government to fund their research and investigations.

All the shows also deal with existential and localized town dread, with specific locations in Washington, Indiana, and Maine, and in various episodes in *The X-Files* all over the continental United States. In the case of

Stranger Things and *Castle Rock*, either through faceless military contractors or twisted townsfolk and the use of them as vessels for evil and supernatural in the woods of Maine, both shows are almost bipolar in their depictions of the beauty of small-town life and then the gnawing dread around or underneath. In *Castle Rock*, it is a more specific evil. In *Stranger Things'* case, it is literally underneath the town. In *Twin Peaks*, it is eating away at the heart of the town. But all four series are political without being political. They showcase places in America where decisions made in Washington, D.C., have a negative or little impact at all. Two of the series are set during optimistic eras and yet that optimism is seen only by the community elites. In *Castle Rock*, it is a town well past deindustrialization and the community is picking off the scraps. In *The X-Files*, it perpetuates the stereotype of rural trailer parks and downtrodden, predominantly white and rural communities, inflicted by dark forces beyond their control. Lynch and Frost's vision in *Twin Peaks* was certainly an influence on these science fiction/horror tropes about rural dread. It raises an interesting question, why are depictions of evil never really in the city despite rural values positioning cities as the centers of sin and immorality? In the cases of *Twin Peaks*, *The X-Files*, *Stranger Things* and *Castle Rock*, it may simply be a geographical choice because as a plot device and in giving the viewer the sense of the area, most towns are surrounded by unpopulated areas and so the evil that lurks in the dark can usefully be employed in the woods and subterranean root systems around and underneath the town.

SEASON TWO OF THE ORIGINAL SERIES

As a result of plot developments in the first season and our understanding of the dynamics in Twin Peaks, culminating with Agent Cooper being shot in the finale, viewers already know the town class divides. The second season then allows Lynch to linger on the complex challenges in the community. Some of these moments simply obfuscate the overall plot and others seem included to give viewers more loose ends to think about but not really tie up. That said, the overall character of the town takes on more shape. But as Albert Rosenfield describes, it still contains "the usual bumper crop of local know-nothings and drunken fly fishermen" (2.2).

The sale of the mill after the fire is a key plot point in Season 2. The discussions between Ben and Jerry Horne are a perfect encapsulation of the greed decade of the 1980s. They have no interest in the well-being of the people who work at the mill and have no longer-term strategy to employ the townspeople at the new development. This is also evidenced by Ben's actions in selling the 350–acre parcel of land owned by the Horne family "to a secretive investment capital group that immediately began construction of a privately owned and operated state prison on the cite," that led to "low-wage, low-skill employment opportunities for many area workers displaced by the shuttering of the local logging industry."[9] This commentary on the lack of any civic engagement and community spirit in the town also includes the Packards and the machinations of how both families are intertwined in destroying the other. Shows like *Dallas* and *Dynasty* suggest narrative models for Lynch and Frost in terms of this superficial soap opera between competing wealthy families.[10] Further, the younger generation, including Audrey, is left out of the discussions about these family-owned businesses. The previous generation seems to be the ones who established these civic entities and the current owners are simply profit maximizing, scamming authorities by not paying federal taxes, hiding money offshore, and being as non-transparent as possible. In the first season, images of the campaigns to say no to the Ghostwood Development Project appear in the diner, but this is not brought to the forefront in the plot. It is unclear if this is townsfolk concerned about the development or Ben Horne's campaign against Catherine Martell (1.5). Lynch perhaps recognizes that these forces are uncontrollable, that the townspeople have no say in any of these decisions. This plays like a metaphor for rural and rust belt narratives and the Reagan-era contradictions that played out in appealing to the values of rural voters but not enforcing or regulating the private sector to be good corporate citizens. In fact, both the mill and the Horne-owned businesses come across as almost an ode to unregulated libertarianism. Meanwhile, the local police and the FBI are investigating nefarious events and murder, but they are not looking at Ben Horne or Catherine Martell for tax fraud, money laundering and embezzlement.

This powerful versus non-powerful is part of mill town narratives. The recent memoirs by J.D. Vance and others have discussed this deindustrialization that had its roots in the 1980s when industry and mills closed, moved labor offshore, and hollowed out communities.[11] Lynch was capturing this hopelessness in *Twin Peaks* by recognizing that the public had no voice in their future. In fact, where this becomes obvious on screen is in the depictions of the class stratifications of the community in the second season. Consider the treatment of Leland Palmer after he confesses to killing Jacques Renault. He gets special consideration by the judge, by the police force and even by Agent Cooper (2.4). The same would not apply had the accused been one of the people who worked at the mill or at the Great Northern. But rather than be explicit about ways in which the people could topple the imbalance or inequality or even root out the corruption, it is treated as a "this is the way it has always been done" mentality. And this is where Lynch is not inherently political. There is no righteous stand made, no fight. It is simply presented as part of small-town life.

By the end of Season 2, Cooper is no longer the voice of reason and rationality in Twin Peaks. We find out his motivations for wanting to escape as his predicament in Pittsburgh is brought up by his FBI superiors. Albert, who is introduced in Season 1 as the malcontent, becomes the voice of reality, albeit cynical, in shattering the myth that Twin Peaks is a nice place. Albert is a voice of experience, having seen this scenario play out before. Amidst the plot convolutions and the metaphysical and dreamlike Lynchian shifts central to the mystery and the murder of Laura Palmer, the second season becomes less about the central characters in the town and more about the forces acting on the people. This is where the science fiction and subconscious trickster elements become the focus. It is also where the plot lost the public and where the television executives did not renew the show. But in those episodes, the idyllic nature of the area, which was a constant for Agent Cooper, undergoes a shift. Even for those who want to get away from it all or live off the grid, the town of Twin Peaks presents the tradeoffs of adopting this lifestyle. With isolation comes weirdness and that weirdness can grow, and the evil that men do is all around us.

THE RETURN: CLASS CONFLICTS IN THE SUBURBS

Lynch's reboot of the series arguably has a better and more relevant story arc than that of Season 2. It also expands the palate of *Twin Peaks*, from the confines of the Pacific Northwest to the remnants of the post–real estate bubble in suburban Las Vegas. That subdivision in which Dougie lives with his wife, in this parallel doppelganger Cooper universe, is a key part of understanding what has happened economically since the original *Twin Peaks* at the beginning of the 1990s. Deindustrialization themes have shifted to mortgage crisis wastelands. What is so striking about *Twin Peaks: The Return* is the class conflicts are demonstrated so clearly through set design. One sees the dilapidated state of the houses in the subdivision, even the paint colors of the walls, where the stains and discoloration of where pictures and art work had hung by the previous owner, presumably forced out of the piece of the American dream as a result of a predatory lender or the collapse of real estate prices. Or the cracks and stains that appear in suburban homes over time, even relatively new ones, where upkeep is not a priority and people have bought them on the backs of other people being forced out.

Without even discussing it in the plot, Lynch is making a point about American consumerism and the American dream. Rancho Rosa Estates, the subdivision that is lingered on in *The Return*, becomes a metaphor for the boom, bust and echo of the promise and empty follow through of the Reagan era. It says as much about the previous era than it does about the Trump years to come. More importantly, it moves that small-town resentment of both elites and urban outsiders, from a place like Twin Peaks to the suburbs. Over the course of *The Return*, elements from outside the suburban enclave increasingly show up in the subdivision. While these key plot points relate to the doppelganger Agent Cooper personas, in both Las Vegas and the Dakotas, on screen this feels like the rural dread invading the suburbs. Ironically, it is these two geographical demographic groupings that form the base of both the Reagan and subsequent Bush and Trump coalitions. But in Lynch's almost dystopic look at the suburbs, they are turning on each other as well. The underlying messages of optimism that Reagan, George W. Bush, and Trump used so well in campaigns expose fragility in the American psyche that Lynch sees in these subdivisions and towns.

In almost every scene in which Lynch and Frost use Rancho Rosa as the backdrop, there are at least four for sale signs and one or two boarded up houses (3.5). This is indicative of the housing bust following the 2007 real estate bubble crash. These depictions of 2016 America, however, are a culmination of selling that same American dream in new bottles. Where Reagan sold that confidence and "morning again" optimism in the 1980s, the George W. Bush years, by way of the Clinton-era policies aimed at the middle class, encouraged home ownership and improving tangible economic indicators for the middle class. Unfortunately, that was accompanied by low regulation on mortgages and home loans and led to the most home foreclosures since the Great Depression.[12] The lingering effect

Figure 3.1. Episode 3.5 "Case Files"
Twin Peaks

of that was houses that decreased dramatically in value and ordinary middle-class subdivisions became unaffordable in the sense that they have been partially abandoned and because those who could afford a new house would not want to move to such a dilapidated area. It is that anxiety, economic and social, where people feel as if forces are acting on them with little ability to control their destiny, that Trump was able to parlay into a successful message. The people of Twin Peaks, and subsequently, those in counties outside of Clark County where Las Vegas is located, are susceptible to political appeals that play on those anxieties. That might explain why the politics at play in *The Return* are more obvious than the original series. The economy did not bounce back after the 2008 financial crisis to large swaths of the United States, most notably rust belt and small towns in the northern United States and subdivisions and developments badly hit by the crisis where house values declined dramatically.[13] That David Lynch chose Rancho Rosa suggests he was willing to let viewers draw conclusions about the political motivations of the characters.

As an insurance salesman, Dougie Jones likely does not make enough to afford a better area to live. So, we see the veneer of respectability in a nice looking home but inside the house, you see how dated, drab and functionally lower middle class the furnishings and interior design are, befitting a family who is only living there because those homes became affordable as a result of other people's economic strife. Janey-E's use of the old yellow dial-up phone inside a home full of early 2000s budget décor belays this point. Even the Lucky 7 Insurance offices have 2010s accouterments but with business values and meetings stuck in the 1980s. Where the politics are more obvious is within the dynamics of the insurance company itself. The traditional male and female roles in employment hiring still exist here; salesmen are hucksters angling how to sell their wares to a public that does not know any better. Anthony Sinclair, amoral and calculating, is Dougie's foil. Sinclair is motivated by greed; his bending of regulations fits with an ethos throughout *Twin Peaks*. Like the Horne brothers, Sinclair gets away with it for so long because it fits with general prosperity. Bushnell Mullins, the owner of Lucky 7, is largely unaware of Sinclair's dealing because Anthony is his best salesman. The same can be said as to why no one investigated the shady dealings of the Great Northern. It was an income generator for the area and so rocking the boat could jeopardize the livelihoods of all kinds of people. This is rather a negative portrayal of small and medium sized businesses in America, but Lynch sees value in showcasing both that entrepreneurship ethos with the shady, underground economy hucksterism that can accompany it. Benjamin Horne is his most complete character in both series. He is at once the embodiment of the American dream and, at the same time, rather perversely the unhappy by-product of a world that has not hemmed him in. While it is subtler in the reboot of the series, Horne's motivations in the first have no altruism or substance beyond profit.

CONCLUSION

David Lynch's film oeuvre is decidedly non-political. He makes movies and series that do not explicitly offer any political angle whatsoever. This contrasts with both liberal and conservative or even issue-oriented "message" filmmaking. Even in terms of social changes that have occurred, if David Lynch addresses them, it is usually only as a by-product of the era in which the film is realized, or where it is meant only for observation. But *Twin Peaks*, whether Lynch and Frost intended, is inherently political. Underneath the soap opera/horror science fiction veneer of the various plots are political observations that are difficult to ignore. The town of Twin Peaks and the social stratification offer viewers a complex world of social interaction and community culture. It is in those verbal and non-verbal cues we see on screen that Lynch says a lot politically without being political. That is an emotional response we as viewers get from watching Agent Cooper navigate Twin Peaks.

Lynch's suburban and small-town dread is a theme throughout many of his films. In *Blue Velvet*, the ear in the grass of the backyard was such a profoundly disturbing moment that when out of character weirdnesses is presented on screen in films since, critics and observers label those moments "Lynchian." *Twin Peaks* allows "Lynchian" moments to linger, with many episodes turning on a dreamlike sequence or culminating in something disturbing or unusual.[14] And yet on a parallel plane, *Twin Peaks* plays out as a straight-ahead crime drama and soap opera. Even for those familiar with Lynch's dialogue, there is an unspoken commentary about big business, consumerism and the politics since Reagan, especially those of George W. Bush, Barack Obama and Donald Trump. Clinton and Bush encouraged the kind of investment in home ownership that led to the subprime mortgage crisis.[15] Obama spent the next eight years helming an economy in which a key element was trying to stabilize home values. Trump then played on those concerns and fears of instability by harkening back to the very same themes of the Reagan years. That is one of the central connecting themes between the original series and *The Return*.

NOTES

1. David Andrews, "An Oneiric Fugue: The Various Logics of Mulholland Dr.," *Journal of Film and Video* 56, no. 1 (Spring 2004): 25.

2. Howard Hampton, "David Lynch's Secret History of the United States," *Film Comment* 29, no. 3 (May 1993): 38.

3. Philip Bump, "Donald Trump Got Reagan-like Support from Union Households," *Washington Post*, last modified November 10, 2016, https://www.washingtonpost.com/news/the-fix/wp/2016/11/10/donald-trump-got-reagan-like-support-from-union-households/?utm_term=.076e4bd8e988

4. Warren E. Miller and J. Merrill Shanks, "Policy Directions and Presidential Leadership: Alternative Interpretations of the 1980 Presidential Election," *British Journal of Political Science* 12, no. 3 (Jul. 1982): 325.

5. See Amanda DiPaolo, " Is It Future or Is It Past?: Nostalgia in *Twin Peaks*," in *The Politics of Twin Peaks* (Lanham, MD: Lexington Books, 2019), 35–52.

6. Scott Pollard, "Cooper, Details, and the Patriotic Mission of Twin Peaks," *Literature/Film Quarterly* 21, no. 4 (Jan 1993): 296.

7. See Garry Wills, *Reagan's America: Innocents At Home* (New York: Penguin, 2000); Sean Wilentz, *The Age of Reagan: A History, 1974–2008* (New York: Harper, 2008).

8. Michael Beschloss, "The Ad that Helped Reagan Sell Good Times to an Uncertain Nation," *New York Times*, last modified May 7, 2016, https://www.nytimes.com/2016/05/08/business/the-ad-that-helped-reagan-sell-good-times-to-an-uncertain-nation.html

9. Mark Frost, *Twin Peaks: The Final Dossier, A Novel* (New York: Flatiron Books, 2017) 31–34.

10. See Ben Kruger Robbins, "The Owls Are Not What They Seem: Retaking Queer Meaning in *Twin Peaks*," *The Politics of Twin Peaks* (Lanham, MD: Lexington Books, 2019), 117–141.

11. J.D. Vance, *Hillbilly Elegy: A Memoir of a Family and Culture in Crisis* (New York: Harper, 2016).

12. Jeff Cox, "US Housing Crisis is Now Worse Than Great Depression," *CNBC*, last modified June 14, 2011, https://www.cnbc.com/id/43395857

13. Sarah Holder, "American's Most and Least Distressed Cities," *City Lab*, last modified September 26, 2017, https://www.citylab.com/equity/2017/09/distressed-communities/541044/

14. Nicholas Barber, "Blue Velvet Is Terrifying, Seductive, and Ahead of Its Time," *BBC*, last modified September 20, 2016, http://www.bbc.com/culture/story/20160920–blue-velvet-is-terrifying-seductive-and-ahead-of-its-time

15. Jo Becker, Sheryl Gay Stolberg, and Stephen LaBaton, "Bush Drive for Home Ownership Fueled Housing Bubble," *New York Times*, last modified December 21, 2008, https://www.nytimes.com/2008/12/21/business/worldbusiness/21iht-admin.4.18853088.html?mtrref=www.google.ca

WORKS CITED

Andrew, David. "An Oneiric Fugue: The Various Logics of Mulholland Dr.," *Journal of Film and Video* 56, no. 1 (Spring 2004): 25–40.

Barber, Nicholas. "Blue Velvet Is Terrifying, Seductive, and Ahead of Its Time," *BBC*, last modified September 20, 2016, http://www.bbc.com/culture/story/20160920–blue-velvet-is-terrifying-seductive-and-ahead-of-its-time.

Becker, Jo, and Sheryl Gay Stolberg, and Stephen LaBaton, "Bush Drive for Home Ownership Fueled Housing Bubble," *New York Times*, last modified December 21, 2008, https://www.nytimes.com/2008/12/21/business/worldbusiness/21iht-admin.4.18853088.html?mtrref=www.google.ca.

Michael Beschloss, "The Ad that Helped Reagan Sell Good Times to an Uncertain Nation," *New York Times*, last modified May 7, 2016, https://www.nytimes.com/2016/05/08/business/the-ad-that-helped-reagan-sell-good-times-to-an-uncertain-nation.html.

Bump, Philip. "Donald Trump got Reagan-like Support from Union Households," *Washington Post*, last modified November 10, 2016, https://www.washingtonpost.com/news/the-fix/wp/2016/11/10/donald-trump-got-reagan-like-support-from-union-households/?utm_term=.076e4bd8e988.

Frost, Mark. *Twin Peaks: The Final Dossier, A Novel*. New York: Flatiron Books, 2017.

Hampton, Howard. "David Lynch's Secret History of the United States." *Film Comment* 29, no. 3 (May 1993): 38–41, 47–49.

Holder, Sarah. "American's Most and Least Distressed Cities," *City Lab*, Last modified September 26, 2017, https://www.citylab.com/equity/2017/09/distressed-communities/541044/.

Miller, Warren E. and Shanks, J. Merrill. "Policy Directions and Presidential Leadership: Alternative Interpretations of the 1980 Presidential Election." *British Journal of Political Science*, 12, no. 3 (Jul. 1982): 299–356.

Pollard, Scott. "Cooper, Details, and the Patriotic Mission of Twin Peaks." *Literature/Film Quarterly* 21, no. 4 (Jan 1993): 296–304.

Vance, J.D. *Hillbilly Elegy: A Memoir of a Family and Culture in Crisis*. New York: Harper, 2016.

Wilentz, Sean. *The Age of Reagan: A History, 1974–2008*. New York: Harper, 2008.

Wills, Gary. *Reagan's America: Innocents At Home*. New York: Penguin, 2000.

Four

"Dirty Bearded Men in a Room!"
Twin Peaks: The Return *and the Politics of Lynchian Comedy*

Martin Fradley and John A. Riley

"HAS MY WATCH STOPPED, OR IS THAT ONE OF THE MARX BROTHERS?": COMEDY, SCHOLARSHIP AND *TWIN PEAKS: THE RETURN*

A short, easily overlooked scene in one of the more relentlessly bizarre episodes of *Twin Peaks: The Return* effectively summaries the humorous dynamic of Lynchian comedy. Set in a Las Vegas police department, two sibling cops, Detectives T. Fusco and "Smiley" Fusco, discuss their mother's invitation to Sunday dinner. "She hopes there's no murders this weekend," giggles Smiley. *"Fat chance of that happening!"* As the two detectives burst into laughter over the remote likelihood that their weekend will remain free of homicidal violence, off-screen voices are clearly audible. "Hey!" shouts a police officer, "she can't piss on the floor! Get her out of here!" A woman screams. "Get her out of here, Phil!" An angry woman's voice can clearly be heard. "Cocksuckers! I'll shit in your mouth!" "She's got a knife!" shouts another cop. "Fuck you, Twinkies!" yells the woman, "I'll cut your nuts off!" Following an audible scuffle, the woman screams and groans after being tasered. *"We wanna report a cop!"* shouts a second, comically indignant female voice (3.13).

Throughout this carnivalesque cacophony, both detectives remain studiously indifferent to the chaos occurring out of frame. The scene is funny, then, because their reaction is so incongruous. Whereas the daily inevitability of violent death reduces the professional law enforcers to hysterical laughter, the Fusco brothers show no reaction to the struggle taking place next door. The plight of their colleagues, and the brutal treatment of the would-be felon, is simply ignored. In this way, the scene serves as something of a reflexive mirror image to *Twin Peaks'* (1990–1991) famously

Figure 4.1. Episode 3.13 "What Story Is That, Charlie?"
Twin Peaks

jarring first comic moment. As the plastic-wrapped body of Laura Palmer is unveiled, Deputy Andy Brennan bursts uncontrollably into tears. With his uncanny resemblance to Stan Laurel, Brennan's gurning visage and excessive tears signify an abrupt tonal and generic shift: from bleak crime-drama sobriety, via melodrama, through to absurdist physical comedy. More intriguing, however, are the ideological underpinnings of this gag. Andy's response is, of course, entirely "human" and empathic, his tears physically expressing shock and grief over the brutal murder of a much-loved young woman from a close-knit provincial locale. However, Andy's tears appear *funny* precisely because of the tension between the (gendered) strictures of his job and the unrepressed excess of his emotions. In other words, Andy's affective response is "funny" because, in an inversion of the Las Vegas detectives' jaded apathy, it unveils a brutal truth about the cruel and dehumanizing demands of that most hallowed component of the neoliberal skill-set: *professionalism*.

Despite the inevitable glut of critical work on Mark Frost and David Lynch's belated opus, we remain confident that few scholars will pay much attention to these relatively inconsequential minutes of *Twin Peaks: The Return*. Moreover, it remains a critical truism that, while it likely exists in equal proportion to the dark and disturbingly gothic textures of his work, David Lynch's propensity for comedy has generally been marginalized by film scholars. Even amidst the intimidatingly voluminous critical literature dedicated to Lynch's work, there remains a stubborn—even perverse—refusal to engage directly with Lynchian humor. For example, not one of the five scholarly anthologies dedicated to the critical interrogation of *Twin Peaks* contains a single essay focused specifically on the comedic aspects of the much-loved series.[1] Elsewhere, Franck Boulègue's recent monograph, *Twin Peaks: Unwrapping the Plastic*, completely ignores the series' humor in favor of an idiosyncratic methodological approach combining neo-Jungian symbolism with the philosophical teachings of Maharishi Mahesh Yogi.[2]

Nor is this notable absent-presence restricted to exclusive studies of *Twin Peaks*. A reader glancing across the indices of such varied books as Jeff Johnson's *The Pervert in the Pulpit: Morality in the Works of David Lynch*, Eric G. Wilson's *The Strange World of David Lynch*, Allister Mactaggart's *The Film Paintings of David Lynch*, Anthony Todd's *Authorship and the Films of David Lynch* or the anthologies *The Philosophy of David Lynch* and *David Lynch: In Theory* will find only the most fleeting references to "humor" and/or "comedy."[3] Tellingly, even the most influential studies of Lynch's work follow suit. Michel Chion's *David Lynch* contains barely a handful of allusions to Lynch's surreal wit, while readers of Todd McGowan's important intervention *The Impossible David Lynch*, the anthology *The Cinema of David Lynch: American Dreams, American Nightmares* or Martha Nochimson's exhaustive two-volume treatise *The Passion of David Lynch* and *David Lynch Swerves* might finish each volume almost entirely unaware that Lynch's work is infectiously, if often perversely, *hilarious*.[4]

There are several broad explanations for this sustained critical oversight. Most obviously, there is the traditional, if increasingly anachronistic, critical suspicion of treating comedy *seriously*. Related to this is a somewhat pathological need to find and/or impose baroque narrative logic upon the abrupt tonal shifts and ideologically unintelligible 'weirdness' of the Lynchian aesthetic strategies which tend to critically elide the absurdist comedy of Lynch's work.[5] Finally, in the decade between the abject critical and commercial failure of *Twin Peaks: Fire Walk With Me* (1992) and his belated critical rehabilitation circa *Mulholland Dr.* (2001), Lynch was regularly dismissed as a tedious obscurantist, his work broadly characterized as (at best) stylish exercises in postmodern cynicism or (at worst) deeply politically reactionary. This brand of criticism has cast a long shadow over subsequent re-evaluations of the director's *oeuvre*. It is not difficult, then, to understand the persistent sidelining of Lynch's penchant for comedy as a strategic circumnavigation of his negative association with the philosophical nihilism of Kierkegaardian irony.[6] By contrast, then, this essay proposes *Twin Peaks: The Return* as not only the most politically engaged work of Lynch's career, but also his most concerted attempt at using laughter to engage with contemporary sociopolitical realities.

Take, for example, the scene briefly outlined at the start of this essay. The sequence functions as a microcosm of Lynch's comedic sensibility, entirely amenable as it is to classic (and often overlapping) theorizations of comedy. Most obviously, the scene is unambiguously marked by its *grotesque realism*. The unseen woman's dissent and ferocious rejection of authority is expressed in gleefully corporeal terms: pissing, shitting, threats of castration and a particularly obscene intimation of coprophilia. The scene is also willfully *absurd* on many levels, not least in the rampant disorder taking place within a police station, a space codified as a symbolic nexus of law and order. Anti-social laughter is also invited by the scene's Freudian dramatization of the *"return of the repressed."* The unseen woman rejects the socially sanctioned imperatives of surplus repression, unleashing her raging *id* in the grotesque melee next door. Meanwhile, the Fusco brothers sit silently, mutually complicit in their contemptuous rejection of the demands of the super-ego and the obligations of the very law they metonymically represent. This obscene collapse of order is funny because it relativizes our sense of normalcy: for the Fusco brothers, abject chaos *is*, like daily murder, the quotidian reality of their working day. Finally, the woman's scream signifies the brutal re-imposition of social regulation, triggering a *de facto* punchline—"we wanna report a cop!"—which is saturated with deep critical *irony*, effectively conflating grotesquerie, absurdism and the psychoanalytic return of the repressed in a highly condensed joke which comically savages the fragile house of cards that constitute the dominant social and political order.

Of course, it may seem somewhat counterintuitive to discuss the "politics" of Lynch's output given that the director's films are so often grounded in the dream-logic of Freudian psychodrama. As Todd McGowan points out, "Lynch's films explore the psyche to such an extent that they never seem to touch the ground, to engage the economic and political realities that shape our lives":

> If there has been one sustained theme of criticism of Lynch's work, it has followed these lines: he creates filmic worlds that show little sign of the material world—of class inequality, marginalized people, or economic struggle. In this sense, Lynch is very much a Hollywood filmmaker, unconcerned with the socioeconomic realities of late capitalist life and committed to delivering fantasies to his audience, even if these fantasies do themselves deviate from the Hollywood norm.[7]

As we have argued at length elsewhere, *The Return* explicitly resists accusations of apolitical irony or expressionist solipsism.[8] Nevertheless, discontent with the politics of Lynch's work—and *Twin Peaks* in particular—has retained a certain critical cachet. Nowhere is this more evident than in Linnie Blake's scorched-earth ideological critique of the original series.[9] In Blake's view, *Twin Peaks* functions primarily as a pop cultural metonym for the conjunction of neoliberal economics and postmodern philosophy, an ideological synchronicity that leads, ultimately, to the ethical abyss of Trumpism. Beginning with an evocatively nostalgic anecdote about the bewitching pleasures of first encountering *Twin Peaks* in 1990, Blake's tone shifts abruptly to register the bitter pill of twenty-first-century hindsight:

> Watching *Twin Peaks* again, from the perspective of 25 years, a great deal has become apparent to me that was simply not "there" at the time. I am considerably more troubled by the program's regressive gender and class politics, for example. I am less seduced by its bedazzling epistemological indeterminacy, generic hybridity, and often-absurdist pastiche of available styles. Mostly, I have come to question the ideological function of such representational practices—and this has led me to explore the links between postmodernism's rejection of the certitudes of the Enlightenment and the social malaise of the new millennium ... As an avowedly postmodern text from the period in which neoliberalism came to dominate global economics, *Twin Peaks* offers us a superb exemplification of the relation between postmodern representational practice and the coming into being of our own horrific world.[10]

In contradistinction to Blake, in this essay we argue that *The Return* should be understood as a revisionist project which replaces the "stylish artificiality"[11] of the 1990–1991 series with a political commitment to the exploration of the social, cultural and economic disquiet of the 2010s. Negotiating Lynch's patented tonal ambiguity, we contend that Lynch's employment of a distinctive comedic mode serves in *The Return* to build a picture of a contemporary United States not only fractured by social, economic, and ideological divisions, but a world that is often comically—and uncannily—unaware of those selfsame fissures and divisions.

"JADE GIVE TWO RIDES!": DOUGIE JONES AND THE GROTESQUE

Russian theorist Mikhail Bakhtin's groundbreaking 1965 study, *Rabelais and His World*, is remembered for two vital concepts: the carnivalesque, an enduringly anarchic literary mode that celebrates transgression and the (temporary) dissolution of social hierarchies; and the grotesque, a concept which limns much of *The Return*'s tonal shifts, its focus on violence, abjection and scatology, and its parodic tone.[12] The grotesque, as conceived by Bakhtin, involves taking elevated characters and their associated values such as moral authority, nobility and honor, subsequently inverting and degrading them in parodic fashion. In a contemporary context, the grotesque can be seen to mock neoliberal shibboleths such as individual agency and self-reliance, portraying the human condition as characterized instead by disempowerment and—as in the aforementioned case of Deputy Brennan's tears or the unseen woman's pissing—the primacy of bodily urges.[13] This inverted emphasis gleefully displaces the sacred with the profane, celebrating the democratic pleasures of indecorous language, physical appetites and bodily excretions.

Needless to say, grotesquerie and corporeal excess abounds in *The Return*. Dougie Jones is discovered lying prone next to a pile of his own vomit (3.3). Bile oozes from the mouth of a zombie-like young woman in a car (3.11). A bizarre frog-moth crawls into a pubescent girl's mouth while she sleeps (3.8). Bill Hasting's head is graphically severed from the mouth upwards (3.11). A drunk incarcerated in a jail cell drools blood while a huge abscess bulges on the side of his face (3.14–15). Agent Cooper and Carrie Page politely ignore a bloodied corpse slumped in a nearby armchair (3.18). A paunchy, decapitated male body is discovered crudely juxtaposed with the severed head of a woman (3.1). An aggressively sexist hauler sports a t-shirt bearing the legend "TRUCK YOU" (3.15). "I gotta take a leak so bad," winces a pained Deputy Briggs, "my back teeth are floating!" (3.4) "Oh, you're nice and wet," deadpans Mr. C, referring to a woman's state of sexual arousal (3.2). Such dialogue and grotesque imagery borrow from the spirit of carnival, wherein bodily humor provokes laughter precisely *because* laughter is the culturally inappropriate response. Yet the grotesque does not need to rely on so-called toilet humor for its political affects. Indeed, *Twin Peaks'* various grotesque parodies—Lynch's trademark mockery of police and other authority figures, for example—all revolve around the series' pivotal thematic reversal, that is, the inversion of the middle-class home from an ideologically sanctified realm into a defiled gothic space. This inversion is enacted primarily by the grotesque paternal figure of Leland Palmer—a respected husband, father and legal practitioner who simultaneously commits sustained incestuous abuse and, ultimately, filicidal violence.

We are, of course, scarcely the first scholars to point to Lynch's embrace of the grotesque and carnivalesque modes. In an early article on *The Return*, Jonathan Foltz argues that Lynch's often mournful reprise of *Twin Peaks* is best understood as a "carnivalesque anthology" of stories about death and mortality, a collection of oblique, fragmented meditations on *The Return*'s own "untimeliness."[14] We would go further, arguing that *The Return* is not simply a grotesque parody of its original incarnation—as Foltz argues at length—but of many other aspects of contemporary American culture. Elsewhere, Justus Nieland invokes the concept of grotesque comedy in his insightful 2012 monograph, *David Lynch*. "Lynchian black humor depends on a kind of self-mockery of human propriety. It acknowledges the human's carnal absurdity or impotence, our inability to simultaneously *be* bodies—animal-like, unthinking—and *have* them, as reflective beings."[15] Although Nieland—one of the few scholars to offer a sustained engagement with the dynamics of Lynchian humor—is discussing comedy in the carnivalesque road movie *Wild at Heart* (1990), his comments are entirely pertinent to *The Return*. Nowhere is this more apparent than in the bizarre reincarnation of Special Agent Dale Cooper as the soporific Dougie Jones.

Dougie's provenance is absurd even by the standards of *Twin Peaks'* dense mythology. A decoy doppelganger apparently manufactured by Mr. C and subsequently inhabited by Agent Cooper, the latter finding himself robbed of all agency and "living" Dougie's former life as an insurance broker in Las Vegas. Whatever the ontological implications of this conflation of previously individuated subjects, Cooper's boyish enthusiasm, folksy charm and all-consuming concern for justice—familiar, of course, to viewers of *Twin Peaks'* original run—have, in *The Return*, been replaced by monosyllabic verbal mimicry and the basest of physical urges.[16] While Cooper was valiant, spiritual and prone to intuitive flashes of preternatural insight, Dougie is a grotesque parody of the much-loved special agent. In playing an infantilized idiot-savant, Kyle MacLachlan's torpid performance is poised unsteadily between deep pathos and broad camp, often evoking Boris Karloff at his most child-like in *Frankenstein* (1931) and *Bride of Frankenstein* (1935). Like James Whale's expressionist classics, *The Return* mobilizes comedy as a strategic veil for caustic social commentary. Dougie's somnambulistic demeanor is overlooked by his wife, Janey-E, who casually packs her dutiful husband off to work at the "Lucky 7" insurance company. Dougie subsequently becomes a walking parody of white collar office work and bourgeois normalcy more broadly. This is exemplified by his near-mute interactions with family and colleagues, situations where mimicking the behavior of his co-workers and repeating fragments of their conversation signals a degree of sentience sufficient for Dougie's lobotomized personality to go largely unnoticed.[17]

Mimicry and parody are key components in the sociopolitical armory of the carnivalesque, allowing the mode to challenge and ridicule established power structures. In *The Return*, however, this sense of political resistance is given a bleakly humorous twist. Dougie, like Cooper, is prone to flashes of metaphysical insight, but here they are rendered as grotesque parody. Guided by mystical dancing lights, the unwitting Dougie becomes a prodigious slot machine-*savant*. Unthinkingly mimicking another punter's four-syllable celebration, "*hell-oo-oo-oo!,*" Dougie transforms into the unaccountably lucky "Mister Jackpots": a grotesque inversion of his famously lateral crime solving methods, his spirituality and intuition put solely to the service of base material gain (3.3). Dougie is guided to similarly materialistic ends when working through a series of insurance case files (3.5). Transfixed by their half-remembered resemblance to his FBI case workload, Dougie's incoherent scribblings ultimately expose corruption both within and without the "Lucky 7" offices. This leads to a vast payout for neo-Mafioso casino owners Bradley and Rodney Mitchum. Where Cooper's deductive idiosyncrasies functioned as a counter-hegemonic challenge to rationalist logic in 1990, in *The Return* Dougie is ultimately in the service of a deeply corrupt neoliberal status quo. *The Return* repeatedly draws comic parallels between the Mitchums' illicit business practices and the would-be wholesome pragmatism of Bushnell Mullins' insurance firm. This reaches its *nadir* with the Mitchums' grotesque celebratory conga through the "Lucky 7" offices when their insurance claim is belatedly sanctioned (3.13). With tellingly discordant music playing in the background, Dougie—ever the amenable blank slate—happily joins in.

In *Twin Peaks'* original run, Cooper's wholesomeness was underscored by his appreciation of quotidian physical pleasures and a devout love of black coffee and cherry pie. In *The Return*, however, this boyish enthusiasm becomes comically grotesque, with Dougie grinning maniacally at the mere mention of his favorite hot beverage. As McGowan points out, *Twin Peaks* interrogates the psycho-social conflation of "fantasy" and "reality" which constitutes our sense of normality. *Twin Peaks* often feels comically "unreal," he argues, because it uncannily separates characters from the cultural fantasies which sustain them:

> In the case of Dale Cooper, the series not only presents him as psychically flat, but it also stresses his fantasmatic investment in coffee and pie. That is to say, the show seems unrealistic because of its excess of realism—its depiction of the social reality detached from its fantasmatic supplement. Characters appear strange because their fantasy life has its own isolated position in their lives—like Dale's love for coffee and pie.[18]

For McGowan, then, the political significance of *Twin Peaks* lies in its repeated unveiling of the psychological props and cultural fantasies that structure our otherwise fractured relationship with late-capitalist social conditions. These unveilings strike us as humorous precisely because we (unconsciously) recognize our own alienation rendered hyper-visible in *Twin Peaks'* array of comic grotesques. Alongside Cooper's infatuation with coffee and pie, McGowan highlights Margaret Lanterman—better known as the "Log Lady"—and police receptionist Lucy Moran as illustrative examples which find clear echoes in *The Return*. Like Lucy, *The Return*'s Candie displays a humorously overdetermined investment in her mundane and demeaning job, while Wally Brennan's wholesale reinvention of himself as Marlon Brando circa *The Wild One* (1953) mirrors Lanterman's comically surreal devotion to her mystical log (3.4). Stripped of all ontology beyond his fetishistic stake in coffee and pie, the laughter invited by Dougie's monomaniacal behavior encourages recognition of our shared complicity in the fantasmatic pathologies necessitated by the psycho-social demands of late capitalist culture.

Alongside his idiosyncratic working methods and authoritarian heroics, many aspects of Cooper's personality—his anally retentive character and unhealthy fixation on professional sublimation, for example—were the object of gentle ridicule throughout *Twin Peaks'* original run. However, Cooper's ebullient love of food, drinking coffee and *al fresco* pissing also mark him out as emblematic of the grotesque.[19] "The grotesque's emphasis on bodily functions and excreta is exemplified by Dougie's near-orgasmic pleasure when he urinates. Dougie is more interested in his urge to relieve his bladder than he is in Rhonda, his beautiful colleague who, seemingly unaware of his near-catatonic status, tries unsuccessfully to seduce him (3.5). This bizarre scenario is replicated with Janey-E, who is effectively forced to toilet train her middle-aged husband. In carnivalesque fashion, grotesque humor is repeatedly mobilized in *The Return* as a comic mechanism through which to mock male heroism and undermine patriarchal authority. This reaches its apogee when, after belatedly becoming aware that Dougie has lost fifty pounds in weight, Janey-E lusts over her newly buff husband while he happily devours chocolate cake. In a farcical staging of the Freudian primal scene, Janey-E, entirely happy to instigate vigorous sex with a man who consistently displays the mental capacity of a two-year-old child, straddles Dougie "cowgirl-style" while a bewildered Sonny Jim is awoken by his mother's vocal moans of pleasure (3.10). Significantly, the sex scene functions as a gendered inversion of Dougie's masculine fixation on the statue of a gun-toting cowboy outside the "Lucky 7" offices, reinforcing the comical depiction of their relationship as a grotesque parody of suburban married life. Despite the joyous mutuality of their physical coupling, however, there is none of the cyclical fecundity of Bakhtin's model. When Cooper later ensures that a purposefully "manufactured" replica of Dougie is reunited with Janey-E and Sonny Jim, an ironic tableau rendered in cloyingly sentimental soft focus, *The Return* positions the bourgeois family unit as an ideologically sterile mechanism, the very notion of rebirth parodied as the pro-hegemonic flipside to carnival.

"GOOD THING WE MADE *SO MANY* SANDWICHES!": IRONY, ABSURDISM, AND THE WORKPLACE

In one of the few scholarly essays to engage directly with the cultural politics of Lynchian humor, Bernadette Loacker and Luc Peters emphasize the role absurdism plays in the specific comicality of *Twin Peaks*. Drawing on Michel Foucault's concept of heterotopia, Loacker and Peters argue that the surreal illogic of *Twin Peaks* often serves as "a source of subversion of dominant order, structures and relations of power":

> [T]he absurd is usually understood as a matter or phenomenon that a) contradicts or goes beyond *formal logic* and reason; b) is not in accordance and alignment with *common sense* and commonly held values and expectations; and c) is linked to *ridicule*, foolishness and laughter ... While it is, on that basis, commonly argued that absurdity's intermingling of different, seemingly unreasonably and contradictory orders and conventions provokes the perception of meaninglessness and nonsense ... we claim that the absurd is not solely about lack of meaning and order, but about *other* orders and logics of ordering [original emphasis].[20]

In other words, *Twin Peaks'* absurdist comedy revolves around the tension between plausibility and implausibility, the ontological challenge posed by gleeful illogic subsequently inviting (uneasy) laughter. In political terms, the counter-rationalist thrust of laughter tacitly registers the tenuousness of hegemonic definitions of social normalcy. Examples of this in *The Return* might include: FBI agent Phillip Jeffries' perplexing transmogrification into a steam-emitting machine (3.15); Gordon Cole's rejection of rationalist logic in the straight-faced account of his "Monica Bellucci dream" (3.14); or Jerry Horne arguing with his sentient, and hilariously contrarian, foot (3.9). Such moments illustrate the epistemological incertitude ambivalently celebrated in pre-millennial accounts of *Twin Peaks*, the same "incertitude" later condemned for its "playful" vacuity in Blake's mournful twenty-first-century critique.[21] However, the regular employment of absurdism in *The Return* is also densely comingled with the ambiguous politics of Lynchian irony.[22] Take, for example, Dougie Jones' nonsensical conflation of infantile passivity with a broad range of revered adult competencies. Despite Dougie's inability to function on little more than a primal level—eating, drinking, pissing—he was also widely loved and respected by friends and colleagues, proving himself to be preternaturally adept over a broad-ranging skill set: parenting, gambling, detecting organized crime, fending off would-be assassins, and bringing his previously unhappy wife to ecstatic orgasm.

Of course, Dougie's laughable omni-competence, perhaps *the* definitive neoliberal fetish, is nonsensical and deeply ironic, his effortless travails corresponding with Jerry Palmer's structuralist definition of absurdist comedy.[23] To briefly recap: firstly, there is a surprise (the sharp-witted Cooper returns as an intellectually emaciated man-child); second, there is a logical contradiction (nobody notices that Dougie's psychologically lethargic personality has dramatically altered overnight); and thirdly, there is a hidden logic which imbues the nonsensical situation with a degree of humorous plausibility. In the case of *The Return*, this covert logic stems from the ironic depiction of the corporate workplace and suburban domesticity: middle-class environments in which near-mute passivity and drone-like obedience are unremarkable quotidian norms.

The dichotomy between capitalist mythologies and the humiliating indignities of paid labor have long been a staple of absurdist comedy. Mobilizing absurdism in conjunction with irony, the humor in *The Return* is often at its most unsettling in its depiction of the normalized humiliations of the neoliberal workplace. A telling scene in an early episode sees a welcome cameo appearance from transgender FBI boss Denise Bryson. "I'm speaking more as a woman now than the chief of staff of the entire Federal Bureau of Investigation," Denise tells Gordon Cole (3.4). The humor here lies not in a crudely transphobic joke at Denise's expense, but instead in *The Return*'s ironic depiction of meritocracy as a social reality rather than—a *la* Todd McGowan—a cultural fantasy. Telecast during the first year of Donald Trump's presidency, *The Return* ironically flips Loacker and Peters' thesis on its head. Denise's professional standing raises the utopian possibility of a heterotopic social order—one in which, for example, a trans woman can rise to the upper echelons of the FBI— only to then reaffirm the absurdity of that scenario under the hegemonic strictures of contemporary U.S. culture. As such, Denise's confident reconciliation of two incongruous identities (transgender woman/FBI chief of staff) is a darkly comedic example of misrecognition that is both ironic *and* absurd.

Despite their status as parodic manifestations of crime movie archetypes, the Mitchum brothers are perhaps *The Return*'s most reliable barometer of the absurd, repeatedly pointing out the preposterous nature of events with the comic brevity of a finely honed one-liner. "What kind of fucking neighborhood *is* this?!" exclaims Bradley observing the slaughter of Hutch and Chantal at the hands of an inexplicably angry and outrageously heavily armed accountant (3.16). "People are under a lot of stress, Bradley," counters his brother with comical gravitas. *The Return*'s ironic take on the quasi-empathic banality of twenty-first century "mindfulness," itself little more than a reified brand of ethical capital, is here thrown into sharp relief not only by the ultraviolent suburban bloodbath, but also by the quotidian brutality of the Mitchums' vicious business practices. The Mitchum brothers' skewed morality is mirrored in Hutch and Chantal, the couple's comedic status underscored by the incongruity between their murderous labor and their penchant for ethical deliberation. During regular late-night conversation, for example, the couple greedily devour fast food and admire the beauty of the night sky while philosophizing on organized religion and the hypocrisy of the United States' foundational moral authority. "Government does it all the time," muses Hutch on the ethics of murder. "People get paid for it, just like us ... Christian nation? Might as well be: thou *shalt* kill, show *no* mercy, forgive *no-one—fuck' em all in the ass"* (3.15). Despite this self-awareness about the symptomatic amorality of their labor, Hutch and Chantal's hilariously self-justifying conclusion—brazenly killing for cash trumps being a sanctimonious "two-faced fuck"—serves as a weary summary of these interminably nihilistic pathologies.

The ideological brutality of the contemporary workplace becomes a recurrent thematic motif. One-time teenage delinquent Mike Nelson needlessly humiliates a prospective employee in a job interview (3.5). A casino employee is viciously beaten after Dougie's winning streak (3.5). An inexplicably apoplectic FBI boss relentlessly bullies his junior colleague (3.14, 16). In another ironic parody of the employer/employee paradigm, Hutch and Chantal devote themselves entirely to Mr. C's will, the latter enthusiastically submitting to sexual demands of the "boss man" while her grinning husband looks on. The light comedy provided by FBI double-act Albert Rosenfield and Gordon Cole, together forming a classic straight man/funny man pairing, is repeatedly undercut. An absurdly inappropriate mural of an atomic mushroom cloud in Cole's office highlights the ideological continuum between the FBI's patriotic legitimacy ("to the Bureau!") with genocidal ultraviolence. Elsewhere, the elderly Cole and Rosenfield joke while staring lecherously at the youthful hour-glass figure of up-and-coming FBI agent Tammy Preston (3.4).[24] Yet what seems like an exemplar of the male gaze is shrewdly denaturalized by the formal employment of blue-tinted day-for-night lighting. This anachronistic and visually jarring anti-naturalistic technique underscores the rhetorical insincerity of the scene, employing ironic distanciation to critique the everyday realities of workplace sexism and undermine the paternalistic condescension of the FBI hierarchy.

The Return mobilizes comedy to underscore the dehumanizing imperatives of free market fundamentalism. The interchangeable pink-clad trio of Candie, Mandie and Sandie are absurdist hyper-feminine automatons employed by the Mitchums as decorative menial workers, providing a comic mirror to the highly educated middle-class professionalism of Agent Preston in their blank-faced sublimation to the dictates of contractual labor. Yet even in *The Return*'s lightest scenes economic precarity is never far away. Following a farcical slapstick episode in which she accidentally hits Rodney, Candie is tearful and distraught, terrified of her employment being terminated after accidentally hitting one of her employers in the face. "If we fire her she's got nowhere else to go," offers Bradley with a resigned shrug (3.10). Conversely, in Mr. C's coolly Randian demeanor we witness the pitiless conjunction of neoliberal tyranny and toxic masculinity. Treating his various employees as little more than disposable "resources," Cooper's grim-faced doppelganger is more often disturbing than he is humorous. Nevertheless, a surreal arm wrestling contest serves as a comically literalist staging of the regressive logics of socioeconomic Darwinism (3.13). In a crudely masculinist parody of "healthy" meritocratic competition, Mr. C is portentously informed that he will become "our boss"—the neoliberal accolade *par excellence*—if he wins the contest. Played out in front of a braying horde of low-rent hoodlums, the unsmiling Mr. C humorlessly toys with his rival before casually breaking his arm, subsequently killing him with a single punch.

In keeping with the series' sustained streak of black humor, the return of Agent Cooper proves to be the grim punchline to the painfully protracted joke that is Dougie Jones. Brimming with the messianic self-belief that will ultimately be eviscerated in *The Return*'s abyssian conclusion, Cooper grins as he proclaims, "I *am* the FBI!" (3.16). The psychoanalytic joke here, of course, is that Cooper's hubristic avowal of metonymic authority boldly misrecognizes the special agent's penis for the phallus. Casually oblivious to the Mitchums' obvious criminality ("I am witness to the fact that you both have hearts of gold!"), Cooper's judgment and moral conviction is wildly misplaced, in turn signalling *The Return*'s tonal shift towards outright absurdism (3.16). When BOB appears from Mr. C's abdomen as a floating beach ball, what was once a terrifyingly supernatural manifestation of repressed trauma becomes uncomfortably risible (3.17). BOB is swiftly vanquished with a few well-placed punches from the ludicrous Freddie Sykes and the entire "climax" becomes re-staged as bathetic fantasy, an ironic *mise-en-scene* of (thwarted) nostalgic desire. This absurd phantasmagoria is suitably rounded off with a painfully ironic hat-trick: a bewildered Mitchum-ism ("One for the grandkids!"); Candie's beautiful, dead-eyed smile; and—in what serves as the last thing resembling a "joke" in *The Return*—a serendipitous abundance of sandwiches.

"I DON'T UNDERSTAND HOW THIS KEEPS HAPPENING ... *OVER AND OVER AGAIN*": COMEDY, REPETITION AND THE NEOLIBERAL UNCANNY

The ironic battle with Mr. C and BOB serves as a thematic segue to the oblique final 90 minutes of *The Return*. This unsettling episode-and-a-half concludes with a confused and defeated Agent Cooper, a haunting scream and a profound sense of irresolution. The excessive unreality of Freddie's triumph is only appropriate in a saga which, from the outset, has emphasized the fundamental impossibility of emotional "closure" in the wake of sustained trauma. *The Return* is thus *uncanny* in the sense that it repeatedly teaches us a lesson from the past. In Sigmund Freud's well-known phrasing, the uncanny is an unsettling affective response to "something which ought to have remained hidden but has come to light,"[25] a bipolar structure which, like comedy, has the potential to destabilize our (illusory) sense of social normalcy and ontological coherence. This unnerving return of repressed knowledge creates a sense of disorientation, a feeling that the uncanny object or event is simultaneously strange *and* familiar—a feeling only too familiar to viewers of *The Return*.

Moreover, the uncanny is always in some sense *political*, haunting us with the ghosts and amnesiac specters of our repressed psycho-social baggage. As several critics have pointed out, however, the uncanny is also intimately linked to two conjoined phenomena: comedy and repetition.[26] Indeed, Henri Bergson's classic observation that humor arises when a living creature behaves in a mechanical fashion bears a close kinship with Freud's emphasis on automata—machines which resemble human beings—as emblematic uncanny phenomena.[27] Think, for example, of the virtually interchangeable Candie, Mandie and Sandie, whose photogenic appearance and conventional femininity are all too familiar, but whose dehumanized hollowness and mechanical demeanor also render them strange and humorously alien. Or recall Ike "the Spike" Stadtler, a grotesque parody of the emotionless Randian hitman of crime movie mythology. Ike's diminutive stature, apoplectic rage and pathologically repetitive behavior—we are given no cause to imagine the solitary Ike has *any* social existence outside heavy drinking and frenzied killing—defamiliarizes a generic character who should otherwise be familiar from popular crime fictions. More pointedly, the comic-uncanny in *The Return* invites laughter because characters like Candie and Ike bring uncomfortably into the light those unsettlingly mechanical aspects of social existence we normally disavow: obedient conformity, the repetitive obligations of everyday life, and the imperative to suppress "inappropriate" emotions or desires.

To illustrate this point, we turn to an illustrative scene from *The Return*. In episode 10, the perpetually furious Richard Horne makes an unexpected visit to his family home, intending to extort money from his grandmother, Sylvia. Within the house a severely developmentally disabled figure, Johnny Horne, stares vacantly at a talking teddy bear. Richard arrives and aggressively demands money from Sylvia, becoming violent when she refuses. "*Cocksucking bitch!*" Richard rants, his fury laced with trademark misogyny. "*Give me some fucking money!*" However, this otherwise disturbing scene is laced with discordant humor. Johnny is tied to a chair, clad in padded clothing to protect him from injuring himself. The "bear" is a decapitated parody of a child's toy, a transparent plastic bowl with crudely rendered eyes and mouth replacing his missing head. As a lightbulb flashes inside the bowl, the bear jovially repeats a friendly greeting: "Hello, Johnny! How are you today?" While Richard robs his distraught grandmother, Johnny becomes increasingly upset, eventually rocking his chair until it topples over. The scene ends with a distraught Johnny lying on the floor with Sylvia, their tears accompanied by a mechanically cheerful mantra. "Hello, Johnny! How are you today? *Hello, Johnny! How are you today?*"

On a surface level, the unsettling black comedy of this scene is produced by the incongruity between the bear's unendingly upbeat incantation and the traumatized tears of his victims. However, the fusion of comedy and uncanniness in the scene has greater resonance. The toy is an unthinking automaton, positioned as a "friend" for the incapacitated Johnny. Johnny's vacant features at the start of the scene not only mirror those of the mutilated bear, they also *bear testament* to the latent cruelty of this tableau. Just as Steven's violent domestic rampage has clearly occurred before, so too does the bear's endless mechanical greeting serve to taunt Johnny, a man whose daily life is ultimately as grimly predetermined and mechanically repetitive as that of the toy bear itself. Imprisoned in a perpetual state of pre-socialized infanthood, Johnny becomes, like Dougie, a grotesquely one-dimensional parody of the neoliberal consumer-citizen, all primal instinct with no perceptible autonomy outside of the bear's reified imperative to *enjoy*. The irrepressibly cheerful toy becomes increasingly uncanny as the scene plays out: a grotesquely repetitive embodiment of compulsory optimism and the obligation to pursue happiness—a mechanized metonym, in other words, for what Judith Halberstam has astutely dubbed "the toxic positivity of contemporary life."[28]

As we have argued elsewhere, the often bleak thematic terrain of *The Return* should be understood—at least in part—as an uncanny refraction of the repetitive social, cultural and ideological conditions that ultimately paved the way for the rise of Trumpism.[29] As such, the bear's interminably de-empathized cheerfulness serves as something of a microcosm of *The Return*'s darkly comic politics and its emphasis on repetition, social paralysis and ideological stasis. As the bathetic showdown with BOB demonstrates, it is not the gothic presence of an amorphous supernatural evil that makes *The Return* uncanny, but the fact that it is *itself* a "return." Thus, phrases from the original series—"damn fine coffee!," "the policeman's dream!," "let's rock!"—are repeated in new contexts, these dislocated and half-remembered catchphrases creating an uneasy sense of *deja vu*.

During the 1990–1991 series, characters were often seen watching show-within-a-show *Invitation to Love*, a chintzy daytime soap opera that seemed to provide an oblique meta-commentary on events in *Twin Peaks*. In the intervening years, however, viewers have flocked to alternative media outlets beyond network television. Dr. Lawrence Jacoby's transformation into "Doctor Amp" parodies alt-right conspiracist Alex Jones and other online gurus. Amp's furious populist dissent provokes laughter because, paradoxically, it is both preposterously exaggerated and uncannily familiar. "It's 7 o'clock," Jacoby ritually begins his show, "do you know where your freedom is?":

> And the fucks are at it again! These giant multinational corporations are filled with monstrous vermin: poisonous, vile murderers! And they eat, drink and shit money! They buy our politicians for a song as we gag and cough, sold down the river to die! (3.12)

By some distance the most unambiguously political voice in *The Return*, Dr. Amp's would-be "truther" offers comically repetitive and increasingly incoherent diatribes that lurch unsteadily between anti-globalist fervor and paranoid lunacy, from corrupt politicians to the existential threat posed by poisoned waffles ("What's lurking in that toaster waffle? … Poison! Cancer! Leukemia! Autoimmune disorders! Pulmonary embolism! Warts! Psoriasis, eczema! Cardiac arrest!" 3.5). Aside from Jacoby's descent into monomaniacal psychosis, much of the humor here lies in the good doctor's self-serving remedy to this twenty-first-century malaise. "Shovel your way out of the shit … and into the truth!" he proclaims, hawking cheaply spray-painted gold shovels ("only $29.99!") as a lucrative self-help stratagem. Jacoby's cynically monetized conflation of bastardised psychotherapy and the tragic remnants of counter-cultural politics is echoed by neo-hippy Jerry Horne, a one-time international playboy who now trades in the United States' de-criminalized marijuana market. Perpetually high on his own supply and, along with the equally unhinged Nadine, one of Jacoby/Amp's handful of loyal viewers, Jerry wanders aimlessly round and around in the woods outside Twin Peaks, arguing with his feet and getting angry with his binoculars, a man as lost in narcotic solipsism as Jacoby is in self-defeating conspiracist fervor.

Although it is certainly a comic highlight of *The Return*, Jacoby/Amp's political anger is ultimately impotent. This tragic sense of righteous futility is echoed in another scene which serves as a comedic refraction of *The Return*'s emphasis on post-2008 economic precarity. The seemingly apolitical Janey-E angrily refuses to pay a high interest on Dougie's gambling debts, spitting furious verbal invective toward the bewildered debt collectors.[30] "My husband has a job, he has a wife, he has a child, he does *not* make enough money to pay back $52,000 for *anything*":

> We are *not* wealthy people! We drive cheap, terrible cars! We are the 99 percenters and we are shit on enough! And we are certainly *not* gonna be shit on by the likes of you! … What kind of world are we living in where people

can behave like this? Treat other people this way without any compassion or feeling for their suffering? We are living in a dark, dark age, and *you* are part of the problem. Now, I suggest you take a good, long look at yourselves because I never want to see either of you again! (3.6)

If the debt collectors' awestruck response to Janey-E's apoplectic monologue, ("tough dame!,") serves as the punchline to this particular extended gag, her invocation of that most banal of populist slogans ("we are the 99 percent!") ultimately underscores its political impotence, not least when the economic struggles of the Jones' comfortable middle-class existence are thrown into sharp relief by the abject poverty of many of Twin Peaks' residents.

Repetition, stasis and stagnation become ever more insistent motifs as the series progresses. Deputy Briggs looks dumbstruck when a pre-pubescent boy adopts the same belligerent posture as his identically dressed, NRA-supporting father (3.11). Sarah Palmer becomes paralyzed by dread when she spots a new brand of jerky at her local grocery store (3.12) but remains comically oblivious to the televised 1950s boxing match playing—like her tragically dipsomaniacal existence—on eternal repeat in her lounge (3.13). James Hurley, once Twin Peaks' answer to James Dean but now working as a low-paid security guard, reprises his impossibly saccharine ballad "Just You and I," at the Roadhouse (3.13). Repeating events from the first series, James is later arrested and thrown in Twin Peaks' jail cells (3.15). In keeping with *The Return*'s downbeat revisionism, the space previously occupied by barking juvenile delinquents Bobby Briggs and Mike Nelson is now filled by a grotesque, belligerent drunk who sardonically repeats everything he hears in an uncanny repetition of Dougie's half-conscious mumblings. Audrey's interminable argument with Charlie is painfully repetitive, more the dramatization of an overwrought internal conflict than it is a depiction of marital discord. More pointedly, her tautological reprise of "Audrey's Dance" is one of the series' most uncanny moments, a deceptively slinky jazz-scored meditation on the mortal dread underpinning nostalgic reverie (3.16).

Even the most innocuous of *The Return*'s numerous reprisals carry barbed political resonance. Retrieving a part-eaten box of chocolate bunnies last seen in *Twin Peaks'* pilot episode, Deputy Chief Hawk encounters the same ignorance and casual racism from his colleagues that he wearily tolerated in 1989. "You're an *Indian*," muses Lucy. "Do chocolate bunnies have anything to do with your heritage?" Admitting that she ate the missing bunny, Lucy's amusingly counterintuitive logic moves into full flow: "I only ate one. And I never did it again. But I had a problem at that time with … a bubble of gas. And I had read that sometimes chocolate—which

I *love*—can be used as a remedy, maybe by indigenous people. Is that true, Hawk? Do you use chocolate as a remedy for gas?" (3.1) What is uncanny about this seemingly light-hearted sequence is the way it points to racism as an unchanging and historically recurring phenomena, the laughter invited by this impossibly banal exchange itself an acknowledgment of our own complicity with the thoughtlessness of Western culture and the low-level structural violence of its racist legacies. The joke, in other words, is that as much as we might want to identify with the ever-patient Hawk, who, along with Carl Rodd, acts as the *de facto* ethical centre of *The Return*, it is more likely, and altogether more discomfiting, that *Lucy* "is us."

This sense of paralyzing repetition and the inescapability of socio-economic logics finds its uncanny apogee in what appears to be *The Return*'s solitary conventional emotional payoff. The belated coupling of "Big" Ed Hurley and Norma Jennings plays out against the backdrop of a minor storyline concerning the mooted franchising of the Double-R diner. Told that she is "the face of the franchise," Norma is clearly bewildered by the reifying impetus of business jargon—the *lingua franca* of the neoliberal present—and ultimately opts to retain control of her diner in Twin Peaks. Refusing to take short cuts on quality, Norma asserts the wholesome essence of her beloved cherry pies. "All my ingredients are natural, organic, local," she asserts with defensive pride (3.13). Clearly there is a contemporary discourse about "authenticity" in play here, but this is yet another late-capitalist impasse. Norma rejects franchising, branding and the commercial imperatives of profit over quality, but in its place she valorises the "authentic," "independent," "artisanal," "local," "organic"—all of which are consumerist tropes beloved of middle-class taste cultures. In a cruelly mirthless joke, the Double-R, with its heaven-sent coffee and cherry pie, is the apotheosis of the twenty-first-century "experience economy." On the surface the scene appears as heartwarmingly "wholesome" as Norma's pastries but, like *The Return* as a whole, this is underscored by a fatalistic resignation to the abyssian machinations of neoliberal culture. In Twin Peaks in 2017, the all-too-knowing "joke" is that the cherry pies are stale, the coffee is laced with arsenic and the fish is *still* in the percolator. *Been loving you too long*, indeed.

CONCLUSION: "FUCK GENE KELLY, YOU MOTHERFUCKER!"

Two twenty-something women, Chloe and Ella, drink in a booth at the Roadhouse. Over beers Ella recounts how, after being caught taking drugs at work, she recently lost her job at a local burger bar. "Got *fired*," she complains, "fucker *fired* me" (3.9). Pointing to the irony that she could undertake her menial labor perfectly adequately regardless of how high she was, Ella scratches furiously at a grotesquely inflamed rash in her armpit. When Chloe asks where she's working now, Ella replies with appropriately black humor. "Across the fuckin' street," she laughs maniacally, "serving burgers!" Although only a minor character, Ella's laughter is metonymic: the compensations of a masochistic joke about the inescapability of her socio-economic situation serving as a neat synopsis of *The Return*'s uncompromising fatalism more broadly.

Like the absurdly grotesque spectacle of Leland Palmer launching himself onto his daughter's coffin and riding it like a morbid mechanical bull (1.3), humor in *The Return* is laughter at a funeral, laughter which repeatedly signifies the often nihilistic politics of the unconscious. A grim parody of Francis Fukuyama's "end of history" which rejects the insidious tyranny of "positivity" and its hopelessly individualized genuflections, *The Return*'s gallows humor serves as an uncanny—and entirely deserved—jolt to the vapidity and complacent nostalgia of our twenty-first-century collective unconscious. Pushing aside the facile compensations of happy endings and narrative resolution as the cruellest of bad jokes—*fuck Gene Kelly*, indeed!—*The Return* offers an unblinking look into the abyss with a malevolent smile. As both Bushnell Mullins and the Mitchum brothers, two sides of the same tawdry ideological coin, know all too well, *the house always wins*. Despite (or perhaps because of) its humor, the unmistakably depressive tone of *The Return* is entirely symptomatic of a cultural moment in which comedy has proved its catastrophic political impotence all too clearly.[31] As Carl Rodd, that the wisest and most wizened of *Twin Peaks*' residents, succinctly notes, in what might well be the series' ultimate punchline, "fuckin' *nightmare*."

NOTES

1. See David Lavery, *Full of Secrets: Critical Essays on* Twin Peaks (Detroit, MI: Wayne State University Press, 1995); Marisa C. Hayes and Franck Boulègue, Twin Peaks: *Fan Phenomena* (Bristol: Intellect, 2013); Jeffrey Andrew Weinstock and Catherine Spooner, *Return to* Twin Peaks: *New Approaches to Materiality, Theory, and Genre on Television* (London: Palgrave MacMillan, 2015); Eric Hoffman, *Approaching* Twin Peaks: *Critical Essays on the Original Series* (Jefferson, NC: McFarland & Co., 2017); and Richard Greene and Rachel Robison-Greene. Twin Peaks *and Philosophy: That's Damn Fine Philosophy!* (Chicago, IL: Open Court, 2018).

2. Franck Boulègue, Twin Peaks: *Unwrapping the Plastic* (Bristol: Intellect, 2017).

3. Jeff Johnson, *The Pervert in the Pulpit: Morality in the Works of David Lynch* (Jefferson, NC: McFarland & Co, 2004); Eric G. Wilson, *The Strange World of David Lynch* (London & New York: Continuum, 2007); Allister Mactaggart, *The Film Paintings of David Lynch* (Bristol: Intellect, 2010); Anthony Todd, *Authorship and the Films of David Lynch* (London: I.B. Tauris, 2012); William J. Delvin and Shai

Biderman, *The Philosophy of David Lynch* (Lexington, KY: University of Kentucky Press, 2011); Francois-Xavier Gleyzon, *David Lynch: In Theory* (Prague: Litteraria Pragensia, 2011).

4. Michel Chion, *David Lynch* (London: British Film Institute, 2006); Todd McGowan, *The Impossible David Lynch* (New York: Columbia University Press, 2007); Erica Sheen and Annette Davison, *The Cinema of David Lynch: American Dreams, Nightmare Visions* (London: Wallflower Press, 2004); Martha Nochimson, *The Passion of David Lynch* (Austin, TX: University of Texas Press, 1997); Martha Nochimson, *David Lynch Swerves* (Austin, TX: University of Texas Press, 2014).

5. See Greg Haines, "Red Velvet: Lynch's Cinema(tographic) Ontology," in *David Lynch: In Theory*, ed. Francois-Xavier Gleyzon (Prague: Litteraria Pragensia, 2011), 25. Hainge astutely notes, much of the abundant critical literature on Lynch is unified by a "refus[al] to let Lynch's films *not* make sense [emphasis added]."

6. For a broader discussion of comedy and "Kierkegaardian irony," see Matt Sienkiewicz, "Speaking Too Soon: SNL, 9/11 and the Remaking of American Irony," in *"Saturday Night Live" and American TV*, eds. Nick Marx, Matt Sienkiewicz and Ron Becker (Bloomington: Indiana University Press, 2013) 93–111.

7. McGowan, *The Impossible David Lynch*, 26–7.

8. Martin Fradley and John A. Riley, "'It is happening … again': Trumpism, Uncanny Repetition and *Twin Peaks: The Return*," in *Make America Hate Again: Trump-Era Horror and the Politics of Fear*, ed. Victoria McCollum (Abingdon: Routledge, 2019).

9. Linnie Blake, "Trapped in the Hysterical Sublime: *Twin Peaks*, Postmodernism, and the Neoliberal Now," in *Return to* Twin Peaks: *New Approaches to Materiality, Theory, and Genre on Television*, eds. Jeffrey Andrew Weinstock and Catherine Spooner (London: Palgrave MacMillan, 2015), 229–44.

10. Blake, "Trapped in the Hysterical Sublime," 230.

11. Blake, "Trapped in the Hysterical Sublime," 232.

12. Mikhail Bakhtin [1965], *Rabelais and His World*, trans. Helene Iswoksky (Cambridge, MA: MIT Press, 1968). *The Return* is often overt about its (ironic) debt to the spirit of Bakhtin's carnival. "Looks like a fuckin' circus parade!" exclaims Chantal as the Mitchum brothers' entourage arrives to set up an anachronistic and absurdly spot-lit "gym set" in a quiet Las Vegas suburb (3.16).

13. For a detailed discussion of grotesque realism as a subversion of neoliberal imperatives, see Martin Fradley, "'Al fresco? That's up the anus, innit?': Shane Meadows and the Politics of Abjection," in *Shane Meadows: Critical Essays*, eds. Martin Fradley, Sarah Godfrey and Melanie Williams, (Edinburgh: Edinburgh University Press, 2013), 50–67.

14. Jonathan Foltz, "David Lynch's Late Style," *L.A. Review of Books*, last modified 12 November 2017, https://lareviewofbooks.org/article/david-lynchs-late-style/#!

15. Justus Nieland, *David Lynch* (Urbana-Champaign, IL: University of Illinois press, 2012), 77.

16. In one of *The Return*'s many intertextual jokes, Dougie's verbal mimicry itself replicates the unthinking vocal repetitions of Waldo, the doomed mynah bird in the first season of *Twin Peaks* (1:5–6).

17. The "Lucky 7" offices resemble the functional, hypermodern environs of *Playtime* (1967), directed by Lynch's comedic hero Jacques Tati—an alienating space which leaves Dougie's *naif* awkwardly adrift.

18. Todd McGowan, "Lodged in a Fantasy Space: *Twin Peaks* and Hidden Obscenities," in *Return to* Twin Peaks: *New Approaches to Materiality, Theory, and Genre on Television*, eds. Jeffrey Andrew Weinstock and Catherine Spooner (London: Palgrave MacMillan, 2015), 145.

19. In Scott Frost's official para-textual spin-off, *The Autobiography of FBI Special Agent Dale Cooper: My Life, My Tapes* (London: Penguin, 1992), the young Dale Cooper meticulously records memorable episodes of urination. In one entry from 1975, he soberly avows the pleasures of delayed urination as an entirely satisfactory substitute for sex (88).

20. Bernadette Loacker and Luc Peters, "'Come on, get happy!': Exploring Absurdity and Sites of Alternate Ordering in *Twin Peaks*." *Ephemera: Theory & Politics in Organization* 15, no. 3 (2015): 625.

21. Jimmie L. Reeves, "Postmodernism and Television: Speaking of *Twin Peaks*," in *Full of Secrets: Critical Approaches to* Twin Peaks, ed. David Lavery (Detroit, MI: Wayne State University Press, 1995), 173–95.

22. For a succinct and usefully nuanced discussion of Lynchian irony, see Nieland, *David Lynch*, 62–64.

23. Jerry Palmer, *The Logic of the Absurd: On Film and Television Comedy* (London: British Film Institute, 1988), 39–44.

24. As embodied by Bell's performance, the character of Tammy Preston is strongly coded as being as absurdly fantastical as Denise's career trajectory. As Bell notes, Lynch "had a vision of the character ... He kept honing in until he had this Jessica-Rabbit-as-an-FBI-agent look." See David Lynch and Kristine McKenna, *Room to Dream* (Edinburgh: Canongate, 2018), 483.

25. Sigmund Freud, "The Uncanny," in *The Standard Edition of the Complete Psychological Works of Sigmund Freud, Volume XVII*, trans. and ed. James Strachey (London: Hogarth, 1955), 222–23.

26. See Alenka Zupančič, *The Odd One In* (Cambridge, MA: MIT Press, 2008), and Carsten Bagge Lausten and Rasmus Uglit, "Uncanny Repetitions: Abu Ghraib in Afterthought," *Journal for Cultural Research* 61, no. 1 (2012): 81–102. In their insightful essay, Lausten and Uglit use the uncanny potential of both comedy and repetition as a critical lens through which to interrogate the ongoing moral, ethical and political failings of modern Western society. Using the notorious images of U.S. troops laughing at their humiliation of prisoners at Abu Ghraib as an illustrative example, the authors underscore their analysis with a powerful evocation of ideological stasis. "[M]ore than anything, the true surprise and scandal of the surfacing of the Abu Ghraib photographs could be said to be the lack of impact they had on politics and society ... There was a great deal of media attention and some public debate as a result of the publication of the pictures, but in the end the political effect of Abu Ghraib was generally non" (82).

27. Henri Bergson, *Laughter: An Essay on the Meaning of the Comic*, trans. Cloudesley Brereton and Fred Rothwell (New York: MacMillan, 1914).

28. Halberstam, *The Queer Art of Failure*, 3.

29. Martin Fradley and John A. Riley, "'It is happening ... again.'"

30. Although space dictates that we cannot develop this point further, it is indicative of the comedic richness of *The Return* that Janey-E, alongside Audrey, Chantal and Diane, can easily be interpreted as "unruly women," an enduring comic archetype discussed in detail by Kathleen Rowe Karlyn, in *The Unruly Woman: Gender and the Genres of Laughter* (Austin, TX: Unversity of Texas Press, 1995).

31. Slavoj Žižek, "Hegel on Donald Trump's 'Objective Humor,'" *žižek.uk*, last modified 15 January 2018, https://zizek.uk/hegel-on-donald-trumps-objective-humor/. Žižek notes President Trump exists *beyond* comedy: "[W]hat are even the best jokes on Trump compared to the joke that is Trump's actual politics? Imagine that, a couple of years ago, a comedian were to perform on stage Trump's statements, tweets and decisions. That would have been experienced as a non-realist exaggerated joke. So, Trump already is his own parody, with the uncanny effect of the reality of his acts being more outrageously funny than most parodies … Remember how many times the liberal media announced that Trump was caught with his pants down and committed a public suicide (mocking the parents of a dead war hero, boasting about pussy grabbing, etc.). Arrogant liberal commentators were shocked at how their continuous acerbic attacks on Trump's vulgar racist and sexist outbursts, factual inaccuracies, economic nonsense, etc., did not hurt him at all but maybe even enhanced his popular appeal. They missed how identification works: we as a rule identify with the other's weaknesses, not only or even not principally with the strengths. Which means that the more Trump's limitations were mocked the more ordinary people identified with him and perceived attacks on him as condescending attacks on themselves. The subliminal message of Trump's vulgarities to ordinary people was: »I am one of you!«, while Trump supporters felt constantly humiliated by the liberal elite's patronizing attitude towards them."

WORKS CITED

Bakhtin, Mikhail. [1965]. *Rabelais and His World*. Translated by Helene Iswoksky. Cambridge, MA: MIT Press, 1968.

Bergson, Henri. *Laughter: An Essay on the Meaning of the Comic*. Translated by Cloudesley Brereton and Fred Rothwell. New York: MacMillan, 1914.

Blake, Linnie. "Trapped in the Hysterical Sublime: *Twin Peaks*, Postmodernism, and the Neoliberal Now." In *Return to* Twin Peaks: *New Approaches to Materiality, Theory, and Genre on Television*, edited by Jeffrey Andrew Weinstock and Catherine Spooner, 229–44. London: Palgrave MacMillan, 2015.

Boulègue, Franck. Twin Peaks: *Unwrapping the Plastic*. Bristol: Intellect, 2017.

Chion, Micheal. *David Lynch*. London: British Film Institute, 2006.

Devlin, William J., and Shai Biderman. *The Philosophy of David Lynch*. Lexington, KY: University of Kentucky Press, 2011.

Fradley, Martin, and John A. Riley "'It is happening … again': Trumpism, Uncanny Repetition and *Twin Peaks: The Return*." In *Make America Hate Again: Trump-Era Horror and the Politics of Fear*, edited by Victoria McCollum. Abingdon: Routledge, 2019.

Fradley, Martin. "'Al fresco? That's up the anus, innit?': Shane Meadows and the Politics of Abjection." In *Shane Meadows: Critical Essays*, edited by Martin Fradley, Sarah Godfrey and Melanie Williams, 50–67. Edinburgh: Edinburgh University Press, 2013.

Freud, Sigmund. [1919] "The Uncanny." In *The Standard Edition of the Complete Psychological Works of Sigmund Freud, Volume XVII*, translated and edited James Strachey, 217–56. London: Hogarth, 1955.

Frost, Scott. *The Autobiography of FBI Special Agent Dale Cooper: My Life, My Tapes*. London: Penguin, 1992.

Foltz, Jonathan. "David Lynch's Late Style." *L.A. Review of Books*. Last modified 12 November 2017. https://lareviewofbooks.org/article/david-lynchs-late-style/#!.

Greene, Richard, and Rachel Robison-Greene. Twin Peaks *and Philosophy: That's Damn Fine Philosophy!* Chicago, IL: Open Court, 2018.

Gleyzon, Francois-Xavier. *David Lynch: In Theory*. Prague: Litteraria Pragensia, 2011.

Hainge, Greg. "Red Velvet: Lynch's Cinema(tographic) Ontology." In *David Lynch: In Theory*, edited by Francois-Xavier Gleyzon. Prague: Litteraria Pragensia, 2011.

Halberstam, Judith. *The Queer Art of Failure*. Durham, NC: Duke University Press, 2011.

Hayes, Marisa C., and Franck Boulègue. Twin Peaks: *Fan Phenomena*. Bristol: Intellect, 2013.

Hoffman, Eric. *Approaching* Twin Peaks: *Critical Essays on the Original Series*. Jefferson, NC: McFarland & Co, 2017.

Johnson, Jeff. *The Pervert in the Pulpit: Morality in the Works of David Lynch*. Jefferson, NC: McFarland & Co, 2004.

Karlyn, Kathlyn Rowe. *The Unruly Woman: Gender and the Genres of Laughter*. Austin, TX: Unversity of Texas Press, 1995.

Lausten, Carsten Bagge, and Rasmus Uglit. "Uncanny Repetitions: Abu Ghraib in Afterthought." *Journal for Cultural Research* 61, no. 1 (2012): 81–102.

Lavery, David. *Full of Secrets: Critical Approaches to* Twin Peaks. Detroit, MI: Wayne State University Press, 1995.

Loacker, Bernadette, and Luc Peters. "'Come on, get happy!': Exploring Absurdity and Sites of Alternate Ordering in *Twin Peaks*." *Ephemera: Theory & Politics in Organization* 15, no. 3 (2015): 621–49.

Lynch, David, and Kristine McKenna. *Room to Dream*. Edinburgh: Canongate, 2018.

Mactaggart, Allister. *The Film Paintings of David Lynch: Challenging Film Theory*. Bristol: Intellect, 2010.

McGowan, Todd. "Lodged in a Fantasy Space: *Twin Peaks* and Hidden Obscenities." In *Return to* Twin Peaks: *New Approaches to Materiality, Theory, and Genre on Television*, edited by Jeffrey Andrew Weinstock and Catherine Spooner, 143–157. London: Palgrave MacMillan, 2015.

———. *The Impossible David Lynch*. New York: Columbia University Press, 2006.

Nieland, Justus. *David Lynch*. Urbana-Champaign, IL: University of Illinois Press, 2012.

Nochimson, Martha. *David Lynch Swerves: Uncertainty from Lost Highway to Inland Empire*. Austin, TX: University of Texas Press, 2014.
———. *The Passion of David Lynch: Wild at Heart in Hollywood*. Austin, TX: University of Texas Press, 1997.
Palmer, Jerry. *The Logic of the Absurd: On Film and Television Comedy*. London: British Film Institute, 1988.
Reeves, Jimmie L. "Postmodernism and Television: Speaking of *Twin Peaks*." In *Full of Secrets: Critical Approaches to* Twin Peaks, edited by David Lavery, 173–95. Detroit, MI: Wayne State University Press, 1995.
Sheen, Erica, and Annette Davison. *The Cinema of David Lynch: American Dreams, Nightmare Visions*. London: Wallflower Press, 2004.
Sienkiewicz, Matt. "Speaking Too Soon: *SNL*, 9/11 and the Remaking of American Irony." In *"Saturday Night Live" and American TV*, edited by Nick Marx, Matt Sienkiewicz and Ron Becker, 93–111. Bloomington: Indiana University Press. 2013.
Thorne, John. *The Essential Wrapped in Plastic: Pathways to* Twin Peaks. Dallas, TX: John Thorne, 2016.
Todd, Anthony. *Authorship and the Films of David Lynch: Aesthetic Receptions in Contemporary Hollywood*. London: I.B. Tauris, 2012.
Weinstock, Jeffery Andrews, and Catherine Spooner. *Return to* Twin Peaks*: New Approaches to Materiality, Theory, and Genre on Television*. London: Palgrave MacMillan, 2015.
Wilson, Eric G. *The Strange World of David Lynch: Transcendental Irony from* Eraserhead *to* Mulholland Dr. London & New York: Continuum, 2007.
Žižek, Slavoj. "Hegel on Donald Trump's 'Objective Humor.'" *žižek.uk*. Last modified 15 January 2018. https://zizek.uk/hegel-on-donald-trumps-objective-humor/.
Zupančič, Alenka. *The Odd One In*. Cambridge, MA: MIT Press, 2008.

III

IDENTITY, REPRESENTATION, AND THE POLITICAL

Five

Violence, Representation, and Girl Power

Twin Peaks' *Female Characters and Third Wave Feminism*

Stacy Rusnak

There is little doubt that *Twin Peaks* (1990–1991) left a lasting mark on television history. Claimed to be the series that "single-handedly refigured the conservative, ratings-led conventions of the television soap opera,"[1] *Twin Peaks* was indicative of a new wave in 1990s postmodern television. It broke general television rules through its aggressively eclectic style: surreal juxtapositions, disturbing sounds and visual aesthetics, and unbalanced compositions. Additionally, it blurred the boundaries between television and film, combing narrative conventions from genres as varied as the soap opera, the detective film, the melodrama, the gothic, horror, science fiction, and the hospital drama. Some critics complained that the excessive use of generic conventions made the series an ambivalent parody and campy trash TV.[2] Moreover, such misuse of conventions challenged the viewer to take some scenes seriously, especially the most violent ones. However, there is no denying that the brutal murder of Maddy by Leland Palmer, possessed by BOB, is one of the most difficult scenes to watch. Yet, Maddy and most of the other girls of *Twin Peaks* have received far less attention than Laura Palmer in feminist scholarship.

In her critique of *Twin Peaks*, Diane Hume George states, "Prime time business as usual, only a little worse because even feminists let it go by, behaving like charmed backsliders involved with a man so charismatic that we just couldn't think straight."[3] Arguably, the series portrayed some rather objectionable sexual ethics regarding the treatment of women, and it is for this reason that I find it so surprising that little scholarship exists on the series' female characters. Interestingly, the series aired at a particularly tense moment in feminist history with the backlash towards women in full swing and the rise of third wave feminism on the horizon. It is within this context that I reconsider some of the series' most well-known female characters, demonstrating how their representations denaturalize and deglamorize the popular media's definition of control over the individual female and notions of femininity. I begin with an overview of some of the principles of third wave feminism. Then, I analyze the constructions of violence suffered by three of the series' women: Laura, Maddy, and Shelly, making the argument that each woman is more than a victim. Afterward, I consider how Nadine, Lucy, and Norma challenge normative assumptions of femininity, giving rise to new positions of power. I end with a brief discussion of the reception of Audrey and Donna as examples of third wave girl culture and girl power. Such a re-reading of these characters through a third wave lens allows for a more multifaceted understanding of the series' representations of gender, violence, agency, and power.

SITUATING THIRD WAVE FEMINISM

There is no clear-cut chronology of when second wave feminism ends, and the third wave begins. Generally, the former is associated with the political activism of women during the 1960s and 1970s, and the latter is identified as a new way of feminist thinking that emerges in the 1990s. There is no time here for an exhaustive history of feminism, but I do acknowledge that the metaphor of *waves* is controversial as it carries with it implications regarding generational differences, which are problematic in their own right. Thus, I am using the terms *second* and *third* wave similarly to Amber E. Kinser, who regards the second wave as an *"era of feminism rooted in and shaped by the 1960s–1980s political climate* and 'third wave' to suggest the *era of feminism rooted in and shaped by the mid '80–new millennium political climate."*[4] This usage of terms permits an understanding that each era has its constraints and possibilities for change and that a feminist might align themselves with the ideals of either.

By the 1980s, the second wave seemed to recede with the rise of the new conservative right and the beginning of the Reagan era. The neoconservatives sported a moral agenda with roots in "myths regarding traditional family values, individuality, national strength and the importance of technical progress."[5] This resulted in a heated backlash towards feminism and the hard-won victories that women had achieved during the 1960s and 1970s. According to Susan Faludi, this backlash utilized popular media notions about the second wave to turn women against feminism. She states:

> Women are unhappy precisely *because* they are free. Women are enslaved by their own liberation. They have grabbed at the gold ring of independence,

only to miss the one ring that really matters. They have gained control of their fertility, only to destroy it ... The women's movement, as we are told time and again has proved women's own worst enemy.[6]

Feminism had become the dirty *f-word*, and as a means of distancing themselves from the backlash, feminist scholars in the 1980s identified a new condition called postfeminism, which became associated with those feminists who were "said to view that earlier movement as embodying and advocating a style of femininity/femaleness with which they do not want to be associated."[7] In the 1990s, third wave feminism embraced a similar agenda of alienation from the second wave, citing that it was outdated and did not reflect women's everyday lives.

In the introduction to *Catching a Wave: Reclaiming Feminism for the 21st Century*, Rory Dicker and Alison Piepmeier suggest that one of the reasons why third wave feminists distance themselves from their predecessors is that they see feminist gains as fundamental rights and fail to recognize the efforts that went into securing them.[8] Despite their dissimilarities, the third wave contains elements of the second such as the critique of beauty culture, sexual abuse, unequal power structures, and the use of the male gaze as a weapon to hold women in their place. Where the two diverge the most is in the third wave's postmodernist orientation towards both consumer and popular culture. The rise of the third wave coincided with the rise of neoliberalism in the 1990s, which promoted free-market individualism. This directly countered the second wave notion of collectivity, seemingly at the expense of political activism. Furthermore, the second wave decried the power of the media and consumerism to shape women according to the patriarchy's desire, thereby denying them agency.

Third wave feminists are particularly interested in how the media frames issues related to sex, gender, and identity. In general, they do not see the same contradictions between female power and assertive sexuality and are attentive to girl culture's reclamation of femininity. Kathleen Rowe Karlyn states that for the third wave, "popular culture is a natural site of identity formation and empowerment, providing an abundant storehouse of images and narratives valuable less as a means of representing reality and more as motifs available for contesting, rewriting and recoding."[9] Additionally, Leslie Heywood and Jennifer Drake discuss how popular cultural representations have the potential to reveal much about contemporary society and social constructs. They write, "third wave activists are well aware of the power of representations to promote or contest domination. Since we understand the "'real' as an effect of representation and understand that representational effects play out in material spaces and in material ways, we take critical engagement with popular culture as a key to political struggle."[10] These sites provide opportunities for women to work out relationships between girl culture and real empowerment, and they allow for representations of feminist agency and resistance.

WOMEN, VIOLENCE, AND REPRESENTATION: LAURA, MADDY, AND SHELLY

The world of *Twin Peaks* is a microcosm of a mythic America under Ronald Reagan, a nostalgic reverie that never existed and that the series unravels to its most vile core. As a cultural product of that decade, *Twin Peaks* is steeped in the same nostalgic rhetoric of Reaganism with its popular expressions of a return to the so-called good old days. Graham Thompson states, "The attempt to recover the 1950s often formed around a rhetoric of contented domesticity and so-called 'family values' of respect, monogamy and simplicity."[11] This moral agenda was joined by an equally important economic one, which encouraged individuals to work hard and spend money. At the heart of American capitalism is a system that enforces conformity and clear-cut roles for family members. In *Twin Peaks*, Laura, Maddy and Shelly all suffer physical abuse within this system, demonstrating the dark side of the American family and the American Dream.

On the surface, the Palmers project the image of the perfect middle-class family. Mr. Palmer is a lawyer for the Great Northern Hotel, and Mrs. Palmer is a stay at home mother. Laura is homecoming queen, helps organize Meals on Wheels, tutors Audrey Horne's mentally disabled brother Johnny, and instructs Josie in English speaking classes. By day, Laura conforms to the demands of the patriarchal authority. By night, her world is much grimmer as she hides many secrets, one of which is an incestuous affair with her father. In season 2, episode 1, Ronette Pulaski, who was with Laura when she was murdered, has a nightmare of Laura's death. As the dream sequence begins, there are cuts back and forth between Ronette in the hospital and BOB and Laura in a dark room. BOB wears jeans, a dark shirt, a jean jacket, and has long grey hair. His appearance connotes a working-class background, which is reminiscent of the 1960s hippie culture that conservatives in the 1980s hoped to erase from the cultural imaginary. His presence is like a stain—a vulgar threat to the sanctity of the middle-class family. When the scene cuts back to a close up of Laura, she is bathed in a reddish-orange light. Her eyes are wild and her mouth is agape as she lets out guttural screams. BOB appears again and raises a rock over his head several times, pounding her with it. We do not see the blows, but Laura's screams of agony flood the soundtrack. Finally, there is silence as the camera pans slowly over Laura's lifeless body and then tilts up in the darkness to show BOB standing over her.

Despite the scene's brevity, it packs a powerful punch, especially since we now know that BOB is really Leland. What may have seemed like gratuitous violence on the night the episode aired, in retrospect, can be read as a much more complex reaction to the 1980s conservative moral and economic agenda. Lisa McGirr contends that the emphasis placed on the nuclear family was a departure from previous notions of family. She states, "Calls for strengthening the family meant shoring up parental (and particularly patriarchal) authority within this smaller family unit and did not encompass a vision of larger, extended networks that had been the cornerstone of earlier understandings of the family."[12] Such *shoring up* places huge tension on the nuclear family to project the ideal image of the perfect family. For this reason, Leland cannot discuss his dark desires for fear of being judged as a weak father. Laura cannot speak either, for doing so will tarnish the myth of the textbook middle-class family. Although the term is never used in the series, the father-daughter incest motif has entered popular culture in *Twin Peaks*.

The series is unique in that it makes explicit Leland's desire without merely displacing it onto a substitute daughter, which is more common in popular narratives. In general, the father-daughter motif is associated with the Seductive Daughter trope, which makes the father the victim because he cannot fend off his daughter's sexual desires. It often appears in popular representations when masculinity and/or family values are perceived as in crisis. Karlyn states, "incest provides a discourse or established set of conventions available for examining—and usually reasserting—male authority perceived to be under siege."[13] In *Twin* Peaks, Leland is not conceptualized as a victim to his daughter's sexual prowess. In fact, the repression of his own victimization as a child perversely resurfaces and is manifested in his abuse of Laura. Secondly, Leland's confession does not absolve him from the murder, nor does it reassert patriarchal control. Instead, it demonstrates how the tradition of American capitalism engenders a myth based on the incompatibility between freedom and family, and thus contests the traditional family hierarchy that places the power of the father at its core.

Ironically, Laura proves to be the most powerful challenge to both her father and the idealization of patriarchal authority through her death, as she continues to *speak* loudly from the grave through the entire series. In "Arbitrary Law," Laura writes an entry into her diary that foreshadows her own death (read out loud by Donna): "February 23rd, tonight is the night that I die. I know I have to because it is the only way to keep BOB away from me. The only way to tear him out from inside. I know he wants me. I can feel his fire, but if I die, he can't hurt me anymore" (2.9). I am more than positive that this entry goes unnoticed in most cases, written off as the ranting of a disturbed teenage girl. However, instead of dismissing the diary entry, I propose that Laura may have orchestrated her own death by revealing to BOB/Leland that she was going to expose him. Her assertion of power and confrontation with BOB/Leland marks a kind of radical individualism that coincides with the third wave, which "pretends the power of self-definition is all about being 'in control' and 'making choices,' regardless, it seems, of who controls the 'choices available.'"[14] Laura's diary entry seems to suggest that she is taking control of her circumstances and is willing to sacrifice her own life in order to free herself from her abuser. When she provokes BOB/Leland and is punished through death, her murder becomes politicized because it disrupts the social order that privileges patriarchal authority. Likewise, it drives home the point that incest does happen to outwardly *normal* middle-class families, despite attempts to suggest otherwise.

Additionally, underneath her pristine façade, Laura dates both Bobby Briggs and James Hurley, works as a prostitute for Blackie O'Reilly at One-Eyed Jack's, places messages in the pornographic *Flesh World* magazine to hook up with men, and snorts cocaine. Instead of a passive object of male fantasy where she exists only for male pleasure, Laura opts for multiple participatory sex acts with her peers, the elite clientele of One-Eyed Jack's, and regular working-class men that respond to *Flesh World*.

Figure 5.1. Episode 2.9 "Arbitrary Law"
Twin Peaks

In addition to her making her own choices about her sex partners, her actions align with third wave feminism's attitude towards sexuality as more open and less conflicting. Granted, such positioning needs to be taken with caution, as sexual desire, when linked to eroticized disparities of power, can be exploitative and devastating. This is the case with Laura and her father, and some critics might suggest that Laura's sexual behavior *is* the result of her father's incest.[15] Yet, this would indicate that Laura has no agency and that her actions are purely reactive to the abuse she suffers, a point that I refute. Of all of her relationships, only the one with BOB/Leland appears forced upon her. She willingly goes out with Bobby and James. She consciously takes a job at Horne's Department store, where it is clear that she will more than likely end up at One-Eyed Jack's, and she actively utilizes the *Flesh World* services. Hence, her *bad girl* behavior runs counter to the standards expected by her middle-class status, thereby challenging patriarchal authority and traditionalist values.

If Laura is identified as the *bad girl* type, then her cousin Maddy is the quintessential *good girl*. Maddy comes to stay with Leland and Sarah after Laura's death. Her presence serves as a connection for the family with their dead daughter. In season 2, episode 7, Maddy reveals that she will be returning home to Missoula. The camera slowly pans across the Palmer living room, past photos of Laura in the foreground and Leland, Maddy, and Sarah nestled in the background, sitting closely together on the sofa. Louis Armstrong's "What a Wonderful World" plays on the record player, and it appears that domesticity is intact within the Palmer household. Leland assures Maddy that they understand and tells her that she is welcome to visit any time. As the scene comes to a close, the camera lingers on the record player in deep focus, making it appear grotesquely out of proportion. The juxtaposition between Armstrong's song and the surrealistic oversizing of the recorder player visually indicate something other than domestic bliss.

At the end of the episode, there is a return to the Palmers' living room. The record player is featured for the second time, but the only sound is the metronomic repetition of the needle as it passes over a stuck record. There is a cut to Leland looking into the hallway mirror smiling, a cut to an objective POV with the camera looking directly at Leland, and then a cut back to Leland looking into the mirror. This time, the reflection is of BOB's smiling face. We watch as BOB/Leland puts on plastic gloves. There is a cut to the other side of the living room, where Sarah lays face down, drugged and incapacitated. The figure of the mother proves useless in her prescribed space of the domestic sphere. Maddy rushes in, and BOB/Leland chases her off screen as her screams fill the soundtrack. Somewhere in the back of our minds, we know we have already witnessed this horrific scene. Maddy's sobbing takes us back to Ronette's dream, and we are perceptively aware that Maddy's fate is intimately tied to Laura. BOB/Leland punches Maddy in the face several times before picking up her limp, semi-conscious body and moving around in a dance-like circle, repeating, "Laura, Laura, Laura. Laura, my baby" (2.7). The scene shifts back and forth between Leland and BOB. BOB aggressively kisses Maddy's bloody face and neck in a slow-motion effect, with mutated animalistic growling sounds filling the atmosphere. Leland finally puts Maddy down and then slams her face into a framed picture hanging on the wall, resulting in her death.

John Alexander states that Maddy's death is "possibly the most brutal sequence ever made for American prime-time television."[16] The scene's use of slow motion forces the viewer to linger within the now uncomfortable space of the previously idyllic home. The spectacle of Maddy's death returns us to the repressed primal scene of the crime, the family living room, and makes us admit what we have suspected all along but refused to acknowledge—that Leland killed his own daughter. Thus, Maddy's murder reintroduces the traces of incest and family violence and produces an uncanny effect, revealing that the home "is always and already a site which is eminently vulnerable to threats that are conjured from within—and—without—its architectural borders."[17] The home, "understood as an extension of the female body and/or mind,"[18] is not a place of peace where evil is absent, nor is the father figure always the benevolent protector. Furthermore, the scene demonstrates that the power wielded by the father subverts that of the mother, even within the one space that is designated as her own.

The connection between danger and the domestic sphere continues in Shelly Johnson's depiction of domestic violence by her husband Leo. In episode 3 of season 1, there is a long shot of Shelly with a black eye standing in the kitchen. In the background, we hear the popular tagline of the soap opera that figures prominently in the series, "Every day brings a new beginning and every hour holds the promise of ... *An Invitation to Love*." Shelly walks into the living room and sarcastically proclaims, "Yeah, right," as she turns the television off. Later, she nostalgically tells her boss, Norma, why she married Leo, "He was so great at first, you know. Flashy guy in his hot car. We get married and I find out all he was looking for is a maid he didn't have to pay. I feel so stupid" (1.5). Her comments lay bare the false consciousness at work in the mythic vision of the fairy tale fantasy of true love and happily ever after.

Ann Jones states that, "Every day, in fact, four or five women die in the United States at the hands of their current or former husbands or boyfriends."[19] The terror these women experience generally starts with small, private offenses that escalate into physical violence and sometimes death. Shelly's abuse demonstrates this same pattern. Initially, Leo's abuse is verbal. He tells her, "There are two things, Shelly. When I come home this house should be clean, and I mean clean. Number two, you smoke one brand of cigarettes from now on because if I ever see two brands of cigarettes in this house again, I'm going to snap your neck like a twig" (1.Pilot). By episode 2, the threat is physical. Leo grabs a bar of soap off the kitchen sink and places it inside a sock. He stalks Shelly across the kitchen telling her, "I'm going to teach you a lesson now Shelly about taking care of my property" (1.2). He swings the sock over his head and turns on the radio as Shelly cowers in the corner. The screen fades to black, but not before we hear the impact of the blow landing on Shelly. Later, in episode 6, when Leo shoves Shelly to the floor, she pulls a gun on him, claiming, "You're not going to hurt me again. Don't touch me. Don't come near me Leo" (1.6). She pulls the trigger, shoots him, and is momentarily free from his abuse when he flees the home. However, Leo returns to kill Shelly for her insubordination. He ties her up in the Packard Sawmill before setting it ablaze. Showing her a timer, he says, "You hear that? You've got about one hour to think about what you've done to me. And think about it because by then, Bobby Briggs is going to be dead" (1.7). Leo *punishes* Shelly because he can no longer control her. Jones claims, "A man—of any age—threatens, intimidates, abuses and batters a woman to make her do what he wants."[20] Despite the abuse, Shelly has subverted much of the control that Leo believes he has over her by continuing to see Bobby and working outside of the home, where she is generally content. When he realizes that she is not his passive victim, he seeks to destroy her.

On one hand, Shelly's battle with domestic violence criticizes the way in which society often turns a blind eye towards such violence. bell hooks states:

Male violence against women in personal relationships is one of the most blatant expressions of the use of abusive force to maintain domination and control. It epitomizes the actualization of the concept of hierarchical rule and coercive authority ... it is the violence that is most overly condoned and accepted, even celebrated in this culture.[21]

When society accepts this type of violence against women, the cycle continues, making it difficult to control or eradicate. Recall that Shelly never gets help from the authorities, even though both Sheriff Truman and Agent Cooper frequently interact with her in the Double R Diner. On the other hand, bringing the topic out into the public "is an articulation of strength, for to give a name to the injustices that continue to oppress is to adamantly refuse victim status."[22] As a result, we can read Shelly as part of the resistance to discourses that repress the reality of male violence against women or that reduce women to victims without agency. As Jones makes clear, women in abusive relationships are not mere victims; "they are resistance. But they are almost entirely on their own."[23]

NEW NORMS OF FEMININITY: NADINE, LUCY, AND NORMA

Beyond the physical violence enacted upon the bodies of Laura, Maddy, and Shelly, other women in *Twin Peaks* can be said to suffer non-violent consequences of the patriarchal institutions that govern society. These women are not passive either, as they challenge dominant ideologies about gender by playing with traditional codes of femininity. One of the themes of third wave feminism is empowerment for women. Notions of empowerment lead to new femininities that disrupt the conventional idea of women as passive, vulnerable, helpless, and subservient. However, the rise of new femininities "provide far from straightforward subject positions as they produce both possibilities and troubles for young women attempting to manage the difficulties of enacting ideas associated with traditional femininity and masculinity."[24] Although contradictions exist, it is important to look at possible examples of new types of femininities available to women.

In *Twin Peaks*, Nadine performs a new *emancipated* femininity, described by Michelle M. Lazar as that which can be "presented as a form of consciousness or attitude. Following Gill (2009), this involves a transformation of the self, which is less about acting or performing than about remodeling one's interior or psychic sense of self—in this case involving the embracing of an attitude of self-belief."[25] In season 1 of the series, Nadine is living a drab life as a neurotic housewife, whose sole objective is to create an invention for a silent drapery runner. When the patent office rejects her, she attempts suicide; and in season 2, she is awakened from a coma, thinking she is a high school girl. Through her transformation, she takes on a different sense of self and displays confidence in both her masculine prowess and her girly persona. This is not mere performance, as she genuinely believes she is back in high school. For example, in episode 12 of season 2, the high school coach invites her to join the wrestling team (clearly a male-coded activity), mentioning to the all-male team that Nadine has a moral and constitutional right to compete. Nadine stands demurely next to the coach, wearing jean shorts, a red belt, a Twin Peaks High t-shirt, red lipstick, and her hair is pulled back in a ponytail with a coordinating red bow. Her red bow, belt, and lipstick are feminine adornments used to make her appealing to Mike Nelson, the wrestling district champion. To prove her physical strength, she agrees to wrestle Mike. As the match begins, Mike tries to coach Nadine by telling her where to put her hands and how to move. Nadine responds, "Want to go out tonight?" Mike grabs her, and she squeals in delight. She gets Mike in a headlock, and when he complains that she is breaking his neck, she exclaims, "You're right! This is sort of like necking." Then, we witness her body strain and stretch to pick Mike up over her head and throw him to the ground. Finally, she body slams him, throws herself on top of him, and asks in a girly, innocent voice if he will go out with her. Such display of the female body performing more *masculine* tasks, with Nadine squatting and straining against Mike's body, disrupts the conventional notions of the desirable female form.

However, her transformation affords her a new go-getting attitude, which frees her from the rejection and feelings of worthlessness that she possessed as a housewife. The cause of her change is never fully revealed, but this should not undermine her new sense of self, which includes showing off her physical strength, embracing her desire, and transgressing normative feminine behaviors. Karlyn notes that assertive sexuality and female power are symptomatic of the new girl culture that informs third wave feminism. Instead of an analytic or rational strategy (associated with the second wave), third wave feminism uses a mythic approach, "manifesting itself in the symbols, rhythms, and motifs of a media-infused age."[26] As a result, Nadine becomes a symbol for female liberation by remolding the way she sees herself and then acting on her desires, despite the *inappropriateness* of her behavior for a woman nearly in her forties. Her expressions of physicality and aggressive sexuality loosen the straight-jacketing of gender identity prescribed for women as passive and receptive.

The concept of emancipatory femininity is closely related to the notion of *choice* feminism, a term coined by Linda R. Hirshman.[27] Choice feminism is defined as that which "indexes the shift to personal (rather than social and political) choices made by women in domains such as paid work, domesticity, and parenting, sexuality, as well as grooming."[28] In *Twin Peaks*, Lucy exemplifies this position of femininity through the choices she makes about her pregnancy and her partner. The concept of choice is highly debated amongst feminists, primarily because of its relationship to the 1980s U.S. landmark case *Roe vs. Wade*, concerning women's rights to safe and legal abortions. Instead of being framed as a matter of reproductive *rights*, this issue centered on choice.[29] Such a shift in language used by U.S. liberal feminists to talk about abortion made a deliberate turn towards the apolitical and gradually influenced women's decision making in other areas.

Still, choice feminism is a useful concept for considering the character of Lucy, as we are directly concerned with issues of sexuality, reproduction, and parenting. In season 1, episode 7, we find out that Lucy is pregnant and that she has been sleeping with both Deputy Andy Brennan and department store manager Dick Tremayne. She believes the baby is Dick's because Andy has told her that he is sterile, which we later learn is not the case. Dick's initial response is for Lucy to have an abortion, and he hands her $650 to cover the procedure. Despite her squeaky voice and off-handed, airheaded comments at times, Lucy exerts authority over her own body and the baby inside her, telling him, "Richard, here's what you are going to do. Take your money, put it back in your wallet or your pocket, turn around, and walk through both sets of doors ... And never speak to me again" (2.4). Later, in episode 9, after Andy and Dick have been competing over who would be the best dad, Lucy takes control, sitting them both down in the sheriff's station for a talk. She tells them, "Ok. Here's how this is going to work. I'm going to keep my baby. There's only one way to handle this. They have a test to determine the blood type of the father. They won't be doing the test until after the baby is born, during which time I expect complete cooperation from each of you two gentlemen" (2.9). Lucy makes it clear that keeping the baby is *her* choice. Her take-charge attitude dictates the passive position of the men, as the pregnant female body cannot be pressured by the masculine desire to operate on their timeline.

Moreover, Lucy subverts conventional norms regarding the reproductive paradigm for sexuality and gender that denies women the sexual freedom that is generally associated with men. Angela McRobbie states, "On condition that she does not reproduce outside marriage or civil partnership, or become the single mother of several children, the young woman is now granted a prominence as a pleasure-seeking subject in possession of a healthy sexual appetite and identity."[30] This new attitude is reflected through Lucy, who is never judged for being single and pregnant, even though it is the norm for young, unwed middle-class women to refuse motherhood. Within the third wave framework, her choice is one that is considered personal/individual, not social/collective activism, and is premised upon a discourse of rights, which makes clear that she *should* be free to make her own choices about her body. This does not mean that her choice is the *correct* one in all cases; it merely reflects that women deserve equal opportunities to exercise free will and to embrace their sexuality as a form of pleasure.

Both emancipated and choice femininities share affinities with the notion of *successful* femininity, which is embodied by Norma. This new femininity defines the idealized subject as individualized, resilient, driven, confident, flexible, and self-made.[31] Steven P. Schacht and Doris W. Ewing write, "In our society, power is primarily reflected and sustained by how much money one has. Men's traditional role as breadwinner ... provided them with power while placing the homemaker wife in a subordinate, dependent role."[32] In Norma's case, the role is reversed. Her husband, Hank, is in prison, and she is the sole owner of the Double R Diner. It is her testimony at his parole hearing that appeases the board's concern about his re-entry into society and the necessity to work to support himself. When Norma tells the parole board, "I own the Double R Diner. I can give him a job," they promptly release Hank (1.5). The scene demonstrates the power that economic independence wields within society.

Norma's economic empowerment, however, does not equal personal fulfillment, as she is unhappy with her marriage and in love with Ed, Nadine's husband. Shelley Budgeon claims that "maintaining a coherent empowerment narrative requires a denial of the effects that external influences have on the realization of individual success."[33] To resolve such factors requires individualized strategies that do not necessarily work for all women and do not necessitate a shift towards autonomy. In Norma's case, her biggest obstacle is her husband, as she has spent 20 years as the self-sacrificing, nurturing wife. In season 2, episode 16, however, Norma takes a stand against Hank to stop living for him and start living for herself. Norma visits Hank, who is in jail, and tells him she wants a divorce. He agrees only if Norma gives him the alibi he needs to go free. When she refuses, he calls her a whore because of the affair with Ed. Norma retorts, "I'd rather be his whore than your wife," and walks out. For the first time, Norma rejects her role as a caring wife and exerts her sense of self. Third wave feminism promotes self-definition as a means of advancing a politics that makes female ambition an attainable prospect,[34] but it does not force a one-size-fits-all model. Because Norma has acknowledged her ability to support herself, and because she has found the confidence to leave Hank, she reflects what successful femininity might look like in real life.

All three of these femininities: emancipated, choice, and successful, are the result of a global discourse on neoliberalism, supported by capitalist culture and consumer lifestyle choices. For this reason, these discourses remain contradictory, but third wave feminism represents one strategy for negotiating the ambiguities associated with new femininities, asserting that women have gained increasing access to autonomous subject positions in the latter half of the twentieth century, which has allowed women more space for defining their own identities independently from relations with others.[35] Such an agenda of *self-definition* promotes agency and allows for an understanding of the personal realm, which focuses on individual and emotional needs over policy or legislative changes. While collective action is needed, examples of individual empowerment are also essential elements for social transformation.

GIRL POWER AND FANDOM: AUDREY AND DONNA

Fan culture, too, illustrates how consumers make sense of their emotional relationships with popular media representations. When *Twin Peaks* aired in 1990, there were no social media like Facebook, Twitter, Instagram, or blogging. Only a small subset of viewers took advantage of online communities through different bulletin board systems to discuss the series. One of the earliest *Twin Peaks* communities was the alt.tv.twin-peaks group. In Henry Jenkins' study of the community, he discusses how female fans of *Twin Peaks* stayed away from gossipy items, preferring to focus on their display of professional expertise in areas such as psychology.[36] Today, viewers have reinterpreted the series and have gone online to talk about the emotional draw of the characters for their own consumption. And characters such as Audrey and Donna have emerged as figures of girl power.

Girl culture and girl power emerged alongside third wave feminism, reclaiming and embracing girliness and all the many pleasures of female culture. Girl power "encourages girls and women to identify as traditionally feminine objects *and* as powerful female agents."[37] Coded in neoliberal language, girl power proposes that women have the *choice* to decide how they wish to present themselves. As sites of consumption, girl power is expressed through physical adornment: fashion, makeup, jewelry, etc. Emilie Zaslow states, "Girl power focuses on style as a mark of one's autonomy, on sexual expression as a symbol of one's connection with the self, on independence from men rather than from patriarchal systems and relations of power, and on the individual as independent resister rather than as member of collective social change movement."[38] Through their fashion and behavior, Audrey and Donna can be read as examples of girl culture in terms of agency and/or resistance.

In her 1990s feature in *Playboy*, Sherilyn Fenn identifies the cultural significance of her character. She states, "She had made it OK to use the power one has as a woman to be manipulative at times, to be precocious. She goes after what she wants vehemently, and she takes it. I think that's really admirable."[39] Fenn makes it clear that Audrey was different from the demure, vulnerable young girls often portrayed on television. Audrey had feminine styling with a take-charge dynamism associated with girl power. She wore lipstick and tightly fitted sweaters, but she also wore schoolgirl style skirts, socks, and shoes. In her article, "Audrey in Five Outfits," Angela K. Bayout does a textual analysis of some of Audrey's clothes from the series. When commenting on the iconic scene of Audrey at school changing her saddle shoes for a pair of red high heels, she states, "The image may not be popular because of its thematic symbolism, but because it depicts an act that women can relate to. Sometimes it's difficult for teenage girls to express themselves through fashion around their families, especially when the fashions are tight and low-cut."[40] Audrey served as a model for younger women trying to find their own gendered identity through fashion.

Yet, Audrey was more than a sex symbol and style icon. Whelehan writes that the girlie girl "notionally offers a subversion of the pin-up image: she is active rather than passive, and ruthlessly self-seeking in her own pleasures. Outspoken and sometimes aggressive, the new girl has no truck with feminine wiles, yet she looks deceptively like a pin-up."[41] Audrey's look evokes the image of the pin-up with her fitted sweaters and saddle shoes, but she is not passive. For instance, in season 1, episode 6, Audrey devises a plan to work for the perfume counter at her father's department store where Laura once worked, with the sole purpose of helping Agent Cooper solve Laura's case. Audrey, with her short hair pulled back from her face, pouty red lips and big doe eyes, dictates what she wants when she meets the Horne's Department Store manager. She states innocently, "You're going to tell my father that I'm busy as a bee wrapping boxes with the drones. Then, you are going to put me to work this afternoon behind the perfume counter, because if you don't, I'm going to rip my dress in half and scream at the top of my lungs and tell my father you made a pass at me" (1.6). Audrey combines assertiveness with manipulation to get what she wants, which is reflected as a sense of victory over the salacious character of Emory Battis, who we know serves as a go-between for Horne's Department Store and One-Eyed Jack's. Audrey plays tough; she is smart and has control over her own body as a feminine object *and* a powerful female agent. Her girlie display aligns with third wave feminism's insistence that "women can be sexual and stylish without being exploited."[42]

A quick Internet search for "Audrey Horne" today shows that viewers still see her as an example of girl power. For example, in 2011, Danielle Villano wrote in her "Style Icon-Audrey Horne" blog, "Ah, just look at how perfect those brows are! Who wouldn't want to be this girl ... Aside from having great fashion sense, Audrey Horne is cool, intelligent, and confident."[43] Nancy Wilde, in August 2014, posted eighteen photos of Audrey in different outfits, describing her as "Cool, stylish and seductively charming."[44] And, on the Reddit *Twin Peaks* page, one subscriber wrote about Audrey:

> A great deal of Audrey fans are women—they relate to her. In the original series of all the women she had the most adventurous story thread. Despite nearly being killed she was rescued by the man she loved and in return was able to get him information about the people framing him. I ended up liking her—she turned out to be much more than the spoiled brat we saw at the beginning of the series.[45]

These comments demonstrate that Audrey's feminine charm and hardcore determination still ring true as iconic markers of girl power.

Despite her similarity to Audrey, Donna Hayward does not have the same fan following as Audrey, as her expression of girl power is less about her sexual charm and more about her independence and anti-normative performance of femininity. When Bayout talks about Donna's fashion, she does so regarding a *lack* of style. She states, "Even though she looks very similar to Audrey, she sleuths around town in oversized down vests, and awkwardly dons Laura's old sunglasses while picking up smoking."[46] Donna's emulation of Laura's sexy style comes off as inauthentic because it undermines the power of the gaze that is often privileged by the male viewer. For instance, Donna visits James in jail. She wears a blue sweater, thigh length black skirt, black belt, Laura's black shades, red lipstick, and is smoking. Donna speaks in a seductive voice, asking James, who seems perplexed by her transformation, "So don't you want to kiss me?" (2.1). They kiss and Donna aggressively pulls James towards her through the cell bars, but James tugs away. Later, James tells Maddy about the visit, claiming, "It was weird. It wasn't like her" (2.3). Donna's behavior is awkward because it demonstrates the artificiality of the female object put on display for the male gaze. In fact, Donna does not perform for James. She does it for her own pleasure, in the hopes of understanding Laura's secrets and helping to solve her murder.

Donna's true fashion sense comes out in her 1990s grunge aesthetic, a kind of anti-style that favored an unconventional mixing of masculine and feminine elements. In the iconic oversized, baggy clothes of this style, she may have less sex appeal than Audrey, but she is proven to be a strong, independent woman. Even her parents permit her to do what she thinks best. For example, in the pilot episode, Donna gets caught after sneaking out, and her *dad*, Doc Hayward, must pick her up from the police station. Doc begins to chastise her, but then changes his tune, stating, "But, I also know you well enough to know you wouldn't have done it unless you had a good reason" (1.Pilot). The paternal vote of confidence Donna receives is typically reserved for male characters, but Donna is different. Her very lack of desire to be bound by the ideological constructions of conventional femininity (coquettish, sexily dressed) positions her as one who embodies girl power values of independence and selfhood.

Despite her appeal as an autonomous, free spirit, a quick Internet search on Donna makes clear that fans preferred the sexualized charm of Audrey to the nonconformity of Donna. Although there are Tumblr and Pinterest sites devoted to her, and Etsy sites with Donna inspired merchandise, there are few blogs dedicated to her. Still, one blog post reveals the reason why Donna has had such staying power, despite her *lack* of style and sexual prowess:

Donna Hayward's one of the unsung saints, the sweet one, the pensive romantic, the girl with the strongest heart of all and an endearing flair for fantastical drama that often manifested as teary outbursts. Brave when it came to tracking clues to the mystery of her BFF's death, she never stooped to revenge. Oh Donna, you rock back inside our hearts.[47]

Donna is special because she projects a sense of self that is courageous and strong (generally coded masculine), while also being vulnerable and receptive (coded feminine). She is not easily reduced to a stereotype of typical femaleness. Her complexity as a character makes her intriguing as an individual, rather than objectified as a sexual fetish.

CONCLUSION

Despite its short run, *Twin Peaks* clearly left a mark on our cultural imaginary. From its postmodern, offbeat use of generic conventions, to its dismantling of ridged parameters of the televisual narrative, the series challenged its viewers to consider the dark side of human nature below the pristine surface of middle-class American life. In this essay, I have reconsidered the cultural significance of some of the series' women by re-reading their characters through a third wave feminist lens. With its contradictions and focus on inclusivity, the third wave allows us to consider the complexity of these characters without simply dismissing them as victims of the patriarchal institutions that structure society. I have revealed how the series tackled complicated issues such as incest and domestic violence, which had only begun receiving public attention in the early 1990s. Additionally, I argued that normative assumptions of femininity were challenged in the series, giving rise to new positions of power that allow for less rigid constructions of female bodily pleasure, desire, and identification. Finally, I explored how early notions of girl culture and girl power were present in the series, which has led to a continued fan base for young women today. These new considerations support a more multifaceted interpretation of how the series negotiated key issues of gender, violence, agency, and power. *Twin Peaks'* women live on in our hearts and minds not because they are victims, but because they are complex and contradictory characters that deserve more credit than they have been given in the past.

NOTES

1. Anthony Todd, *Authorship and the Films of David Lynch* (New York: IB Tauris, 2012), 86.

2. Jim Collins, "Television and Postmodernism," in *Channels of Discourse, Reassembled*, ed. Robert C. Allen (Chapel Hill: University of North Carolina Press, 1992), 346.

3. Diana Hume George, "Lynching Women: A Feminist Reading of *Twin Peaks*,' in *Full of Secrets: Critical Approaches to Twin Peaks*, ed. David Lavery (Detroit: Wayne State University Press, 1995), 110.

4. Amber E. Kinser, "Negotiating Spaces for/through Third Wave Feminism," *NWSA Journal* 16, no. 3 (Fall 2004): 132.

5. Graham Thompson, *American Culture in the 1980s* (Edinburgh: Edinburgh University Press, 2007), 8.

6. Susan Faludi, *Backlash: The Undeclared War against American Women* (New York: Crown Publishers, Inc., 1991), x.

7. Sherry B. Ortner, "Too Soon for Post-Feminism: The Ongoing Life of Patriarchy in Neoliberal America," *History and Anthropology* 25, no. 4 (2014): 531.

8. Rory Dicker and Alison Piepmeier, "Introduction," in *Catching a Wave: Reclaiming Feminism for the 21st Century*, eds. Rory Dicker and Alison Piepmeier (Boston: Northeastern University Press, 2003), 11.

9. Kathleen Rowe Karlyn, *Unruly Girls, Unrepentant Mothers: Redefining Feminism on Screen* (Austin: University of Texas Press, 2011), 33–34.

10. Jennifer Heywood and Jennifer Drake, "We Learn America Like a Script: Activism in the Third Wave; or, Enough Phantoms of Nothing," in *Third Wave Agenda: Being Feminist, Doing Feminism*, eds. Leslie Heywood and Jennifer Drake, (Minneapolis: University of Minnesota Press, 1997), 51.

11. Thompson, *American Culture*, 104.

12. Lisa McGirr, *Suburban Warriors: The Origins of the New American Right* (Princeton: Princeton University Press, 2001), 302.

13. Rowe Karlyn, *Unruly Girls*, 52.

14. Imelda Whelehan, *Overloaded: Popular Culture and the Future of Feminism* (London: The Women's Press Ltd., 2000), 4.

15. See Randi Davenport's "The Knowing Spectator of *Twin Peaks*," Laura Plummer's "'I'm Not Laura Palmer': David Lynch's Fractured Fairy Tale," and Michail Zontos' "Leland Palmer was Not Alone."

16. John Alexander, *The Films of David Lynch* (London: Charles Letts & Co., 1993), 171.

17. Melanie Waters, "The Horrors of Home: Feminism and Femininity in the Suburban Gothic," in *Women on Screen: Feminism and Femininity in Visual Culture*, ed. Melanie Waters (London: Palgrave, 2011), 67.

18. Waters, "The Horrors of Home," 70.

19. Ann Jones, "Battering: Who's Going to Stop It?," in *"Bad Girls"/"Good Girls": Women, Sex, and Power in the Nineties*, eds. Nan Bauer Maglin and Donna Perry (New Brunswick: Rutgers University Press, 1996), 166.

20. Jones, "Battering," 171.

21. bell hooks, *Feminist Theory: From Margins to Center*, 2nd edition (New York: South End Press, 2000), 120.

22. Deborah L. Siegel, "Reading Between the Waves: Feminist Historiography in a 'Postfeminist' Moment," in *Third Wave Agenda: Being Feminist, Doing Femi-*

nism, eds. Leslie Heywood and Jennifer Drake (Minneapolis: University of Minnesota Press, 1997), 76.

23. Jones, 171.

24. Shelly Budgeon, "The Contradictions of Successful Femininity: Third Wave Feminism, Postfeminism and 'New' Femininities," in *New Femininities: Postfeminism, Neoliberalism and Subjectivity*, eds. Rosalind Gill and Christina Scharff, (London: Palgrave, 2011), 285.

25. Michelle M. Lazar, "The Right to Be Beautiful: Postfeminist Identity and Consumer Beauty Advertising," in *New Femininities: Postfeminism, Neoliberalism and Subjectivity*, ed. Rosalind Gill and Christina Scharff, (London: Palgrave, 2011): 42.

26. Rowe Karlyn, *Unruly Girl*, 35.

27. Linda R. Hirshman, *Get to Work: A Manifesto for Women of the World* (New York: Penguin Group, 2006).

28. Lazar, "The Right to Be Beautiful," 43.

29. Lazar, "The Right to Be Beautiful," 43.

30. Angela McRobbie, "Top Girls?: Young women and the Post-Feminist Sexual Contract," *Cultural Studies* 21, nos. 4–5 (July/September, 2007): 732.

31. Budgeon, "The Contradictions of Successful Femininity," 284.

32. Steven P. Schacht and Deborah W. Ewing, *Feminism with Men: Bridging the Gender Gap* (Oxford: Rowman & Littlefield, 2004), 66.

33. Budgeon, "The Contradictions of Successful Femininity," 285.

34. Budgeon, "The Contradictions of Successful Femininity," 83.

35. Budgeon, "The Contradictions of Successful Femininity," 284.

36. Henry Jenkins, "'Do You Enjoy Making the Rest of Us Feel Stupid?': alt. tv.twinpeaks, the Trickster Author, and Viewer Mastery," in *Full of Secrets: Critical Approaches to Twin Peaks*, ed. David Lavery (Detroit: Wayne State University Press, 1995), 60–61.

37. Emilie Zaslow, *Feminism, INC.: Coming to Age in Girl Power and Media Culture* (New York: Palgrave, 2009), 3.

38. Zaslow, *Feminism, INC.*, 158.

39. Glenn O'Brien, "When '*Twin Peaks*' Actress Sherilyn Fenn Posed for *Playboy*," *Playboy*, last modified June 6, 2017, http://www.playboy.com/articles/sherilyn-fenn-playboy-pictorial.

40. Angela K. Bayout, "Audrey in 5 Outfits," in *Fan Phenomena: Twin Peaks*, eds. Marisa C. Hayes and Franck Boulègue (Chicago: Intellect Ltd., 2013), 23.

41. Whelehan, *Overloaded*, 37.

42. Zaslow, *Feminism INC.*, 27.

43. Danielle Villano, "Style Icon—Audrey Horne," *Her Campus Media*, last modified September 29, 2011, https://www.hercampus.com/school/purchase/style-icon-audrey-horne-0.

44. Nancy Wilde, "Style Icon: Audrey Horne," *The Nancy Wilde Experience* (blog), last modified August 22, 2014, http://nancywilde.blogspot.com/2014/08/style-icon-audrey-horne.html.

45. Topcat1436, July 30, 2017 (10:53 a.m.), comment on u/princeofropes, "[No spoilers] Why is Audrey Horne Such a Fan Favorite Character?," *Reddit*

Twin Peaks, July 30, 2017 (8:28 a.m.), https://www.reddit.com/r/twinpeaks/comments/6qgw96/no_spoilers_why_is_audrey_horne_such_a_fan/.

46. Bayout, "Audrey in 5 Outfits," 23.

47. "Donna Hayward from *Twin Peaks*," *Nasty Galaxy*, September 25, 2012, https://blog.nastygal.com/style/role-model/2012/09/donna-hayward-from-twin-peaks/.

WORKS CITED

Alexander, John. *The Films of David Lynch*. London: Charles Letts & Co, 1993.

Bayout, Angela. "Audrey in 5 Outfits." In *Fan Phenomena: Twin Peaks*, edited by Marisa C. Hayes and Franck Boulègue, 20–29. Chicago: Intellect Ltd., 2013.

Budgeon, Shelly. "The Contradictions of Successful Femininity: Third Wave Feminism, Postfeminism and 'New' Femininities." In *New Femininities: Postfeminism, Neoliberalism and Subjectivity*, edited by Rosalind Gill and Christina Scharff, 279–292. London: Palgrave, 2011.

Collins, Jim. "Television and Postmodernism." In *Channels of Discourse, Reassembled*, edited by Robert C. Allen, 327–353. Chapel Hill: University of North Carolina Press, 1992.

Dicker, Rory, and Alison Piepmeier. "Introduction." In *Catching a Wave: Reclaiming Feminism for the 21st Century*, edited by Rory Dicker and Alison Piepmeier, 3–28. Boston: Northeastern University Press, 2003.

"Donna Hayward from *Twin Peaks*." *Nasty Galaxy*, September 25, 2012. https://blog.nastygal.com/style/role-model/2012/09/donna-hayward-from-twin-peaks/.

Faludi, Susan. *Backlash: The Undeclared War against American Women*. New York: Crown Publishers, Inc., 1991.

Heywood, Leslie, and Jennifer Drake. "We Learn America Like a Script: Activism in the Third Wave; or, Enough Phantoms of Nothing." In *Third Wave Agenda: Being Feminist, Doing Feminism*, edited by Leslie Heywood and Jennifer Drake, 40–54. Minneapolis: University of Minnesota Press, 1997.

Hirshman, Linda R. *Get to Work: A Manifesto for Women of the World*. New York: Penguin Group, 2006.

hooks, bell. *Feminist Theory: From Margins to Center*. 2nd edition. New York: South End Press, 2000.

Hume George, Diana. "Lynching Women: A Feminist Reading of *Twin Peaks*." In *Full of Secrets: Critical Approaches to Twin Peaks*, edited by David Lavery, 109–119. Detroit: Wayne State University, 1995.

Jenkins, Henry. "'Do you Enjoy Making the Rest of Us Feel Stupid?': alt.tv.twinpeaks, the Trickster Author, and Viewer Mastery." In *Full of Secrets: Critical Approaches to Twin Peaks*, edited by David Lavery, 51–69. Detroit: Wayne State University Press, 1995.

Jones, Anne. "Battering: Who's Going to Stop It?," In*"Bad Girls"/"Good Girls": Women, Sex, and Power in the Nineties*, edited by Nan Bauer Maglin and Donna Perry, 164174. New Brunswick: Rutgers University Press, 1996.

Karlyn, Kathleen Rowe. *Unruly Girls, Unrepentant Mothers: Redefining Feminism on Screen*. Austin: University of Texas Press, 2011.

Kinser, Amber E. "Negotiating Spaces for/through Third wave Feminism." *NWSA Journal* 16, no. 3 (2004): 124–153. https://www.nytimes.com/2017/05/17/arts/television/twin-peaks-abc-1990.html.

Lazar, Michelle M. "The Right to Be Beautiful: Postfeminist Identity and Consumer Beauty Advertising." In *New Femininities: Postfeminism, Neoliberalism and Subjectivity*, edited by Rosalind Gill and Christina Scharff, 37–51. London: Palgrave, 2011.

Lynch, David, and Mark Frost, creators. *Twin Peaks*. ABC, 1990–1991. *Netflix*, https://www.netflix.com/search?q=twin%20peak.

McGirr, Lisa. *Suburban Warriors: The Origins of the New American Right*. Princeton: Princeton University Press, 2001.

McRobbie, Angela. "Top Girls?: Young Women and the Post-Feminist Sexual Contract." *Cultural Studies* 21, nos. 4–5 (2007): 718–737.

O'Brien, Glenn. "When *Twin Peaks'* Actress Sherilyn Fenn Posed for *Playboy*." *Playboy*, June 6, 2017. http://www.playboy.com/articles/sherilyn-fenn-playboy-pictorial.

Ortner, Sherry B. "Too Soon for Post-Feminism: The Ongoing Life of Patriarchy in Neoliberal America." *History and Anthropology* 25, no. 4 (2014): 530–549.

Schacht, Steven P., and Doris W. Ewing. *Feminism with Men: Bridging the Gender Gap*. Oxford: Rowman & Littlefield, 2004.

Siegel, Deborah L. "Reading between the Waves: Feminist Historiography in a 'Postfeminist' Moment." In *Third Wave Agenda: Being Feminist, Doing Feminism*, edited by Leslie Heywood and Jennifer Drake, 55–82. Minneapolis: University of Minnesota Press, 1997.

Thompson, Graham. *American Culture in the 1980s*. Edinburgh: Edinburgh University Press, 2007.

Todd, Anthony. *Authorship and the Films of David Lynch*. New York: IB Tauris, 2012.

Topcat1436. July 30, 2017 (10:53 a.m.). Comment on u/princeofropes. "[No spoilers] Why is Audrey Horne Such a Fan Favorite Character?" *Reddit* Twin Peaks. July 30, 2017 (8:28 a.m.). https://www.reddit.com/r/twinpeaks/comments/6qgw96/no_spoilers_why_is_audrey_horne_such_a_fan/.

Villano, Danielle. "Style Icon—Audrey Horne." *Her Campus Media*. September 29, 2011. https://www.hercampus.com/school/purchase/style-icon-audrey-horne-0

Waters, Melanie. "The Heroes of Home: Feminism and Femininity in the Suburban Gothic." In *Women on Screen: Feminism and Femininity in Visual Culture*, edited by Melanie Waters, 58–73. London: Palgrave, 2011.

Whelehan, Imelda. *Overloaded: Popular Culture and the Future of Feminism*. London: The Women's Press Ltd, 2000.

Wilde, Nancy. "Style Icon: Audrey Horne." *The Nancy Wild Experience* (blog). August 22, 2014. http://nancywilde.blogspot.com/2014/08/style-icon-audrey-horne.html

Zaslow, Emilie. *Feminism, INC.: Coming to Age in Girl Power and Media Culture*. New York: Palgrave, 2009.

Six

The Owls Are Not What They Seem

Retaking Queer Meaning in Twin Peaks

Ben Kruger-Robbins

Twin Peaks' movie-length pilot aired on April 8, 1990 to near-unanimous critical praise, both for the show and its network, the American Broadcasting Company (ABC). Reviewers from popular national publications hailed the program as a brilliant, revelatory predictor of television trends in the 1990s. These press outlets, enamored with *Twin Peaks'* cinematic aesthetics, series co-creator David Lynch's "strange" authorial flourishes, and the show's complex narrative and offbeat characters, declared *Twin Peaks* an almost revolutionary event, albeit one destined to ultimately fail. Such critical appreciation involved a comparison between entertainment journalists' superior tastes and those of "mass" audiences whose non-sophistication would inevitably result in *Twin Peaks'* cancellation. Moreover, many critics themselves later soured on episodes not directed by Lynch, describing much of the first season and all the second as derivative, pretentious, and soapy. These perspectives, I maintain, celebrated the "exceptional auteur" and distinguished the first season's "cinematic" presentation from purportedly lesser installments more geared toward television soap opera. Twenty-six years after the pilot's premiere, critics again flocked to *Twin Peaks: The Return,* now airing on the subscription channel Showtime, to valorize what *Twin Peaks* "should have been" all along: *art* on television.

In this chapter, I consider how popular press outlets and industry personnel worked to legitimate, masculinize, and de-queer the show before examining how diverse fan fiction entries responded to and challenged the program's restrictive discursive framing. In contrast to critics' claims about the show's superior construction, many entries expounded on affective, relational knowledge between characters to flesh out the narrative's non/anti/contra-straight possibilities. I contend that such reclamations of gender and sexual non-normativity in *Twin Peaks* and *Twin Peaks: The Return* amended press articles that diminish the show's feminine qualities through gendered and classist laments against an imagined "mass" broadcast viewership.

I first examine how critics discussed *Twin Peaks'* initial run in the early 1990s as being "too groundbreaking" for network broadcast and, therefore, under imminent threat of cancellation. Competition from cable television and the home video market compelled the major networks to "innovate," a prerogative that the popular press championed as necessary and overdue. These views, however, proved incompatible with reviewers' relative disdain for *Twin Peaks'* second season in 1991, wherein the show resolved Laura Palmer's murder and focused more on relationships within the town. I use these same articles to elaborate upon the popular press' erasure and limitation of queerness as a defining attribute of season two, a thematic conceit evident in the show's exploration of non/anti/contra-straight characters such as transgender Drug Enforcement Administration (DEA) agent (and, later, Federal Bureau of Investigation [FBI] chief of staff) Denise Bryson and confounding of straight narrative tropes and expectations. Moreover, many of these same press outlets helped to frame *Twin Peaks'* titular "return" in 2017 as a premium-cable event, presumably too complex and cinematic for network broadcast and mass audiences. Ironically, however, I consider *Twin Peaks: The Return*'s indulgence in narrative "excess" and continued unwillingness to "resolve" earlier season mysteries as queer prerogatives that undercut the show's elite critical positioning.

Secondly, I compare these historically selective press articles with lesbian, gay, bisexual, transgender, queer and questioning, intersex, asexual, and allied (LGBTQIA+) fans' reclamation of queer meaning within *Twin Peaks* through affective personal writing and alternative archival practices. I argue that such entries revel in the show's soap-operatic aspects and serve as counterpoints to more culturally exalted fan practices of "decoding" and "problem-solving" the program's mysteries. Herein, I engage a user profile, Amatara, as one viable case study in curating community dialogue around *Twin Peaks'* relational webs. Amatara's online engagement with queerly explicit "slash" fiction bridges the show's initial run with its 2017 "return" and validates non/anti/contra-straight gravitations toward narrative circularity and irresolution.

HIGH ART, LOW RATINGS, AND COSTS OF "QUALITY"

Within television studies, feminist and queer scholars have long challenged more masculine-oriented definitions of quality as relates to programs, production processes, genres, reception practices, and the ontology of the medium itself. Jane Feuer undertakes questions of legitimation in two seminal works which, respectively, shine a light on how television's notions of "live" programming work to devalue recorded fare[1] and how the moniker of "quality" functions ideologically by permitting niche groups "to enjoy a form of television which is seen as more literate, more stylistically complex, and more psychologically 'deep' than ordinary TV fare."[2] She recognizes here not only a form of targeted branding (in this case the "MTM style" of many 1970s CBS sitcoms) but a differentiation in viewer positioning. Feuer underscores that "the quality audience gets to separate itself from the mass audience and can watch TV without guilt, and without realizing the double-edged discourse they are getting is also ordinary TV."[3] Her argument serves to challenge taste hierarchies that regularly adopt a masculinist and purportedly "objective" view of "better" television.

Despite shifts since the mid-1980s in what television theorist John Thornton Caldwell terms "televisuality," or "stylizing performance … that challenges television's existing formal and presentational hierarchies,"[4] TV historians have marked accompanying changes in how popular press and academia define "quality." Michael Newman and Elana Levine consider more contemporary television legitimation as related to programs' cinematic attributes, auteur status, and narrative "complexity." They argue, citing *Twin Peaks* as a key example, that "the discourses of legitimation [circa 1990] offered something new … a hint that television as a whole might be changing—improving even—with *Twin Peaks* as a harbinger."[5] Herein, the authors mark a shift from the past wherein "this discourse [of quality] had been associated with a particular production company—such as MTM—but more typically linked to a single program like *Hill Street Blues*." By contrast, they determine that "some of the discourse around *Twin Peaks* suggested that its radical departure from the TV norm might have signaled a more significant shift in the medium as a whole."[6] Indeed, both critical and academic infatuation with the show[7] helped to mark *Twin Peaks* as a turning point toward what media scholar Jason Mittell describes as "complex TV."[8] Newman and Levine, however, charge that the popular press' and, more recently, the academe's unbridled celebration of narrative complexity on TV often "[accepts and perpetuates] the logic and interests of the media industries,"[9] thereby tacitly endorsing the commercial incentives of global conglomerates. Additionally, they cite a divergence between these purviews and television studies' investments in delegitimated "feminine" genres like soap operas and examinations of the medium's gendered production, reception, and marketing-based power imbalances.[10]

Twin Peaks' premiere garnered hyperbolic pre-show press. Howard Rosenberg, in anticipation of the premiere, asked in the *Los Angeles Times* on April 6, 1990, "First question: Can this be happening? Second question: Can this be happening on television?"[11] Answering himself "yes and yes," Rosenberg suggested that ABC, unlike its "big three" network competitors, NBC and CBS, offered an alternative to mainstream fare. He compared the commercial network to Channel 4 in Britain concerning its willingness to serve as a "laboratory" for individualistic experimentation rather than a "rest home for tired ideas."[12] Mark Harris of *Entertainment Weekly* similarly acknowledged *Twin Peaks* as necessarily reviving network programming, noting that "ten years ago, the networks didn't need David Lynch. Not only did they not need him—they wouldn't have wanted him. They had *Three's Company* and *That's Incredible*, shows that attracted 9 out of 10 viewers without being innovative, or adventurous, or good."[13] He later projected that "[*Twin Peaks*] could foretell a decade in which network television programmers will have to face many more excursions into the unknown. For TV viewers, that can only be taken as good news."[14] In applauding *Twin Peaks'* distinction from earlier ABC fare, such reviews echo ABC's industrial discourse, most apparent in an ad for *Twin Peaks* proclaiming, "ABC is looking more and more like the network of the '90s,"[15] darker and edgier than the competition, serious and removed from its frivolous reputation for tawdry teen shows.[16] The advertisement includes some of the show's more offbeat images, including a flashing red streetlight, and emphasizes *Peaks'* "cinematic" low-key, high contrast lighting concept. Review excerpts from *Time Magazine* and *The Gannett News Service* proclaimed *Twin Peaks'* pilot as "the most hauntingly original work ever done for American TV,"[17] thereby reinforcing Rosenberg's and Harris' claims about the program's exceptionality.

Such praise, however, carried warnings of impending failure for *Twin Peaks*, fears predicated on ratings and "mainstream" audiences' inability to process narratively and visually complex content. Ken Tucker of *Entertainment Weekly* bluntly prophesized, "Will *Twin Peaks* be a hit? Not a chance in hell. (Well, maybe in hell)"[18] and denigrated viewers for enjoying what he and his colleague, Mark Harris, dismissed as inferior television. Drawing comparisons between *Twin Peaks* and its time-slot competitors, Tucker continued:

> I also recognize that [unsettling drama] is not what most people watch TV for, and I'm guessing that a hefty percentage of the millions who'll tune in out of curiosity won't make it past Peaks' grim first 15 minutes. Groans of "Honey, we're missing *Married... With Children* for this?" will resound throughout this great land, as remote-control trigger-fingers get itchy.[19]

Considering that *Married... With Children* (1987–1997), a staple along with *The Simpsons* (1988–) of the newly emergent Fox network's primetime lineup, already pushed boundaries of content, Tucker's statement seems more predicated on audiences' intolerance for cinematic "artistry" on TV. He lambasted the previously sacrosanct zero-degree aesthetic of 1970s sitcoms to valorize *Twin Peaks'* extra-televisual virtues and chided ABC's audience for unsophistication. Similarly, John O'Connor, interviewing David Lynch for a Sunday edition of the *New York Times* months prior to the show's premiere, wrote, "whether or not a television audience can accept Lynch's weirder ideas, he has movies for his more unbridled fits of imagination,"[20] implying the same intellectual laziness in television audiences. As Newman and Levine note, "television is legitimated when it no longer resembles television; instances of television achieve prominence when they take on the traits of a more culturally validated form."[21] "Failure," as Tucker, Harris, and O'Connor use the term, actually marks *Twin Peaks'* success in breaking with "low" formal conventions and achieving avant-garde status in defiance of a supine viewership content with tried and true generic formulas.

Academics such as Eileen Meehan and Ien Ang, however, challenge invocations of "audience" that perpetuate fictions conjured by rating companies. Ang, channeling cultural critic Todd Gitlin, argues in *Desperately Seeking the Audience* that "the elevated status of research as a means of providing the institution with ... ways to predict success and failure"[22] does not account for actual audience tastes but for abstract market predictions. Meehan, articulating similar concerns, in "Heads of Household and Ladies of the House: Gender, Genre, and Broadcast Ratings 1929–1990" writes that "the interaction of advertisers, networks, and the ratings monopolist generate the definition of the commodity audience, which is then operationalized through the ratings."[23] Critics' perspectives actually reiterate what cultural theorist Michel Foucault terms an "incitement to discourse," which he describes not as "silence itself—the things one declines to say or is forbidden to name" but rather "an element that functions alongside the things said, with them and in relation to them within overall strategies."[24] In blaming audiences for promoting allegedly lower quality programming through choice and poor taste, reviewers rhetorically disavow the power dynamics central to industrial discourse wherein networks, ratings organizations, critics, and viewers enter into a dialogue that maintains, rather than undermines, corporate status quo. These reviewers distinguish their superiority of taste from the crassness of ratings, applauding ABC and David Lynch for the artistic "success" of the program while blaming the audience rather than institutional arrangements for the program's inevitable failure. Invoking ratings as the ultimate determinant of televisual longevity, they work to sustain and reinforce ABC's commodity politics.

TWIN PEAKS' GENRE CONSTRUCTION AND GENDERED POSITIONING IN POPULAR PRESS

While ratings discourse remained consistent across most reviews that I uncovered, most critics also invoked genre to qualify, masculinize, and de-queer *Twin Peaks* despite the show's overt calls to forego masculinist logics. As previously indicated, the serial's soap-operatic positioning worked to denotatively elevate non/anti/contra-straight characters, situations, and visual/aural stylizations, though reviewers either actively diminished the genre's "feminine" elements or (inaccurately) discussed this motivation as parody. A key example of the show's interlocking queer and melodramatic imperatives revolves around the relationship between cisgender/heterosexually coded FBI special agent Dale Cooper and transgender DEA agent Denise Bryson. At the episode's climax, town sheriff Harry Truman dispatches Bryson to intervene in a hostage situation where Cooper is held at gunpoint, the damsel in distress. Bryson entices Cooper's captor, drug lord Jean Renault, with an amusing display of gender performativity, lifting her skirt flirtatiously and allowing Cooper to grab a gun holstered to her thigh; together, in an intimate partnership, Cooper and Bryson take down the captors. As an added aside, when Cooper mentions to Bryson, who expresses sexual interest in a woman, "Denise, I thought you were no longer interested in girls," Bryson responds, "Coop, I may be wearing a dress, but I still put my panties on one leg at a time if you know what I mean," thus inviting ambiguity between gender, biological sex, and sexual object-choice (2.13). Bryson's story arc over the course of four episodes echoes Teresa de Lauretis's determination regarding "the construction of gender as the product and process of both representation and self-representation"[25] rather than simply a biological distinction between male and female.

Bryson's multifaceted identity as a biological male who comfortably identifies as female yet sexually prefers women also reflects queer media scholar Alexander Doty's analysis of George Cukor's film *Sylvia Scarlett* that, "queerly seen it is erotically daring ... seriocomic uses of transvestitism within the conventions of a mistaken-identity plot playfully invite all spectators to experience 'queer feelings' as they move through the range of homo- bi- and heterosexual desires articulated through the text."[26] *Twin Peaks* likewise evokes marginalized sexual and gender positions that also render its genre orientation polymorphous. As Lynch scholar Martha Nochimson writes in *The Passion of David Lynch: Wild at Heart in Hollywood*, the program "alters the conventional structure of gender ... Cooper's crucial receptivity envisions feminine wisdom as necessary to the seeker [and] significantly transforms the pervasive phallocentrism of American screen fiction."[27] During a panel discussion at the 2018 Society for Cinema and Media Studies conference in Toronto, Nochimson also spoke to Lynch's reverence of soap opera form and speculated on his desire to incorporate, not denigrate or mock, the genre in *Twin Peaks*.[28]

The popular press, however, either unflatteringly compared daytime and primetime soaps to *Twin Peaks* or lambasted the show for its melodramatic "detours." Ed Bark's article for the *Dallas Morning News* announced the show as, "*Dallas* with an IQ, *Dynasty* without all that lousy acting … it is so unusual that ABC entertainment president Robert Iger says the network seriously is considering airing it without commercials."[29] The preview, while complimentary toward *Twin Peaks*, ridiculed the explicitly commercial designation of soap opera and the form's purportedly kitschy translation to primetime television in the 1980s. By contrast, John O'Connor's initial review of the pilot unusually and refreshingly attended to and lauded melodramatic excess, surmising that:

> The series slips into the traditional television form of a soap opera, complete with ominous cue music. On the surface, things seem comfortably ordinary, right down to the diner that makes a nifty tuna sandwich and great cherry pie. But as the murder investigation proceeds, all sorts of nasty business are exposed, from betrayals and secret affairs to drugs and pornography.[30]

His later discussion of the second season, however, reviled televisual indulgences and criticized the show for its redundant weirdness. In an October 1991 review, O'Connor wrote:

> Instead of a dancing dwarf, Mr. Lynch this time came up with a strange giant who, in a vaguely German accent, appeared to the wounded and exhausted Agent Cooper with odd clues and warnings. ("The owls are not what they seemed.") It seems that Mr. Lynch's oft-stated belief in the redemptive powers of fantasy will be indulged more openly this season. Intuition and subconscious, do your stuff. In his *Saturday Night Live* appearance, the engaging Mr. MacLachlan had two routines revolving around who really killed Laura Palmer, both of which only served to underscore an obvious thought: who cares? *Twin Peaks* has done enough fiddling. It's time to get on with the show.[31]

These comments spoke to aggravation with the form of soap opera, which, as Tania Modleski observes, employs circularity and defers story information to "undercut the very notion of success by continuously demonstrating that happiness for all is an unattainable goal."[32] Instead, O'Connor craved finite resolution, a cinematic expectation that Newman and Levine cite as a qualifying distinction between serialized primetime dramas and endless soaps. His press remarks, as well as Bark's notion of subpar acting and mindless commerciality in soap operas both, characterize critical disinvestment in *Twin Peaks* as the show broke from conventions of "quality" television.

Television scholar Christine Gledhill, however, emphasizes soap opera's importance to socially marginalized viewers and cites Ien Ang's ethnography of female viewers of *Dallas* to discuss the genre (and its primetime successors) as "permitting emotional enactments within fantasies disallowed by social or cultural convention."[33] She registers the form's basis in "talk" rather than "action" as privileging culturally feminine modes of interaction that Bark's and O'Connor's writings ignored or rejected. Bark, especially, disregarded the sexual politics inherent in shows like *Dallas* and *Dynasty*, programs that highlighted challenges to gender roles and sexual permissiveness. Ang observes the Ewing family's dysfunction and domestic strife as pivotal to *Dallas*'s female viewership while scholars like Stephen Tropiano and Jane Feuer[34] underscore *Dynasty*'s gay following that resulted from its camp theatrics and the introduction of an out character, Steven Carrington, to primetime. As Tropiano notes in *The Prime Time Closet*, *Dynasty* ultimately garnered a cult following, including screenings at gay bars,[35] appending Feuer's recognition that 1980s primetime soaps were industrially coded to appeal to gay men. Feuer writes of *Dynasty* that "very early on, the show's producers were aware of the show's excesses and intended to code them within the plots."[36] In tandem with its "low genre" counterparts, *Twin Peaks* upheld melodrama's ideological implications, celebrated queerness, and posed similar challenges to gender roles and dominant conceptualizations of power.

Indeed, as *Twin Peaks'* second season developed, many of the "distractions" and "interruptions" that O'Connor, Bark, and other entertainment journalists dismissed as overly soapy and narratively unnecessary took on connotatively non/anti/contra-straight form. In addition to Cooper enlisting Bryson's expertise, Cooper and his nemesis Windom Earle, once competing for the affections of Earle's deceased wife Caroline, encounter doppelgangers of themselves in the queerly fashioned alternative space of the Black Lodge. Such "doubles" challenge ingrained ideals of macho competition and heterosexual romantic union.

Additionally, outcast characters such as Margaret Lanterman, a woman who receives vital information from her log, and the sheriff's office receptionist, Lucy Moran, who uncovers clues via her investment in the show's soap opera intertext, *Invitation to Love,* maintain agency and advantage over their "straight-man" counterparts. Bark's sentiment that the second season's premiere amounted to "absurdly abstract swill, a plodding, self-indulgent farce from a director who seemingly has lost his senses, and his sense of direction"[37] condemned these instances of "debased" narrative logic and, by implication, their queer centrality. Most ironically, by abandoning the series and deferring to the wisdom of industrial discourse by season two, reviewers like Bark and O'Connor substantiated the logic of ratings from which they sought exception at the time of *Twin Peaks'* premiere. Bark speculated that:

> The joke may be on Mr. Lynch. By choosing to laugh in the face of any remaining plausibility, he may well have killed *Peaks* ' chances to survive the season. Ratings from Nielsen's 23 "overnight" TV markets, including Dallas/Fort Worth, show sharp audience drop-offs during the show's first 15 minutes. In Dallas/Fort Worth, the Nielsens say that 236,000 homes were tuned to Peaks at 8 p.m. But by 8:15 p.m., 45,000 of those homes had tuned out.[38]

He quite suddenly adopted a populist tone and shifted from his earlier claims about the expendable mass audience's uncouth tastes.

William Grimes of the *New York Times* echoed these implications that *Twin Peaks'* second season "subplots and peculiar characters" deterred "reasonable" viewers but would surely serve as "fodder for the academic trough ... later this month in Chicago, the International Communication Association will chew over topics like 'Sexual Politics at the Double R: A Gender Analysis of the Working Men and Women of Twin Peaks' and 'Twin Peaks' and the Paradoxical Politics of Postmodernist Representation."[39] Both authors reviled the show's queer discourse, first through denigration of "mass television" and later through a tirade against academic elitism. Their contradictory and heteronormatively grounded stances on the show, ultimately, relied on *Twin Peak*'s standing as a commercial "success" or "failure" and rendered their initially assured commitments to its "unlikely" longevity fickle.

Perhaps expectedly, critics returned to herald *Twin Peaks'* television revival twenty-six years later, an "event" wherein Lynch directed all eighteen episodes and brought the program to Showtime, a commercial-free subscription channel. Industrial and popular press journalists, who were initially relieved that the show would not be airing on broadcast television (ABC), still fretted over how premiere cable executives might tarnish Lynch's art, and speculation swirled for weeks over whether or not the director would pull *Twin Peaks* over "creative differences" with Showtime. Maureen Ryan's 2017 feature article for the trade publication *Variety* heavily quoted Lynch as well as Showtime chief executive officer David Nevins and president of programming Gary Levine on the struggle. Ryan's piece retrospectively rehashed how "the revival almost fell apart before production began," ultimately "[taking] delicate negotiations by all parties to rescue the project."[40]

Nevins and Levine reiterated their initial concerns about the project's cost and manageability under Lynch's control, but ultimately ceded to the legitimating framework of superior authorial license. Nevins stated that "once I understood what the issues were from the point of view of the filmmaker, I was like, 'OK, we can figure that out' ... and we did," adding later that "new installments of the drama reflect Lynch's advancement as an artist."[41] Despite Levine's elevation of subscription TV "freedoms," however, Lynch interestingly noted in the same article that changing networks minimally impacted his storytelling approach, considering that permissions for graphic content (nudity and violence) were largely irrelevant to the show. Furthermore, Ryan, in a rare moment of praise for network television, described *Twin Peaks* as indebted to broadcast pleasures, writing that the original run fit "easily into a number of existing TV categories: the classic nighttime soap, the murder mystery, the high school drama and the small-town saga."[42] Ryan's and Lynch's remarks, sandwiched between industry rhetoric, still worked to champion *Twin Peaks'* "non-quality" markers of televisual presentation.

Popular press critics, however, deferred largely to myths of the filmmaker's independent vision and applauded *Twin Peaks* for its canonization as quality TV (which they describe as "superior" to a cinematic landscape dominated by intellectual property-based sequels and remakes). Furthermore, and in the same breath, some television critics continued to herald the original series for its "groundbreaking" appeal, unmatched by *The Return*'s purportedly more contemplative, less "raw" feel. James Poniewozik wrote in the *New York Times* that "as inventive as it was, the 'Twin Peaks' of 1990–91 was also a creature of its time, borrowing elements from prime-time soaps and detective series. To watch its new iteration is to be reminded of what TV has done in its absence."[43] At season's end, however, he and his *Times* co-critics Mike Hale and Margaret Lyons promoted *Twin Peaks: The Return* as one of 2017's ten best shows and professed that it was "a direct download from the subconscious of Mr. Lynch, who directed every episode: part horror story, part slapstick, all twisted fantasy."[44]

Poniewozik's initial slight against *Twin Peaks: The Return* as an inadequate imitation of the quality programming it helped invent, however, also pervaded Ed Bark's review. Bark, writing as a freelance entertainment journalist, surmised that:

> In its glorified early episodes, the original "Twin Peaks" was something to behold. But in the nearly 26 years since it left ABC, a number of other TV auteurs have emerged and surpassed Lynch, who's now well beyond middle-aged crazy at age 71. Vince Gilligan (FX's [sic] "Breaking Bad," "Better Call Saul"), Noah Hawley (FX's "Fargo" and "Legion") and Ryan Murphy (FX's "American Horror Story", "American Crime Story" and "Feud" anthologies) are among those with a talent for blending the absurd with the basically plausible.[45]

His comparison upheld a broader critical consensus about television's "second golden age" and bolstered the auteurist bona fides of showrunners working in cable television. Herein, Bark also applied a cinematic standard to television presentation, which Newman and Levine would likely recognize as part and parcel to "the television set [being] remade in the image of the film screen."[46] While Bark remained consistent in his displeasure with the show's "inferior" qualities through its run and reemergence, however, many film critics prized the new installments as "exceptional" *despite* televisual inadequacies. Perhaps most egregiously, *The New Yorker*'s Richard Brody mentioned *The Return* as an aside to his year-end "best of movies" list, proposing that, "most of what's good in 'Twin Peaks: The Return' is good in movie-like ways—the pacing and framing, the space and time and tone that develop around, and are inseparable from, the realization of certain main characters."[47]

Judith Halberstam, in *The Queer Art of Failure,* indicates that such qualifications work to reinforce a status quo of heterosexual progress, a teleological narrative of "becoming" intertwined with monetary goals but disguised as an artistic process. Halberstam cites Scott Sandage's *A History of Failure in America* to observe that:

> Failure, of course, goes hand in hand with capitalism. A market economy must have winners and losers; capitalism requires that everyone live in a system that equates success with profit and links failure to the inability to accumulate wealth. Losers leave no records, while winners cannot stop talking about it, and so the record of failure is a hidden history of pessimism in a culture of optimism.[48]

In seeking to illuminate queer struggle as "an art of unbecoming," Halberstam argues against forms of remembrance that perpetuate dominant discourses of success. By their logic, *Twin Peaks'* purported shortcomings can be read as queerly influential attributes that challenge popular press perceptions of the show as a failed shot at artistic legitimacy on TV. While national publications evaluated *Twin Peaks* on fluctuating criteria of success and failure, fan responses, as I discuss below, reveled in aspects of the programs deemed frivolous and antithetical to "quality" television. Retrospective *Twin Peaks* "slash" fiction, which subverted or reread the show's purportedly "straight" relationships, explicated the show's queer subtext through romantic interludes and found pleasure in narrative irresolution. These entries derived largely from second-season *Twin Peaks* story lines and navigated intra- and extra-textual timeframes. Through their collection and curation on the www.dreamwidth.org user profile Amatara,[49] they also comprised, in Halberstam's terms, a "silly archive" that served as a corrective to official and legitimated understandings of *Twin Peaks*.

THE QUEER ART OF FANDOM: REVIVING, RECLAIMING, AND REDISTRIBUTING *TWIN PEAKS'* AFFECTIVE PLEASURES

Ann Cvetkovich's *An Archive of Feelings* discusses how queer history, often absent institutionalized memory, relies on "ephemeral and personal collections of objects [that] stand alongside the dominant culture in order to offer alternative forms of knowledge."[50] Her understanding of non-traditional archival practice defines not only fan fiction on Amatara but the series' own narrative investments. *Twin Peaks'* re-airing on the Bravo cable channel in 1994 featured introductions to each episode by Margaret Lanterman, the Log Lady. Margaret's communications with a tree log, as previously indicated, provide her with obscure insights about the mysterious woods surrounding the town of Twin Peaks and allow her to navigate fraught netherworlds that proved perilous to characters employing "traditional," gendered rationality. Introducing the series' second to last episode, Margaret cryptically states:

> There are clues everywhere—all around us. But the puzzle maker is clever. The clues, although surrounding us, are somehow mistaken for something else. And the something else—the "wrong" interpretation of the clues—we call our world. Our world is a magical smoke screen. How should we interpret the happy song of the meadowlark, or the robust flavor of a wild strawberry?[51]

Her ending invocation of pleasure and diversion as a counter-logic to tactical puzzle solving and finding answers provides an apt summation of *Twin Peaks'* second season, which reveled in throwaway plotlines, humorous interactions, red herrings, abandoned mysteries, and fleeting characters.

As an alternative to the popular press' determinations of success and failure, queer fan fiction entries explored these frivolous, meandering, and irresolute objects/spaces of *Twin Peaks*; such accounts emphasized the strawberries and meadowlarks over smokescreens of narrative complexity and celebrated *Twin Peaks* as critical failure, thereby undermining politically fraught notions of quality. In doing so, they both indulged and expanded *Twin Peaks'* less accredited archival effects. Amatara, subtitled "amat aram alterius mundi: loving the refuge of alternate wor(l)ds," served as a user profile within the site www.dreamwidth.org and provided a hub for fan fiction entries that indulged in romance, sex, and beauty in the expanded world of *Twin Peaks*. One way in which this archive explored queer sexual subjectivity was through slash fiction, a form of fan writing that adopts diegetically "heterosexual" characters and reconfigures them in non-straight relationships. Writers featured on this archival forum often adopted the perspectives of marginalized and peripheral characters when composing slash works for other sites such as An Archive of Our Own and ReoCities. Amatara, crucially, offered a queerly explicit space for curating slash-based community dialogue.

Two of the earliest slash fictions on Amatara's page, composed by the author DBKate, developed romantic interactions between FBI forensics expert Albert Rosenfield and Cooper that "happened" at fraught narrative instances between the show's two seasons. The entries' investments in relationships deemed irrelevant or tangential to the show's murder mystery plot, however, rendered their time-placement within the series less consequential than their emphasis on queer memory throughout the series and, especially, at points of its "transition" from quality show to excessive soap. "Coincidence"[52] forefronted Albert's damaged mental state driving from Seattle to Twin Peaks in response to the first season's cliffhanger that Cooper had been shot by an unknown assailant, while "Wonderful"[53] considered a tender exchange between the two lovers wherein Albert dresses Cooper's gunshot wound. Amatara described these works as "short, introspective, and lovely," and noted qualities such as their "acerbic wit" and "sweet" sentimentality, drawing attention to the fictions' privileging of emotional resonance over plot construction.

Both "Coincidence" and "Wonderful" denotatively underscored the affective playfulness that marked the show's second season as it wrapped up the Laura Palmer mystery. Albert, for example, only exceeded the limits of crass archetype, the indignant and sarcastic "big city" expert/lawman, in the third episode of *Twin Peaks'* sophomore "slump" during an exchange with Sheriff Harry Truman. After a quip from Albert about the townspeople's primitive behavior, Truman grabs him by the lapels to issue a litany of verbal and physical threats. In one of the show's most unexpected and touching moments, Albert responds, while locked in an embrace with Truman that moves from tense to tender:

> You listen to me, while I will admit to a certain cynicism, the fact is that I'm a naysayer and hatchet-man in the fight against violence. I pride myself on taking a punch and I'll gladly take another because I choose to live my life in the company of Gandhi and King. My concerns are global. I reject absolutely revenge, aggression, and retaliation. The foundation of such a method is love. I love you, Sheriff Truman (2.3).[54]

The moment, complete with Angelo Badalamenti's swelling orchestral score and a slow tracking shot into Albert and Truman that frames them in tight, intimate medium close-up, admonishes a type of performative masculinity that DBKate's entries similarly reject. Instead, both the show and fictions opt towards displays of same-sex intimacy that subvert narrative expectations out of ideological principle.

Figure 6.1. Episode 2.3 "The Man behind the Glass"
Twin Peaks

As Gary Needham observes in "Scheduling Normativity: Television, the Family, and Queer Temporality," such representations of queer affect manifest through "recourse to anomalous temporalities,"[55] an understanding of television sequencing that applies to both the in-between time frames that DBKate's entries explore and characters' temporally opaque travels within the show itself. The textual space of the Black Lodge in *Twin Peaks*, for example, populated by character doppelgangers, dancing dwarves, disembodied spirits and other manifestations of queerness, presents the possibility of multiple conjoined time frames rather than a singular diegetic "reality" with which fan fiction must cohere. Thus, DB Kate's entries sync with *Twin Peaks'* disregard for "canonical" chronology.

Amatara, likewise, served as an unofficial, out-of-time, and incomplete archive and posed a response to more legitimated fan forums, gelling with Halberstam's interest in "small projects, micropolitics, hunches, whims, and fancies."[56] Unlike alt.tv.twinpeaks, a discussion board that allowed for "real time" exchanges (largely regarding plot developments and textual clues) between white, heterosexual, well-educated men during the program's original airing (1990–1991), Amatara sidestepped officialdom and legitimation. Instead, the retrospective fan fictions on her page, composed after 1999, hint at queer spectatorship during the time of the show's broadcast, and present alternative memory as evident "in flashes and fragments"[57] outside the discourse of narrative linearity and straight television time.

Fan response to *Twin Peaks* arrived simultaneously with the show's original broadcast, largely due to the popularization of online bulletin board systems (BBSs) amongst amateur computer enthusiasts. In "'Do You Enjoy Making the Rest of Us Feel Stupid?': alt.tv.twinpeaks, the Trickster Author, and Viewer Mastery," media scholar Henry Jenkins discusses *Twin Peaks'* online interaction and fandom within the context of heterosexual, upper-class young men's penchant for online communication and computing. He writes that, "net responses reflect the particular cultural interests and strategies of ... college educated, professionally oriented, technologically inclined men,"[58] reading *Twin Peaks* fans' online world as an "interpretive community"[59] invested in "the search for answers to narrative questions."[60] Jenkins briefly nods towards other fan constituencies, stating that "if *Twin Peaks* was a mystery, it was also a soap opera and many female fans of the series focused on the bonding of Harry Truman and Dale Cooper"[61] but then posits the web forums as technological and, therefore, male-coded, white, and presumably heterosexual spaces for the show's most socially/historically dominant fandom.

While Amatara's page provided fans similar leverage to negotiate important narrative moments and reorganize the diegetic chronology of *Twin Peaks*, the site focused less on answers and more on questions, while also complicating gendered categorization of fandoms. In her user profile, Amatara described herself professionally as "formerly a grad student in physics, now in finance and ICT,"[62] interests that might presumably align her with Sherry Turkle's (quoted in Jenkins' chapter) conceptualization of *Twin Peaks'* "male" hacker fans who purportedly "prefer the technical precision of Bach over the emotionalism of Beethoven, the complex discursiveness of Escher over the blurry impressionism of Monet."[63] Rather, the author/curator alluded to moods, feelings, and descriptive adjectives of sensation and pleasure instead of using the "informational economy of the net" to "stake out a claim for superior knowledge of the shared narrative."[64]

Amatara captions one entry, "I Am a Lonely Soul" by Smercy, a "brilliant mindfuck of a fic, circular and confusing and claustrophobic,"[65] thereby posing a counter-logic to the search for narrative answers that Jenkins considers central to alt.tv.twinpeaks. Additionally, the gender/sexual ambiguity of the users on this forum (aside from the site's author, who describes herself as a "girl in a man's world"[66]) complicated the too-regularly reinforced binary between (straight) male and female fans of the show and their correspondent gravitation toward defined online spaces in the early 1990s. Fan fiction on Amatara's site employed a "different, a queer, and more fluid form of knowing that operates independently of coherence, or linearity, or narrative progression,"[67] regularly drawing on tangential, seemingly insignificant narrative moments and maligned characters. While Jenkins quotes an entry on alt.tv.twinpeaks as speculating that, "the first season we set up who was good and who was bad. This season we do a reverse flip and change them entirely: Donna becomes BAD, Josie may turn out to be GOOD,"[68] Amatara's site evoked pleasure in character ambiguity and indulged in "connections between queerness and negativity."[69] "Author ingridmatthews' "Nothing Left to Hide," for example, fashioned a confused romantic triangle between the deceased Laura Palmer, her "good guy" boyfriend, James Hurley, and her "bad guy" ex, Bobby Briggs, that fanned the flames of homosocial tension between the two boys, and explored the emotive logic of their attraction. Rather than "reversing" Bobby and James as "bad" and "good," respectively, "Nothing to Hide" removed characters from the heteronormative world in which Jenkins' puzzle-solving fans placed them to queer their dramatic intentions beautifully.

Once ingridmatthews dislodged Bobby's narratively peripheral subjectivity from the service of propelling the Laura Palmer mystery forward, "unbounded forms of speculation" materialized that "ally not with rigor and order but with inspiration and unpredictability."[70] From this standpoint, the entry's "unexpected and screwed-up POV"[71] extracted a throwaway moment from the diegesis and presented it as pivotal to Bobby's sexual and emotional infatuation with both Laura and James:

> Maybe it's the way Bobby's staring or the loud idling of his car but Hurley turns around, scowling as if he knew Briggs was there all along. Their eyes meet and something sparks, making Bobby's throat turn suddenly dry and tight. He's driving so fast the hood of the car begins to rattle. Screwing with the radio doesn't help, the song sounds distorted, like a girl's laughter. Like Laura's laughter, and that's when Bobby finds himself crying, sobbing as he drives, the world blurring all around him. Fuck you, Laura. I never told you, but I hated you. God, how I hated you. And fuck you, James Hurley. I hate you too.[72]

A heterosexual love triangle morphed into queer adolescent confusion as the author contoured Bobby's comically archetypal "bad boy" persona to render the character tragic and misunderstood, if still petty and jealous. Again, this motivation drew from *Twin Peaks*' own gender/genre play wherein Bobby, long the brash comic relief, revealed a sensitive need for attachment to his surprisingly empathic father, Major Garland Briggs, in season 2 and, having become an introverted lawman in *Twin Peaks: The Return*, soulfully pined for his ex-wife Shelly and their daughter Becky.

Bobby's dramatic resonance, initially readable as parodic, developed in serialized, soap-operatic form as quietly expressive.

Entries like "Nothing to Hide" drew on the *Twin Peaks'* overt investment in melodramatic irresolution and expanded storylines contingent on feelings and moods, loose ends and cyclical complications. Such writings located queer televisual logic through "intensely emotive means"[73] and, in Halberstam's terms, meditated on "desiring and melancholic relations between the living and dead,"[74] all imperatives of the show itself. Another entry, "Victory" by XParrot, opened minutes after *Twin Peaks'* season two cliffhanger, in which Dale Cooper's soul remains incarcerated in the Black Lodge and offered a desperate final exchange between Cooper and Sheriff Truman that prolonged Lynch's promise of inconclusiveness. Rather than allowing for narrative finality or serial continuance by permitting Cooper to either die or escape from the dark spirit BOB's corporeal stranglehold, "Victory" ended with Cooper suspended in an indefinite and irresolute state of madness and supernatural possession.

This work fatalistically informed the reader that the cycle of spiritual usurpation, death, and release would find another body after Cooper's demise and BOB's escape.[75] Halberstam considers how twisted and redundant narrative "spiraling ... becomes a new performance of forgetting and a new (and failed) attempt to advance, progress, and accumulate knowledge" and intones that this "seeming irrelevance of the time loop masks a highly charged narrative in which cause and event continue to switch places until causality ceases to produce the logic for narrative movement."[76] In recognizing and sustaining *Twin Peaks'* narrative suspension, based in romance and emotion, "Victory" and other Amatara fan fiction entries propelled a vital celebration of failure evident in the show's soapiest and most institutionally delegitimated moments. The entry also served as apt prophecy for *Twin Peaks: The Return*'s finale, wherein Cooper, newly animated after a decades-long entrapment in the Black Lodge and, later, in the body of Midwestern insurance adjustor Dougie Jones, reemerged to heroically "rescue" Laura Palmer from the Lodge's Red Room. His enactment of normative masculinity, however, led to miscalculated time travels that likely suspended Laura in a different purgatory.

CONCLUSION

Many fan fiction trends and archival practices continued into the release of *Twin Peaks: The Return* as Amatara contributed "missing pieces" to the show's already complicated temporality. Entry hyperlinks on the earlier www.dreamwidth.org page, like much Internet ephemera, now lead to Error 404 and "domain for sale" messages, though Amatara's Tumblr archive[77] and profile page on An Archive of Our Own,[78] as of this writing, house or link to both authored and shared fan fictions since 2011. Her newer works, however, indicate queer grief for lost opportunities and worlds, in contrast to ecstatic critical reactions. Entries like "In the Wake,"[79] a tale of a young Albert's dead cat, which an online arts magazine, *Stackedd,* describes as Amatara's way of "[showing] us (without telling us!) how different the boy feels at school and in [his] neighborhood ... alluding to his Jewishness, his extreme intelligence, his sensitivity"[80] read like eulogies for the deceased actor Miguel Ferrer and melancholy tributes to marginalized characters. Her story "Safety in Numbers" opens with a caption that the piece is "my last chance to sneak a happy(ish) ending in between the cracks of canon."[81] It reconceives Cooper's emergence from Dougie's persona as a queer reunion with both Albert and his former FBI boss, Gordon Cole (portrayed in the show by David Lynch himself) and ends with a moment of respite if also continued irresolution. Amatara writes, from Cooper's perspective, that "sorrow will come, and death and loss and struggle, and everything else that he can't begin to wrap his mind around ... but it's not coming just yet ... for now, he's real and alive and *found.*"[82]

Queer theorist Lee Edelman might describe the found object as *jouissance,* "a fantasmatic escape from the alienation intrinsic to meaning"[83] that penetrates *Twin Peaks'* narrative, formal, and affective logics. It is only in making *jouissance* "decodable" and artistically legitimate that the show's reviewers and industrial handlers hinder its continued project of unbecoming.

NOTES

1. Jane Feuer, "The Concept of Live Television: Ontology as Ideology," in *Regarding Television: Critical Approaches,* ed. E. Ann Kaplan (Frederick, MD: University Publications of America, 1983), 12–22.

2. Jane Feuer, "The MTM Style," in *Television: The Critical View* (Fifth Edition), ed. Horace Newcomb (Oxford University Press, 1994), 80.

3. Feuer, "The MTM Style," 80.

4. John Thornton Caldwell, *Televisuality: Style, Crisis, and Authority in American Television* (New Brunswick, NJ: Rutgers University Press, 1995), 5–6.

5. Michael Newman and Elana Levine, *Legitimating Television: Media Convergence and Cultural Status* (New York: Routledge, 2012), 27.

6. Newman, *Legitimating Television,* 27.

7. See both Mark Dolan's "The Peaks and Valleys of Serial Creativity: What Happened to/on *Twin Peaks,*" and David Lavery's "The Semiotics of Cobbler: *Twin Peaks'* Interpretive Community" in *Full of Secrets: Critical Approaches to Twin Peaks,* ed. David Lavery (Detroit, MI: Wayne State University Press, 1995) as well

as Martha Nochimson's *The Passion of David Lynch: Wild at Heart in Hollywood* (Austin, TX: University of Texas Press, 1997).

8. Mittell describes "complex" TV as intricately plotted, formally layered, and narratively ambiguous serial programs emergent during the early 2000s. His "poetics-based" methodological approach engages these serials "less [as] linear storytelling object[s] than as a library of narrative content that might be consumed as via a wide range of practices, sequences, fragments, moments, choices, and repetitions." Jason Mittell, *Complex TV: The Poetics of Contemporary Television Storytelling* (New York: New York University Press, 2015), 7.

9. Newman and Levine, *Legitimating Television*, 116.

10. For historical discussion of soap opera form, reception, and production vis-à-vis feminism, see: Charlotte Brunsdon, *The Feminist, the Housewife and the Soap Opera* (Oxford: Clarendon Press, 2000); Sandy Flitterman-Lewis, "All's Well that Doesn't End: Soap Opera and the Marriage Motif," in *Private Screenings: Television and the Female Consumer*, eds. Lynn Spigel and Denise Mann (Minneapolis, MN: University of Minnesota Press, 1992); and Tania Modleski, "The Search for Tomorrow in Today's Soap Operas: Notes on a Feminine Narrative Form," *Film Quarterly* 33, no. 1 (Fall 1979): 12–21.

11. Howard Rosenberg, "TV You've Never Seen Before: Soap Opera: Director David Lynch's *Twin Peaks* is the Kind of Bold Programming that is Setting ABC Apart from the Competition," *Los Angeles Times*, April 6, 1990, http://articles.latimes.com/1990-04-06/entertainment/ca-676_1_twin-peaks.

12. Rosenberg, "TV You've Never Seen Before."

13. Mark Harris, "Why TV Had to Make 'Peaks.'" *Entertainment Weekly*, April 6, 1990, http://ew.com/article/1990/04/06/why-tv-had-make-twin-peaks/.

14. Harris, "Why TV Had to Make 'Peaks.'"

15. "*Twin Peaks* Promo," YouTube, published on August 19, 2006 by user TwinPeaks2007, https://www.youtube.com/watch?v=wsNgxzIs0KM.

16. Elana Levine discusses ABC's willingness to experiment with overt sexually suggestive material in the 1970s as an economically necessary tactic to compete with its more established network rivals, NBC and CBS. She describes ABC as strategically targeting young people with shows like *Happy Days* and *Three's Company* that served as a counterpoint to CBS's more "socially relevant" fare. Elana Levine, *Wallowing in Sex: The New Sexual Culture of 1970s American Television* (Durham, NC: Duke University Press, 2007).

17. Zoglin, Richard. "Like Nothing On Earth," *Time*. April 9, 1990. http://time.com/3476115/like-nothing-on-earth/.

18. Ken Tucker, "TV Review: 'Twin Peaks,'" *Entertainment Weekly*, October 26, 1990, http://ew.com/article/1990/10/26/twin-peaks/.

19. Tucker, "TV Review."

20. John O'Connor, "A Skewed Vision of a Small Town In 'Twin Peaks,'" *New York Times*, April 6, 1990, C34.

21. Newman and Levine, *Legitimating Television*, 29.

22. Ien Ang, *Desperately Seeking the Audience* (New York: Routledge, 1991), 22.

23. Eileen Meehan, "Heads of Household and Ladies of the House: Gender, Genre, and Broadcast Ratings, 1929–1990," in *Ruthless Criticism: New Perspectives in*

U.S. Communications History, eds. William S. Solomon and Robert W. McChesney (Minneapolis, MN: University of Minnesota Press, 1993), 213.

24. Michel Foucault, *The History of Sexuality Volume 1: An Introduction* (New York: Random House, 1978), 27.

25. Teresa De Lauretis, *Technologies of Gender: Essays on Theory, Film, and Gender* (Bloomington, IN: University of Indiana Press, 1987), 9.

26. Alexander Doty, *Making Things Perfectly Queer: Interpreting Mass Culture* (Minneapolis, MN: University of Minnesota Press, 1993), 37.

27. Martha Nochimson, *The Passion of David Lynch: Wild at Heart in Hollywood* (Austin, TX: University of Texas Press, 1997), 88.

28. Nochimson responded to my question about the prevalence of soap operatic motifs and narrative strategies in David Lynch's work (*Twin Peaks, Mulholland Dr., Twin Peaks: The Return*) by citing her in-person and telephone conversations with the director over several decades. She intimated that the soap opera intertext *Invitation to Love* in *Twin Peaks'* original run had been developed by series co-creator Mark Frost and had upset Lynch due to its mocking and parodic tone. Martha Nochimson, Respondent, "Entering the Lynch-verse: Celebrity, Collaboration, and Aging in the Worlds of David Lynch," presented at the Society for Cinema and Media Studies (SCMS) conference in Toronto, Ontario, Canada, March 2018.

29. Ed Bark, "ABC Aims High With 'Twin Peaks,'" *Dallas Morning News*, January 11, 1990, C5.

30. John O'Connor, "Review/Television: Uncertainties May Lurk In 'Twin Peaks' Future," *New York Times*, April 30, 1990, C16.

31. John O'Connor, "Time to Let Go of Laura Palmer," *New York Times*, October 2 1991, C15.

32. Tania Modleski, "The Rhythms of Reception: Daytime Television and Women's Work," *Regarding Television*, ed. E. Ann Kaplan (Frederick, MD: Greenwood Publishing Group, 1985), 72.

33. Christine Gledhill, "Speculations on the Relationship between Soap Opera and Melodrama," *Quarterly Review of Film and Video* 14, nos. 1–2 (1992), 121.

34. Jane Feuer discusses gay men's reading of *Dynasty* as "outrageous camp" in the chapter "The Reception of Dynasty" in her monograph *Seeing Through the Eighties: Television and Reaganism* (Durham, NC: Duke University Press, 1995), 131–148.

35. Discussed in Stephen Tropiano's chapter, "Drama Queens: Homosexuality and Dramatic Series, Mini-Series, and Movies of the Week" in *The Prime Time Closet: A History of Gays and Lesbians on Television* (New York: Applause, 2002), 109–185.

36. Feuer, *Seeing Through the Eighties*, 133.

37. Ed Bark, "'Twin Peaks' Could Lynch Itself Soon," *Dallas Morning News*, October 2, 1990, C5.

38. Bark, "'Twin Peaks' Could Lynch Itself Soon."

39. William Grimes, "Television: Welcome to *Twin Peaks* and Valleys," *New York Times*, May 5, 1991, https://www.nytimes.com/1991/05/05/arts/television-welcome-to-twin-peaks-and-valleys.html.

40. Maureen Ryan, "'Peak' Performance," *Variety*, May 9, 2017, 44.

41. Ryan, "'Peak' Performance."
42. Ryan, "'Peak' Performance."
43. James Poniewozik, "Review: In 'Twin Peaks' an Old Log Learns Some New Tricks," *New York Times*, May 21, 2017, https://www.nytimes.com/2017/05/21/arts/television/twin-peaks-review.html.
44. James Poniewozik, Mike Hale, and Margaret Lyons, "The Best Shows of 2017," *New York Times*, last modified December 4, 2017, https://www.nytimes.com/2017/12/04/arts/television/best-tv-shows.html.
45. Ed Bark, "What Was That? It's Showtime for *Twin Peaks*," Unclebarky.com, last modified May 22, 2017, http://www.unclebarky.com/reviews_files/9d41999230701aa3ee099a5cd2524833-2246.html.
46. Newman and Levine, *Legitimating Television*, 101.
47. Richard Brody, "The Best Movies of 2017," *The New Yorker*, last modified December 8, 2017, https://www.newyorker.com/culture/2017-in-review/the-best-movies-of-2017.
48. Judith Halberstam, *The Queer Art of Failure* (Durham, NC: Duke University Press, 2011), 88.
49. Amatara, "*Twin Peaks* recs: Cooper/Albert & Other Favorites," last modified July 18, 2010, https://amatara.dreamwidth.org/18084.html?thread=140964.
50. Ann Cvetkovich, *An Archive of Feelings: Trauma, Sexuality, and Lesbian Public Cultures* (Durham, NC: Duke University Press, 2003), 8.
51. Included in *Twin Peaks:* Definitive Gold Box Edition (2007; Burbank, CA: Paramount/CBS Video), DVD.
52. DBKate, "Coincidence," Geocities, 1999, http://www.reocities.com/dbkate/twin_peaks/coincidence.txt.
53. DBKate, "Wonderful," GeoCities, 1999, http://www.reocities.com/dbkate/twin_peaks/wonderful.txt.
54. "The Man Behind the Glass," directed by Lesli Linka Glatter, *Twin Peaks:* Definitive Gold Box Edition (2007; Burbank, CA: Paramount/CBS Video, 2007), DVD.
55. Gary Needham, "Scheduling Normativity: Television, the Family, and Queer Temporality," in *Queer TV: Theories, Histories, Politics*, eds. Glyn Davis and Gary Needham (New York: Routledge, 2009), 157.
56. Halberstam, *The Queer Art of Failure*, 21.
57. Halberstam, *The Queer Art of Failure*, 54.
58. Henry Jenkins, "'Do You Enjoy Making the Rest of Us Feel Stupid?': alt.tv.twinpeaks, the Trickster Author, and Viewer Mastery," in *Full of Secrets: Critical Approaches to* Twin Peaks, ed. David Lavery (Detroit, MI: Wayne State University Press, 1995), 53.
59. Jenkins, "'Do You Enjoy Making the Rest of Us Feel Stupid?,'" 52.
60. Jenkins, "'Do You Enjoy Making the Rest of Us Feel Stupid?,'" 56.
61. Jenkins, "'Do You Enjoy Making the Rest of Us Feel Stupid?,'" 60.
62. Amatara, "Profile," September 1, 2010, https://amatara.dreamwidth.org/profile.
63. Jenkins, "'Do You Enjoy Making the Rest of Us Feel Stupid?,'" 55.
64. Jenkins, "'Do You Enjoy Making the Rest of Us Feel Stupid?,'" 56.

65. Amatara, "*Twin Peaks* recs."
66. Amatara, "Profile."
67. Halberstam, *The Queer Art of Failure*, 5.
68. Jenkins, "'Do You Enjoy Making the Rest of Us Feel Stupid?,'" 53, author's emphasis.
69. Halberstam, *The Queer Art of Failure*, 98.
70. Halberstam, *The Queer Art of Failure*, 10.
71. Amatara, "*Twin Peaks* recs."
72. Ingridmatthews, "Nothing Left to Hide," An Archive of Our Own, last modified December 21, 2009, https://www.archiveofourown.org/works/33673?view_adult=true.
73. Needham, "Scheduling Normativity," 153.
74. Halberstam, *The Queer Art of Failure*, 89.
75. XFarrot, "Victory," An Archive of Our Own, last modified March 29, 2005, https://archiveofourown.org/works/6100.
76. XFarrot, "Victory."
77. Amatara, Tumblr, http://amatara.tumblr.com/archive.
78. Amatara, "Profile," An Archive of Our Own, https://archiveofourown.org/users/Amatara/pseuds/Amatara.
79. Amatara, "In the Wake," An Archive of Our Own, https://archiveofourown.org/works/165486.
80. Lilith Wood, "Welcome to Amateur Hour: The Slow Burn of Albert Rosenfield and Dale Cooper in *Twin Peaks* Fanfic," *Stackedd Magazine*, last modified May 15, 2017, http://stackeddmagazine.com/2017/05/15/welcome-amateur-hour-slow-burn-albert-rosenfield-dale-cooper-twin-peaks-fanfic/.
81. Amatara, "Safety in Numbers," An Archive of Our Own, https://archiveofourown.org/works/11901735.
82. Amatara, "Safety in Numbers," author's emphasis.
83. Edelman expounds on Jacques Lacan's psychoanalytical associations between *jouissance* and the death drive in *No Future: Queer Theory and the Death Drive* (Durham, NC: Duke University Press, 2004), 25.

WORKS CITED

Amatara. "Profile." Dreamwidth. Last modified 1 September 2010. https://amatara.dreamwidth.org/profile.

Amatara. "*Twin Peaks* Recs: Cooper/Albert & Other Favorites." Dreamwidth. Last modified 18 July 2010. https://amatara.dreamwidth.org/18084.html?thread=140964.

Amatara. ""Safety in Numbers." An Archive of Our Own. Last modified 25 August 2017. https://archiveofourown.org/works/11901735.

Ang, Ien. *Desperately Seeking the Audience*. New York: Routledge, 1991.

Bark, Ed "ABC Aims High With 'Twin Peaks.'" *Dallas Morning News*. 11 January 1990. C5.

Bark, Ed. "'Twin Peaks' Could Lynch Itself Soon." *Dallas Morning News*. 2 October 1990.

Bark, Ed. "What Was That? It's Showtime for *Twin Peaks*." Unclebarky.com. Last modified 22 May 2017. http://www.unclebarky.com/reviews_files/9d41999230701aa3ee099a5cd2524833-2246.html.

Brody, Richard. "The Best Movies of 2017." *The New Yorker*. Last modified 8 December 2017. https://www.newyorker.com/culture/2017-in-review/the-best-movies-of-2017.

Caldwell, John Thornton. *Televisuality: Style, Crisis, and Authority in American Television*. New Brunswick, NJ: Rutgers University Press, 1995.

Cvetkovich, Ann. *An Archive of Feelings: Trauma, Sexuality, and Lesbian Public Cultures*. Durham, NC: Duke University Press, 2003.

DBKate. "Coincidence." GeoCities, 1999. Accessed 6 December 2013. http://www.reocities.com/dbkate/twin_peaks/coincidence.txt.

DBKate. "Wonderful." GeoCities, 1999. Accessed 6 December 2013. http://www.reocities.com/dbkate/twin_peaks/wonderful.txt.

De Lauretis, Teresa. *Technologies of Gender: Essays on Theory, Film, and Gender*. Bloomington, IN: University of Indiana Press, 1987.

Dolan, Mark. "The Peaks and Valleys of Serial Creativity: What Happened to/on *Twin Peaks?*" *Full of Secrets: Critical Approaches to* Twin Peaks. Ed. David Lavery. Detroit, MI: Wayne State University Press, 1995. 30–50.

Doty, Alexander. *Making Things Perfectly Queer: Interpreting Mass Culture*. Minneapolis, MN: University of Minnesota Press, 1993.

Edelman, Lee. *No Future: Queer Theory and the Death Drive*. Durham, NC: Duke University Press, 2004.

Feuer, Jane. "The Concept of Live Television: Ontology as Ideology." *Regarding Television: Critical Approaches*. Ed. E. Ann Kaplan. Frederick, MD: University Publications of America, 1983. 12–22.

Feuer, Jane. "The MTM Style." *Television: The Critical View* (Fifth Edition). Ed. Horace Newcomb. Oxford University Press, 1994. 52–84.

Foucault, Michel. *The History of Sexuality Volume 1: An Introduction*. New York: Random House, 1978.

Gledhill, Christine. "Speculations on the Relationship between Soap Opera and Melodrama." *Quar. Rev. of Film and Video* 14(1–2) (1992): 103–124.

Grimes, William. "Television: Welcome to Twin Peaks and Valleys." *New York Times*. 5 May 1991. https://www.nytimes.com/1991/05/05/arts/televisionwelcome-to-twin-peaks-and-valleys.html.

Halberstam, Judith. *The Queer Art of Failure*. Durham, NC: Duke University Press, 2011.

Harris, Mark. "Why TV Had to Make 'Peaks.'" *Entertainment Weekly*. 6 April 1990. http://ew.com/article/1990/04/06/why-tv-had-make-twin-peaks/.

Ingridmatthews. "Nothing Left to Hide." An Archive of Our Own. Last modified 21 December 2009. https://www.archiveofourown.org/works/33673?view_adult=true.

Jenkins, Henry. "'Do You Enjoy Making the Rest of Us Feel Stupid?': alt.tv.twinpeaks, the Trickster Author, and Viewer Mastery." *Full of Secrets: Critical*

Approaches to Twin Peaks. Ed. David Lavery. Detroit, MI: Wayne State University Press, 1995.

Jenkins, Henry. "*Star Trek* Rerun, Reread, Rewritten: Fan Writing as Textual Poaching." *Fans, Bloggers, and Gamers: Exploring Participatory Culture*. New York: New York University Press, 2006. 37–60.

Lavery, David. "The Semiotics of Cobbler: *Twin Peaks'* Interpretive Community." *Full of Secrets: Critical Approaches to* Twin Peaks. Ed. David Lavery. Detroit, MI: Wayne State University Press, 1995. 1–21.

Levine, Elana. *Wallowing in Sex: The New Sexual Culture of 1970s American Television*. Durham, NC: Duke University Press, 2007.

Meehan, Eileen. "Heads of Household and Ladies of the House: Gender, Genre, and Broadcast Ratings, 1929–1990." *Ruthless Criticism: New Perspectives in U.S. Communications History*. Eds. William S. Solomon and Robert W McChesney. Minneapolis, MN: University of Minnesota Press, 1993. 204–221.

Mittell, Jason. *Complex TV: The Poetics of Contemporary Television Storytelling*. New York: New York University Press, 2015.

Modleski, Tania. "The Rhythms of Reception: Daytime Television and Women's Work." *Regarding Television*. Ed. E. Ann Kaplan. Frederick, MD: Greenwood Publishing Group, 1985. 67–75.

Needham, Gary. "Scheduling Normativity: Television, the Family, and Queer Temporality." *Queer TV: Theories, Histories, Politics*. Eds. Glyn Davis and Gary Needham. New York: Routledge, 2009. 143–158.

Newman, Michael and Elana Levine. *Legitimating Television: Media Convergence and Cultural Status*. New York: Routledge, 2012.

Nochimson, Martha. *The Passion of David Lynch: Wild at Heart in Hollywood*. Austin, TX: University of Texas Press, 1997.

O'Connor, John. "A Skewed Vision of a Small Town In 'Twin Peaks.'" *New York Times*. 6 April 1990.

O'Connor, John. "Review/Television: Uncertainties May Lurk In 'Twin Peaks' Future." *New York Times*. 30 April 1990.

O'Connor. John. "Time to Let Go of Laura Palmer." *New York Times*. 2 October 1991.

Poniewozik, James. "Review: In 'Twin Peaks' an Old Log Learns Some New Tricks." *New York Times*. Last modified 21 May 2017. https://www.nytimes.com/2017/05/21/arts/television/twin-peaks review.html.

Poniewozik, James, Mike Hale, and Margaret Lyons. "The Best Shows of 2017." *New York Times*. Last modified 4 December 2017. https://www.nytimes.com/2017/12/04/arts/television/best-tv-shows.html.

Rosenberg, Howard. "TV You've Never Seen Before Soap Opera: Director David Lynch's *Twin Peaks* is the Kind of Bold Programming that Is Setting ABC Apart from the Competition." *Los Angeles Times*. 6 April 1990. http://articles.latimes.com/1990-04-06/entertainment/ca-676_1_twin-peaks.

Ryan, Maureen. "'Peak' Performance." *Variety*. 9 May 2017.

Tropiano, Stephen. "Drama Queens: Homosexuality and Dramatic Series, Mini-Series, and Movies of the Week." *The Prime Time Closet: A History of Gays and Lesbians on Television*. New York: Applause, 2002. 109–185.

Tucker, Ken. "TV Review: 'Twin Peaks.'" *Entertainment Weekly*. 26 October 1990. http://ew.com/article/1990/10/26/twin-peaks/.

TwinPeaks2007. "*Twin Peaks* promo." YouTube. Uploaded 19 August 2006. https://www.youtube.com/watch?v=wsNgxzIs0KM

Wood, Lilith. "Welcome to Amateur Hour: The Slow Burn of Albert Rosenfield and Dale Cooper in *Twin Peaks* Fanfic." *Stackedd Magazine*. Last modified 15 May 2017. http://stackeddmagazine.com/2017/05/15/welcome-amateur-hour-slow-burn-albert-rosenfield-dale-cooper-twin-peaks-fanfic/.

XParrot. "Victory." An Archive of Our Own. Last modified 29 March 2005. https://archiveofourown.org/works/6100.

IV

THE POLITICAL AS IT RELATES TO PHILOSOPHICAL, THEORETICAL, AND SPIRITUAL WAYS OF KNOWING

Seven

Zen, or the Art of Being Agent Cooper
Darci Doll

In season 1, episode 3 of *Twin Peaks*, Agent Dale Cooper gathers Sheriff Harry Truman, Hawk, Andy, and Lucy to tell them that he has learned the identity of Laura Palmer's killer. The Twin Peaks locals, expecting to receive a revelation of who committed the murder, are given a brief history of Tibet as a way of describing Agent Cooper's method of deduction. Agent Cooper explains that Tibet has been occupied by China since the 1940s and the Dalai Lama is the source of moral and religious guidance for Tibetans (and Buddhists). He continues by explaining that the Dalai Lama has been in exile for decades, then proceeds to explain how his interest in Tibet has led him to a method of deductive reasoning by way of a dream.[1] Cooper has discovered the ability to discern the truth seemingly effortlessly and the truth is often conveyed to him through dreams. This deductive technique allows Agent Cooper to coordinate the body and mind through the deepest level of intuition. What transpires next isn't anything close to what the audience nor the residents of Twin Peaks expect. In lieu of revealing the name of the murderer, Cooper engages in a process of throwing a rock at a bottle while reciting names, having Lucy record whether the rock hit and/or broke the bottle. Cooper maintains that this process will divulge pertinent information about Laura's killer. However, despite Cooper's assertion that he was explaining his method and what he learned in a dream, we are left wondering how this process is related to (let alone can reveal) Laura Palmer's murderer. We're left feeling disappointed; we thought we were learning who killed Laura Palmer, but we're (rightfully) more confused than before. At best we've learned that Cooper has confidence that his intuition and deductive method will lead him to the identity of the murderer. However, despite his confidence, one might question Agent Cooper's qualification and process. After all, he

Figure 7.1. Episode 1.3 "Zen, or the Skill to Catch a Killer"
Twin Peaks

claims to know who the killer is but is unable to produce the name and instead, must continue the investigative process.

By way of understanding Agent Cooper's method and the events connected to Twin Peaks, I am going to have to tell you about Eastern philosophy as it relates to Cooper. There are three main tenets to the Tibetan Buddhism Agent Cooper focuses on: the three universal truths of causation, the four noble truths, and the eightfold path.[2] The first of the three universal truths holds that nothing in the universe is accidental; everything has a path and a purpose. The second is that everything changes and the third is the law of cause and effect.[3] These three truths, when combined, identify a universe that is ordered, balanced, and in a state of harmonic flux. We want to accept that change is natural and ought to understand that harmony requires taking responsibility for the effects of our actions. Additionally, this means that we should understand that there are changes, causes, and effects that may be out of our control and that are necessary to attain a balance in the universe. We ought not be overly concerned with change nor should we ascribe false values into the world around us; the balance between dark and light is fundamental to the nature of cause and effect. We might be tempted to dwell on the more negative aspects of the universe, but we ought to appreciate that the light is not possible without the dark, good without evil, etc. Once we accept the role of nature we will be more likely to find the path to enlightenment.[4]

The four noble truths focus on suffering—a key concept that allowed the Buddha to attain enlightenment. Born a wealthy prince protected from the unpleasant of life, Prince Siddhartha escaped from his home and was introduced to the suffering that exists in the world.[5] This experience caused him to understand the first of the four noble truths: suffering exists in the world. Buddhism requires that we not try to shield ourselves from this realization. We ought to recognize that suffering is a necessary component of the balance of the universe. Just as with the three universal truths, we cannot have pleasure without the existence of suffering in the world. The second noble truth is that there is a cause to the suffering, specifically, attachment and desire. Third, suffering can end by letting go of attachment. We can alter our perceptions to accept the natural flow of existence and the universe, to find harmony, and to stop ourselves from having attachment. The fourth noble truth notes that following the eightfold path is the way to end suffering. The eightfold path is a set of rules that focus on wisdom, virtue, and meditation. For each of these paths, one is to identify the right, or correct, attitude pertaining to one's existence. One should have: Right understanding of the four noble truths; Right thinking and following the right path in life; Right speech; Right Action; Right livelihood; Right effort, good thoughts; Right mindfulness and awareness of one's body and mind; Right concentration, or a means of attaining higher understanding.[6]

While Agent Cooper did not explain the three universal truths of causation, the four noble truths, nor the eightfold path, understanding them helps one discern how Cooper's deductive technique is working. Cooper has demonstrated an ability to follow the eightfold path. We can see several examples where he thinks, acts, meditates, and even makes his livelihood, with right intention and understanding. Cooper meditates daily and in his comments to Diane, he notes that it improves how he feels and clarifies his understanding of human potential (2.21). He conducts himself in a manner befitting the standards of the bureau as well as *dao*; he acts above reproach when responding to Audrey Horne's advances as well as when he courts Annie. He takes care of the townspeople of Twin Peaks, protecting them from the harshness of his long-term friend and coworker, Albert. When Leland realizes what he has done, Agent Cooper is gentle and supportive; he explains to Hawk and Harry what had happened, but relates it in a calm, sympathetic manner (2.9). During the sting operation at One Eyed Jack's, Cooper takes the paths of least harm (1.6). The way Cooper interacts with everyone is one of harmonious balance. He understands that suffering is a part of life yet he takes effort to not intentionally engage in acts that promote suffering. Cooper seems to be aware that attachment is the root of suffering; he doesn't get attached to material possessions, he appreciates the good around him but doesn't get discouraged at a lack of material pleasures, he abstains from anger, careless sexual activity, he approaches others from a place of positive intent. Agent Cooper is living a life consistent with the tenets of Tibetan Buddhism and *Daoism* and, as a result, has established more harmony with the world than most people around him. He is happy with reasonable lodgings, coffee, and pie. He doesn't require a life of excess; Agent Cooper lives a life of moderation and balance.

Agent Cooper may not have articulated this, but it is clearly fundamental to the core of his being. This adherence to the eightfold path may be the reason that Agent Cooper was able to survive twenty-five years in the Black Lodge and to survive and live according to *dao* after escaping the Lodge, despite an inability to communicate and act as well as before. Because he understands suffering, balance, and the importance of right effort and thought, he is able to be immersed in the darkness of the Black Lodge without getting corrupted himself.

VARIATIONS ON *DAOISM*

Although Agent Cooper suggests he is relying specifically on Tibetan Buddhism, it's worth saying more about the history of Eastern philosophy, specifically on Daoism, to fully explain Cooper's deductive process.[7] The similarities between the philosophies are notable; both focus on balance between opposites, freeing oneself from attachment and finding the Way to truth. Daoism can provide further insight into the lore of *Twin Peaks*, the White and Black Lodges, the doppelgangers, and tulpas. The Log Lady says that there is a one leading to the many and that the one is Laura Palmer.[8] Daoism can help us see *how* Laura is the one as well as the general connection between the one and the many. In a phone call, the Log Lady tells Hawk, "Now the circle is almost complete. Watch and listen to the dream of time and space. It all comes out now, flowing like a river. That which is and is not. Hawk. Laura is the one (3.10)." Throughout the series the Log Lady is reinforcing the idea that Laura is the one, that she is part of the balance, an opposite comprising of a whole. In *Twin Peaks: The Return*, the Log Lady is making sure that Hawk is aware of this to ensure that Laura's importance is not neglected.[9]

Dao is an inherent feature of many Eastern philosophies and there are many different types of *Daoism*. We first get the most cohesive account of *dao* and *Daoism* from Laozi.[10] *Dao* refers to the Way and a reflection of how things are, how the universe is ordered. It's the blueprint for the cosmic order, so to speak. *Dao* is the natural order of things and one achieves harmony when they are able to act in ways consistent with *dao*, or the proper order of nature. This reflection of harmony refers to the natural balance between dark and light, negative and positive, action and inaction. When there is balance, when people's actions (or inactions) are consistent with the *dao*, harmony, peace, enlightenment are possible. When there is discord, these things cannot happen and suffering and discord are likely to be present. In this sense, *Daoism* bears a similarity to the Tibetan connection to suffering, intention, cause and effect. When one acts or thinks incorrectly, or strays from the natural path, harmony is not possible. It's common to say that where there is harmony it is good, while the presence of discord is bad. And this is not entirely incorrect; harmony indicates that things are as they should be, discord is that they are contrary to the natural order. We ought to be careful when making these types of categorizations, however. We need to make sure that we're reserving the normative, or moral, claims of good and bad for situations that are specifically warranting that classification. In *Daoism*, one can have discord in a way that's not consistent with what we'd call *morally* bad. Darkness, bad weather, non-harmonious music, etc. are all components that we may identify as negative. This doesn't mean that they're wrong in the same sense that we may identify murder as being morally bad. Often the discussion of harmony is more of a discussion of whether things are balanced than a moral prescription about how we ought to behave. *Daoist* discussions tend to be more about classifying opposites than identifying moral claims as such. What we're recognizing is different ends, or parts, of pairs. When we try to elevate one part of the pair and devalue the other, we're pursuing what Ivanhoe calls an impossible goal "because of the mutual dependence of such conceptual dichotomies."[11] *Daoism* acknowledges that to know or consider a concept requires the inherent consideration of its opposite. Ideally, Daoists would prefer that we see these entities as a whole and not as separate parts; if we cannot attain this ideal we ought to seek to have harmony and balance between these pairs. By understanding the ways in which dichotomies are interdependent, we will be able to understand the bigger picture and find *dao*.

Perhaps the most important dichotomy in *Daoism* are those of *wei* and *wu-wei*; intentional action and intentional non-action respectively. When one takes intentional action in a way that is in accordance with *dao*, it is said they have attained *wei*. Sometimes for Daoist balance to be attained, intentional inaction is required, which is known as *wu-wei*. A person who has endured proper meditation, consideration, and has attained knowledge about *dao* will know when she ought to act versus when inaction is required. The juxtaposition of these two opposites makes following *dao* possible.

Zhuangzi gave us a more robust understanding of *Dao* and discussed how a layperson can learn *dao* as well as attain ethical excellence.[12] For Zhuangzi, the morally ideal person will be so well in tune with nature that they will possess *wei* and *wu-wei*, will know no fear, will be able to survive in harsh conditions, and will find no need for plans; they will be able to naturally follow *dao* and act (or take non-action) harmoniously without requiring forethought.[13] Zhuangzi used several parables to explain how *dao* is a practice; that if one practices right thought and action often enough they will intuitively know what to do without trying or without thinking. Perhaps the most famous parable is that of the butcher: When first starting out, a butcher has to invest a lot of thought and effort into cutting and cleaning the meat; he only sees the ox. When the butcher masters the skill, he can act relying only on instinct and only sees the way.[14]

THE MAN BEHIND THE *DAO*

What Agent Cooper has described and demonstrated is that he has mastered *wei* and *wu-wei*. He is able to act on instinct, he sees the truth in a situation without having to take overt conscious effort to over-analyze, complicated truths reveal themselves to him in a dream. While he may not immediately *understand* the truths, he has faith that if he takes the right action, or inaction when appropriate, he will be able to understand and articulate the truth. Agent Cooper does not try to force his understanding; instead, he relies on his mastery of *dao* to allow the understanding to be revealed in due time.

Agent Cooper's deductive method learned through the dream is *Daoism* in practice and it has enabled him to be in tune with *dao*. Cooper is able to intuitively recognize the way things are; he is able to identify truth and is able to have harmony between his physical body and his intellect. His method in episode 1.3 is a demonstration of this; Agent Cooper's intuitive understanding of harmony has enabled him to know when to intentionally act versus when he should be passive. Additionally, Cooper's patience demonstrates his commitment to the *dao*. When Cooper wakes from the dream where he learns the name of Laura's killer, he remembers learning the name but doesn't remember the actual name. In the middle of the night, he immediately calls Sheriff Truman but tells him the matter can wait until morning; there's no rush (1.3). Agent Cooper knows that he is on the right path and that the truth will be (re-) revealed in due time. His willingness to wait may seem confusing to some, but to Cooper, it makes total sense; this is an instance where the quest for the truth requires intentional inactivity.[15] He can use *wei* to help narrow down the information (e.g., his rocks and the bottle), but he mostly has to rely on *wu-wei* to allow the information to reveal itself. Throughout his time in Twin Peaks, Agent Cooper is demonstrating a Daoist intuition. He seems to know things without evidence, like James Hurley's innocence with respect to Laura Palmer's murder. He, seemingly instantly, knows about Harry's affair with Josie and that Big Ed Hurley is in love with Norma. Yet, in Daoist fashion, Agent Cooper doesn't judge people based on what he knows; he accepts the world as it is and understands that it's all part of a bigger, harmonious whole. Because Agent Cooper is internally and externally harmonious, he emits a trustworthy, knowledgeable calm; it comes from his awareness of *dao*. This results in his securing the trust of the residents of Twin Peaks, being permitted to work on Project Blue Rose, and ultimately allows him to follow the *dao* to successfully fulfill his duties and help restore balance.

THE PATH TO THE WHITE AND BLACK LODGES

A fundamental component of *Daoism* is this recognition of opposites that comprise a whole.[16] Harmony is only possible when there is balance within this dichotomy; when the whole is complete. A part of this that has only thus far been alluded to is the balance between light and dark forces. Our discussion so far has involved how there is a natural state of opposites that are a necessary part of *dao*. The town of Twin Peaks exemplifies the necessary balance of many of these dichotomies. At a basic level we have symmetry demonstrated by the twin mountains mirroring each other. However, the stories behind *Twin Peaks* teach us that there are more levels of light and dark than neutral natural occurrences that *dao* is primarily concerned with such as good versus bad weather, beautifully harmonious Douglas Fir trees. Sheriff Truman and Hawk explain to Agent Cooper that there are a lot of good things about Twin Peaks; in many ways they're blessed. The good in Twin Peaks is such that Agent Cooper has a desire to stay in Twin Peaks after the case is solved. There definitely seems to be something special about the small town of Twin Peaks (something more than damned fine coffee). Truman and Hawk caution Cooper, however, that there are also parts that are darker, and the following conversation transpires:

> Harry: Twin Peaks is different, a long way from the world. You've noticed that.
>
> Cooper: Yes, I have.

> Harry: That's exactly the way we like it, but there's a ... back end to that that's kind of different, too. Maybe that's the price we pay for all the good things.
>
> Cooper: What would that be?
>
> Harry: There's a sort of evil out there, something very, very strange in these old woods. Call it what you want—a darkness, a presence. It takes many forms, but it's been out there for long as anyone can remember, and we've always been here to fight it (1.3).

The Book House Boys specifically exist to help maintain this balance and to make sure that the darker components don't overpower the good.[17] There has to be balance; for all of the good things that Twin Peaks possesses, there will also be proportionate opposites. In joining forces with the Book House Boys, Agent Cooper is committing himself to the task of combating the evil surrounding Twin Peaks for the sake of the good.

We ultimately learn that Twin Peaks is home to the White and Black Lodges: the former is inhabited by good beings, the latter inhabited by bad.[18] These lodges represent the dark and light but to a stronger degree than what we've seen with the discussion of *Daoism*. The inhabitants of both lodges have characteristics that we associate with good and bad (and with the Black Lodge, we may go so far as to say evil). While *Daoism* is typically taking a value neutral discussion of opposites, these two lodges appear to have a stronger cosmic role with respect to light and dark. From *Fire Walk with Me* and *The Return*, we're led to believe that these lodges may contribute to the generation of good and evil in the world (in the moral sense of the words). The two lodges are inherently connected, and we see throughout the series that the existence of one is only possible because of the existence of the other. The harmonious balance between the two lodges helps create balance; the evil is possible because of the good, the good is understandable because of the comparison to the evil. When the universe is aligned a certain way, the White Lodge can be accessed with love, the Black Lodge with fear. To have balance there must be equal proportions of light and dark. The inhabitants of the White Lodge seem to be aware of this; they observe the world and strive for balance. The inhabitants of the Black Lodge, however, are constantly trying to destroy the balance to have an excess of darkness.

DAOISM IN *TWIN PEAKS*

In Part 8 of *The Return* we see the Black Lodge's creation of BOB and other dark forces.[19] The dark cosmic forces that contribute to BOB's development, creation, and release are depicted in a way that is viscerally unsettling. The event is depicted in an unharmonious, ugly, chaotic manner. We watch anxiously aware that something bad is being created, and when we realize it's BOB, our fears are confirmed.

In this same episode, we see the inhabitants of the White Lodge observe the creation of BOB. In response, they facilitate the creation of a force that appears to be more pure, good, the opposite of the darkness unleashed on the world in 1947. We see here the image of Laura Palmer; a sign that Laura is the light that is meant to balance the dark. In contrast to BOB's creation, Laura's is serene, organized, and in a sense beautiful. She is the proportionate opposite of BOB. *Dao* requires balance, so for every dark force there must be a proportionate light force. It stands to reason, then, that Laura is designed to bring balance to the world after the creation of BOB. Her existence creates the potential for harmony; she may not be able to cancel out the darkness, but she has the potential to bring about an equal light to restore and protect the harmony BOB threatens. Laura Palmer is cosmically valuable; this one person has the power to bring balance to many. Laura's importance has the unfortunate consequence of making her the prey of BOB. BOB's possession of her father, his abuse of her throughout her life are likely means to corrupt her and prevent her from fulfilling her duty. Throughout her life, BOB has put her on a path that challenges her potential to do good and we learn that BOB was desperate to get Laura to let him in (2.9, *Fire Walk with Me*). Her final act of defiance was to die with the ring on, sending her to the Black Lodge. By corrupting and then killing Laura, BOB sets into motion a chain of unharmonious events. He has allowed the dark to potentially overpower the good. BOB and the inhabitants of the Black Lodge desire pain, fear, suffering, garmonbozia; they seek the chaos that would allow them to maximize these qualities and are seeking to destroy the balance that would prevent (or minimize) them. To that end, Laura is indescribably important to them. If she cannot be possessed by BOB, the next best thing is to allow her to die letting chaos ensue. While we can see that Agent Cooper exemplifies harmony and acting in accordance with *dao* creating harmony, the inhabitants of the Black Lodge demonstrate the opposite; they crave discord and are insatiable.

TWO COOPERS

In the final episode of *Twin Peak*'s original run, Agent Cooper enters the Black Lodge to rescue Annie Blackburn and to stop Windom Earle (2.22). While there, we learn about the existence of doppelgangers; the apparent natural opposites of other characters. With the introduction of this information, Major Briggs' message of two Coopers starts to make more sense; it wasn't just a repetition, it may have been a warning that there is more than one Cooper. When the episode concludes, the series ends with Cooper leaving the Black Lodge and returning to Twin Peaks. We're left wondering, though, whether it's *our* Cooper or Cooper's doppelganger. The signs point to the latter, but it's unclear; perhaps the time in the Black Lodge traumatized Cooper.

THREE COOPERS

Early in *The Return*, after twenty-six years of waiting, the answer is revealed. Cooper's doppelganger, henceforth referred to as Mr. C, escaped the Black Lodge and Cooper has been trapped in the Black Lodge for a quarter of a century. Throughout the progression of the series we see that Mr C is truly the opposite of Cooper; he is resourceful and intelligent but uses his abilities for cruelty and evil. He has a clear understanding that at a certain date and time, he will return to the Black Lodge and Cooper will return to the world we know. In the sense of Daoist balance, the two cannot exist in the same place at the same time. For balance, they must be in their respective dimensions. Mr. C sets into motion several contingency plans to ensure that Cooper stays in the Black Lodge, securing his own place in this dimension. One of these contingencies involves tulpas, specifically, Dougie Jones. Dougie Jones is a tulpa that is made from the biological material of Mr. C; he is similar in mannerisms and character. He's not *evil* like Mr. C, but he does tend to err on the side of immorality. Dougie lies to his coworkers (and it's reasonable to believe his clients, too), cheats on his wife, gambles excessively. He is the epitome of vice, a clear indication of the influence of his origin. When the time comes for Dale to return, Mr. C is able to resist the return to the Black Lodge. Dale is able to return to his world because of the existence of Dougie Jones; Dale returns to Las Vegas and Dougie returns to the Black Lodge. While in the Lodge Mike tells Dougie he was manufactured, and he no longer serves a purpose; the tulpa dissolves and Mike pockets the seed for a later use (3.3). This is further demonstration of the balance of the *dao*. Two Coopers are balanced because they're opposites; dichotomies of a whole. Dougie skews the balance (in part because he's a manufactured thing, in part because of his behavior) and his removal helps restore *some* of the balance. That being said, there's still the problem of two Coopers in one dimension and to restore the balance one needs to return to the Black Lodge. Agent Cooper is back physically, but he's not acting like himself and is disoriented. It's unclear if this is solely because of the presence of Mr. C, the fact that he spent twenty-five years in the Black Lodge, that he returned to a tulpa of his doppelganger and not in place of his own doppelganger, or a combination.

However, despite his disorientation and utter lack of an ability to communicate, Cooper can function in the world. Without effort, he still manages to let his instinct lead him to the truth. While at the casino he's able to see which machines will pay money thanks to Mike's guidance; he doesn't seem to comprehend the situation, but he is compelled to follow the signs (3.3). Despite the hindrances he's facing, Cooper still possesses sufficient understanding of *dao* to be able to practice *wu-wei* (and to some extent *wei*). In fact, in this state, Cooper seems to thrive with inaction. He passively follows the natural path, the assistance of others, and his instinct without putting intentional effort or thought into his actions. He's able to see the signs and patterns of the way and by following them instinctively, he is able to accomplish amazing things (despite being unable to master tying a tie). Cooper knows when a colleague at the insurance company he works at is lying (3.5). He can swing into action when his life, as well as the life of Janey-E, is threatened by an assassin sent to kill him (3.7). While many things have changed, the nature of Agent Cooper is constant; like the butcher who no longer sees the ox, Cooper only sees the path. When Cooper gets electrocuted and ends up in a coma, he finally fully wakes up; his cognitive abilities have been restored and he's now capable of fully acting intentionally; his *wei* has been restored (3.16).

Cooper now realizes, with more clarity, what he needs to do and how to do it. Again, this is intuitive understanding of the *dao*. We do not see Cooper engage in a proper deductive technique. Instead, he seems to have an inherent understanding of the bigger picture and follows the steps needed to attain the balance. Without being taught (at least as far as we can tell), Cooper understands that he needs to go to long-lost FBI agent Philip Jeffries, and that he will return to Twin Peaks through the very spot where he entered the Black Lodge twenty-five years ago. He knows what he must do to restore the balance and understands the role everyone has to play in eradicating Mr. C and returning his body to the Black Lodge. He also seems to have learned the balance the White and Black Lodges play, the role of Laura Palmer, and the harmony that will be restored once Mr. C is returned and BOB's plan is thwarted.

LET'S ROCK

Cooper, Mr. C, and Dougie Jones are not the only examples of doppelgangers or tulpas. In the Black Lodge we see the doppelgangers of the arm, Leland Palmer (the one who *didn't* kill anyone), Annie, Caroline, and Laura. In *The Return* Part 16, we learn that Diane is a tulpa of Mr. C's making; she's one of the contingencies he's had in place to help secure his position and thwart Cooper's return. This tulpa has the memories, characteristics, and personality of Diane. She is visibly shaken at the thought of seeing Agent Cooper again yet is able to tell that the person they see in the federal prison isn't the Agent Cooper she knew (3.7). She doesn't know who or what he is, but she knows he's not *the* Agent Cooper. In this sense, we see that Diane likely has some awareness of the *dao*, too; she's able to read what's natural and detect when something is off even if she can't give a clear explanation for it.[20]

The existence of Diane's tulpa reinforces the concept of harmonious balance; the real Diane is sent elsewhere, known to the viewer as Naido. Diane can only return after her tulpa is destroyed. As Naido, Diane is in a similar state as Cooper when he's replaced Dougie Jones. She intuits, she cannot communicate nor see, but she has a clear sense of what to do and the ability to follow through. She is following the natural way and is seeking harmony. She seems to understand the importance of returning Cooper to his world. And even though Cooper can't recognize her, he is able to sense that she is a helpful resource and that he should put some trust into her; despite many years in the Black Lodge (or because of it), Cooper is still able to be one with the Way.

When Diane's tulpa is destroyed, Naido returns to Cooper's world. She is still incapacitated in many ways (3.14). Yet, we can tell that she is instinctively aware of the world, what's going on, and what she must do. She communicates to the best of her ability, for example, when Mr. C arrives at the Twin Peaks sheriffs' station; even though she cannot see him, she is in tune with *dao* enough to *sense* him and understand what his presence means. She does the best she can to verbally warn others of his arrival and appears to try to help communicate during the confrontation in Sheriff Frank Truman's office (3.17).

Agent Cooper makes his timely return to the sheriffs' office during this confrontation. Again, he is able to maneuver through the situation apparently relying on instinct alone; he immediately reads the situation, knows the role that each person is to play. He knows when he needs to practice *wu-wei* and *wei,* and he instructs others to help them fulfill their individual roles. His guidance, and the intervention of Freddie (thanks to the Fireman), allows them to defeat BOB and return Mr. C's body to the lodge. When the dust has settled, and balance has been restored, Cooper sees Naido, recognizes her for who she is, and Diane is able to return to her former state.[21] As the pieces are falling in place and harmony is being restored, Cooper, Diane, and Gordon move on to the next phase; they seek out Jeffries and Agent Cooper makes the decision to go back to the night of Laura Palmer's murder.

LAURA IS THE ONE

When Agent Cooper goes back to the night of Laura's murder, he is able to intercept her and prevent her from going down the path that leads to her death. By saving her, Cooper is allowing balance to potentially be restored; he's allowing Laura to fulfill her cosmic function of maintaining balance. However, there's a bit of a (potentially unfortunate) paradox here. By saving Laura, Cooper has undone the destruction of BOB which means that Leland (or whomever BOB possesses) will still be able to do bad acts and collect garmonbozia. This could be deemed unfortunate because it means that BOB will continue to do bad things without an end in sight, especially since Laura disappears right after Cooper interferes and it's decades before he locates the woman he believes is Laura Palmer. The best answer I can generate is that, first, BOB's bad won't outweigh the bad that Mr. C conducts. Second, Laura Palmer is the key, the one that leads to the many. For there to be the attainment of a true balance, she has a function to fulfill. Likely, that function is not just to balance and/or destroy BOB, but Jouday. In *Fire Walk with Me* and *The Return* we learn that Jouday is the true, ultimate evil (3.16). Further support for this is that when Agent Cooper finds Carrie, the woman whom he believes to be Laura Palmer, he wants to take her to her home to her mother, Sarah Palmer (3.18). At first glance, this may seem to be because Cooper wants to help Laura remember who she is. Looking at the bigger picture, though, Agent Cooper has a broader understanding of the role of all the principal characters. If we accept that Laura isn't just to offset the evil of BOB but also his creator Jouday, we can surmise that Agent Cooper has a bigger goal in store than just helping her remember her identity. We again see him towing the line of *wei* and *wu-wei* with Laura/Carrie; he seems to have an intuitive clear idea of what must transpire. Likely, Cooper understands that Jouday is inhabiting Sarah Palmer and that Laura is the key to negating this negative force. In *Daoism* there is a natural order, a path to that order, and wholes that are comprised of opposites. Agent Cooper's understanding of *dao* allows him to be a facilitator in restoring balance to the world; he is the means by which Laura can fulfill her role as the one that leads to the many.[22]

CONCLUSION

An apparent paradox of *Daoism* is that the more one tries to understand, to force knowledge, the less likely it is that one will attain it. What one needs to do instead is to convene with the natural order and harmony of the universe and to try to (please forgive the cliché), go with the flow.

Understanding comes through experience, intuition, and internal balance. It seems appropriate, then, to end with a comment on understanding David Lynch and Mark Frost. Lynch and Frost are famously difficult to understand; there's reason to believe that the duo has an intent, a plan, and that there is a connection and meaning in all that they choose to do. The problem, much like with *Daoism,* is that people try to force the understanding of their bodies of work. We *feel* that there is a meaning and a message. We desire to understand it completely, and we tend to overanalyze the corpus to attain full understanding. The problem is that when we try too hard, we miss the message and the meaning. We cannot force this type of understanding any more than we can force the understanding of the way that the universe harmonizes. We need to absorb and receive the message they are providing, but we have to accept that there may be some components about which we can't force understanding. That is, at least in part, the appeal of Lynch/Frost; there's a mystery behind (and within) the brilliance of their work. To force understanding is to miss the point.

NOTES

1. While Agent Cooper identifies this as a deductive process, what he describes doesn't quite meet the typical definition of deduction. Deductive reasoning often requires the meticulous collection of facts and generating a logical inference from them. Cooper's method, on the other hand, seems to more closely follow intuitive understanding of a situation. He does use deductive reasoning, but the particular method that appeared to him in the dream is probably closer to induction. For simplicity I will continue to refer to this as a deductive technique.

2. United Nations High Commissions for Refugees, *The Buddhist Core Values and Perspectives for Protection Challenges,* last modified 12 November 2012, http://www.unhcr.org/50be10cb9.pdf.

3. Jean Smith, *Radiant Mind: Essential Buddhist Teachings and Texts* (New York: Riverhead Books, 1999): 13.

4. Smith, *Radiant Mind: Essential Buddhist Teachings and Texts,* 15

5. Smith, *Radiant Mind: Essential Buddhist Teachings and Texts,* 3–6; Dendo Kyokai Bukkyo, ed *The Teaching of the Buddha* (Tokyo: Kosaido Printing Co., 1966): 2–18.

6. Smith, *Radiant Mind: Essential Buddhist Teachings and Texts,* 85–102; Bukkyo, *The Teaching of the Buddha,* 74–88.

7. A note on translation: Daoism and Dao may also be translated as Taoism and Tao. The difference stems from whether the translation is coming from pinyin or wade-giles respectively.

8. *Twin Peaks,* Pilot. Log Lady Introduction.

9. Henceforth, I'll refer to this just as *The Return.*

10. It should be noted that Laozi is the name attributed to the author of the *Daodejing;* however, there is speculation about the veracity of this. There is sub-

stantial evidence that indicates the *daodejing* is the culmination of many authors and that there wasn't a singular author.

11. Philip Ivanhoe, *The Daodejing of Laozi* (Indianapolis: Hackett, 2003), XIX.

12. Burton Watson, trans. *The Complete Works of Chaung Tzu* (New York: Columbia University Press, 1968).

13. Watson, *The Complete Works of Chaung Tzu*, 197–208.

14. Watson, *The Complete Works of Chaung Tzu*, 50–53. Zhuangzi noted that the butcher may experience reason to pause when encountered with a new situation. Attaining *dao* of his craft does not mean the butcher will never need to give intentional thought to a situation. Rather, it means that he will not have to think about the things that he's mastered. When a new situation arises he'll be better suited to master it quickly, but the mastery still needs to commence.

15. This is likely the reason that Cooper didn't give a more thorough technique to the Twin Peaks locals. He explained to them that he has a technique through which he's able to learn truth. However, he knows that he can't force the understanding and that to try to give too much more information would likely not help them understand more. The best he can hope for is to gain their trust and help them see a glimpse of the method behind his apparent madness.

16. It may help to consider the concept of yin-yang; there is an interdependent relationship between light and dark, male and female, and all other opposites.

17. We see this reinforced in *The Secret History* in the discussion of the Nez Perce as well as other discussions of the lore of the local indigenous tribes. There is discussion about white and dark tribes or entities; the map we see in the series and *The Secret History* demonstrates the dichotomy of feast and famine, life and death, fertility and infertility, life sustaining corn and garmonbozia. Mark Frost, *The Secret History of Twin Peaks* (New York: Flatiron Books, 2016), 33.

18. In *The Return* we see indication that the lodges, the gas station, etc. exist in another dimension and there may be multiple entrances to these places. Twin Peaks may be just one of many entrances to the lodges, but there does seem to be a consistent connection between the lodges and Twin Peaks, even if the lodges are only accessible at certain times and when specific conditions are met.

19. It's worth noting the connection to Jouday; a much darker, more evil force. Throughout most of *Twin Peaks*, the emphasis is on BOB and the inhabitants of the Black Lodge as being the evil with which we should be most concerned. However, through the series and in the *The Final Dossier* we see hints that there's something bigger than BOB. When given the opportunity to join Blue Rose, Tamara Preston is told that Judy (originally Jouday) is the ultimate negative force that they are combating.

20. This inference is based on the presumption that since the tulpa mimics Diane's characteristics and abilities, what that demonstrates indicates what Diane would be capable of.

21. Here is an anomaly as this scene unfolds. We see an image of Agent Cooper superimposed, apparently observing what is going on. There is ample room for speculation here and a variety of probable theories. At the very minimum it seems sufficient to say that this is a demonstration of Cooper's observing the events from an external, and perhaps enlightened, perspective.

22. In 3.16 Agent Cooper gives a tuft of his hair to Mike and asks him to use the seed to make a new Dougie for Janey-E and Sonny Jim. We can infer that because of Cooper's DNA, this Dougie will be good whereas the previous one was bad. The presumption is that Cooper's tulpa will not be disruptive to the harmony or the balance of light and dark, especially since he will err on the side of morality. However, it's also possible that this will be a moot point because Dale's returning to the night of Laura Palmer's murder means the course of events that will create Dougie Jones won't have occurred. In true Lynch/Frost fashion, we've been given a puzzle that may not be resolved.

WORKS CITED

Bukkyo Dendo Kyokai, eds. *The Teaching of the Buddha.* Tokyo: Kosaido Printing Co., 1966.
Frost, Mark. *The Secret History of Twin Peaks.* New York: Flatiron Books, 2016.
———. *Twin Peaks: The Final Dossier.* New York: Flatiron Books, 2017.
Ivanhoe, Philip. *The Daodejing of Laozi.* Indianapolis: Hackett, 2003.
Smith, Jean. *Radiant Mind: Essential Buddhist Teachings and Texts.* New York: Riverhead Books, 1999.
Watson, Burton, trans. *The Complete Works of Chaung Tzu.* New York: Columbia University Press, 1968.

Eight

The Transmigration of Cooper

Echoes of Plato's Recollection in Twin Peaks

Jean-Philippe Ranger

Some parts of *Twin Peaks* remind me of Plato's theory of recollection. In *Twin Peaks: The Return*, we follow Special Agent Dale Cooper as he finds his way out of the Red Room of the Black Lodge and is "reborn" in Las Vegas (3.2–3). There, he takes the place of one Dougie Jones, but with no recollection of his previous life as Agent Cooper. It is not until the end of the third season that he succeeds in recovering all of his memories and regains his full identity as Agent Cooper. In the pages that follow, I will argue that some aspects of Cooper's journey are reminiscent of Plato's myths of reincarnation and theory of recollection. I also show that these stories, both in Plato and in *Twin Peaks*, point to deeper philosophical questions about learning and discovering. I proceed in three steps: first, I draw parallels between Cooper's metaphorical rebirth and Plato's use of myths of reincarnation and theory of recollection. Second, I suggest that for Plato, reincarnation and recollection are his response to a classical philosophical puzzle about learning and discovering: Meno's paradox. Finally, in the third and last section of this chapter, I discuss how these outlandish stories—both in *Twin Peaks* and Plato's dialogues—might encourage us to think more carefully about what it means to discover, to learn, and ultimately, to know.

COOPER RECOLLECTS

Twin Peaks: The Return opens with two otherworldly scenes featuring Agent Cooper. The first is a flashback to the Red Room from the second season of the show. Laura Palmer tells a young Cooper that they will meet again in 25 years (2.22). The second is a short exchange between Cooper and the Fireman:

> Fireman: It is in our house now.
>
> Cooper: It is?
>
> Fireman: This cannot be said aloud now. Remember 430. Richard and Linda. Two birds with one stone.
>
> Cooper: I understand.
>
> Fireman: You are far away (3.1).

This enigmatic exchange sets the stage for a theme that is closely related to the central issue of this chapter: memory. Indeed, memory plays an important function in Cooper's character arc throughout all three series. In the world of *Twin Peaks*, certain characters travel through what could be described as different places or dimensions, where time and space work differently than they do for us in the real world. This makes for great television. The way David Lynch and Mark Frost construct their narrative is very intriguing and exciting. But there are some equally exciting insights we can glean from this show, and these relate to some elements in Plato's philosophy.[1] In *Twin Peaks*, the Fireman urges Cooper to remember certain things once he is out of this "other place." Remembering is an essential part of learning and discovering, and Cooper himself goes through such a process. To accurately describe someone as having learned something implies that this person remembers what was learned. And we often are said to progress in our learning by relating or connecting this newly learned thing with our memory of other things.

If we forget, we have effectively unlearned this thing. In *Twin Peaks: The Return*, Cooper goes through a process of learning, forgetting, and relearning. He has learned many things in the other place. Yet when he first comes back to Las Vegas as Dougie Jones, he has forgotten everything. To recover this knowledge, he needs to go through a process of relearning who he is and what he is trying to achieve. This process is reminiscent of Plato's myths of reincarnation, and his amnesia is cured through a process that seems similar to steps in Plato's theory of recollection. Let us begin with the issue of reincarnation.

One myth that we find through a number of Plato's dialogues suggests that the soul is an immaterial thing that goes through a cycle of reincarnation. The soul undergoes a transmigration (i.e., goes through a cycle of successive births and deaths). For this to be possible, Plato first needs to accept that while death is something that happens to us, it is not really the end of what we are. Using his vocabulary, death is "the separation of the soul from the body ... the body comes to be separated by itself apart

The Transmigration of Cooper

from the soul, and the soul comes to be separated by itself apart from the body."[2] For Plato, when a person dies, the body decomposes and is destroyed. The soul, on the other hand, goes to another place, to an underworld of sorts.[3]

Here, we have two parallels with *Twin Peaks*. The first is that Cooper's disappearance and imprisonment in the Red Room of the Black Lodge seems to be like a death for him. The second parallel is on the view of death itself. It is presented in a poignant scene where Margaret Lanterman calls Hawk to let him know that she is dying.

> Margaret: You know about death, that it's just a change, not an end. Hawk, it's time. There is some fear, some fear in letting go. Remember what I told you. I can't say more over the phone, but you know what I mean, from our talks, when we were able to speak face to face. Watch for that one, the one I told you about, the one under the moon, on Blue Pine Mountain. Hawk, my log is turning gold. The wind is moaning. I'm dying. Good night, Hawk (3.15).

According to Margaret's view, death is the passage of a soul from one place to another. She is referring to a process similar to the one that Plato discusses in the *Phaedo* and mentions in the *Apology of Socrates*: the soul and body separate and the soul "goes to another place." For this to be possible, the soul has to outlast the body. In the *Phaedo*, Plato further argues that the soul is something immortal.[4]

In the *Meno*, Plato examines his claim that the soul is immortal. This claim is expressed in a myth.

Figure 8.1. Episode 3.15 "There's Some Fear in Letting Go"
Twin Peaks

> Socrates: I have heard wise men and women talk about divine matters ...
>
> Meno: What did they say?
>
> Socrates: What was, I thought, both true and beautiful.
>
> Meno: What was it, and who were they?
>
> Socrates: The speakers were among the priests and priestesses whose care it is to give an account of their practices. Pindar too says it, and many others among our poets. What they say is this; see whether you think they speak the truth: They say that the human soul is immortal; at times it comes to an end, which they call dying; at times it is reborn, but it is never destroyed, and one must therefore live one's life as piously as possible.[5]

One notable point is that Plato connects the immortality of the soul with the claim that the soul gets successively reincarnated. Furthermore, the fact that the soul is immortal and goes through cycles of reincarnation is supposed to justify the fact that we must be pious. This is the moral lesson associated with myths of reincarnation. To ensure that we will come back on earth with a greater chance of a good life, we ought to be the best person we can be in our current incarnation.[6]

There is, however, a second lesson that comes from the myths of reincarnation and this lesson is *epistemic* (i.e., it deals with questions surrounding knowledge). This epistemic lesson is in three parts. First, before we were born, in our previous incarnations *and in between our incarnations*, we *knew* a great many things. Second, when we were reborn, we *forgot* these things that we knew before. Third, the process through which we relearn is called *recollection*—a recovery of our prenatal knowledge. Let us examine the three parts of this epistemic lesson in detail and see how they relate to Agent Cooper's journey.

To begin, here is the relevant passage:

> As the soul is immortal, has been born often, and has seen all things here and in the underworld, there is nothing which it has not learned; so it is in no way surprising that it can recollect the things it knew before, both about virtue and other things. As the whole of nature is akin, and the soul has learned everything, nothing prevents a man, after recalling one thing only—a process we call learning—discovering everything else for himself, if he is brave and does not tire of the search, for searching and learning are, as a whole, recollection.[7]

In between our incarnations on earth, according to this myth, we knew a great many things since our soul "has seen all things here and in the underworld."[8] Our disincarnated soul, devoid of its senses, could more easily access the truth.[9] In the case of Agent Cooper, each time he travels to this other place, whether it be the Red Room of the Black Lodge or the place where the Fireman resides, he learns something more about Laura Palmer's case. For example, early in the first season, he finds himself in the Red Room and learns the identity of Laura Palmer's killer (1.3). He wakes up and calls Sheriff Harry Truman and tells him that he knows who killed Laura Palmer. Other examples of such information available in these "other places" include the various messages from the Fireman, the "help" he gets to win at the slot machines (3.4), and to find errors in the insurance claims (3.5). Other examples include all that he can glean from his time in the Red Room with Mike and the Arm, and what he must do to find Laura (3.1). Agent Cooper is not the only one privy to such information from "other places." Major Garland Briggs and Phillip Jeffries have also learnt a great many things there. Dreams have a prophetic quality in the show, and some characters have access to this special knowledge because they are somehow attuned to these other places.[10] These other places are where these characters have gathered information.

The second part of what Plato is getting at in the epistemic versions of his reincarnation myths is that when we are reborn, we *forget* all that we knew. This includes what we knew in our previous lives and what we knew in between our incarnations.[11] When Agent Cooper first returns to Las Vegas as Dougie Jones, he has forgotten everything he knew about being Agent Cooper. He is childlike and innocent, to the point where he hardly remembers to put on shoes when he leaves the vacant house with Jade (3.3) or why he enjoys coffee and cherry pie so much. He also has no recollection of the reason why he has a key to his room at the Great Northern Hotel in Twin Peaks. In fact, he does not even seem to understand what a key is. He has forgotten everything. So when we are born, we forget everything. We might ask whether we can recover any of this information. Plato's answer is that we can, and it is through what he calls recollection.

The theory's main purpose is to reveal something about our ability to relearn those things that we knew before we were born. According to Plato, what we call "inquiring" and "learning" in everyday language is actually a kind of recollection. To make sense of this, we need to turn to a more rational and philosophical account of recollection. This account is found in the *Phaedo*.

In the *Phaedo*, one of the characters of the dialogue claims that we have knowledge inside of us, and that if we go through the proper training, we can access this knowledge.[12] More specifically, we access this knowledge through a process of recovery. We relearn the things we knew before we were born—those things we forgot at birth. The explanation Plato is using is that if we can recognize a claim or a statement as true, it must somehow mean that we knew it before. For example, when Cooper as Dougie first goes to work and meets his co-worker Phil in the lobby, he does not recognize him (3.5). This implies he has never met him before. However, he does seem to recognize the coffee. He recognizes that he loves it. According to Plato's point, if he does recognize it, it means that he must have known it at a prior time. This point is expressed in modern language when we use the term "recognize." To recognize is to "know once again." We can only know something again if we knew it before. In terms of the example, Cooper as Dougie already knows that he loves coffee. That is how he can recognize it. This is the first condition of recollection for Plato: in order to correctly say that someone has recollected something, this person must have known it as some time before. The second condition of recollection is worded in a way that is a little more complex:

> When someone sees or hears or in some way perceives one thing and not only knows that thing but also thinks of another thing of which the knowledge is not the same but different, are we not right to say that this person recollects the second thing that comes into the mind?[13]

This condition states that if, when I perceive something, I am not only thinking about that thing, but also about something else, then I am recollecting that other thing. To recollect is to associate two separate things, following the perception of one of these. As an example, when Ben Horne gets Cooper's Great Northern key in the mail, he sees the key and he is reminded of Dale Cooper (3.7). Perceiving the key makes him think of Dale Cooper. Another example of recollection of this kind is a scene in the process of Cooper's rebirth that triggers recollection for me. It happens after Naido has been projected off the black room that seems to float in the void (3.3). Cooper climbs down the ladder to re-enter the room. I perceive two things: a couch and a woman sitting on it. The couch is made of blue velvet, and the woman sitting on it is named "American Girl" in the closing credits. She is played by actress Phoebe Augustine. At the same time as I perceive these, I think of two other things, that are *different* from what I perceive: I think of David Lynch's 1986 film *Blue Velvet*, and of Ronette Pulaski, who was with Laura Palmer on the night of her murder. Since I perceive something, yet also think of something else in both these cases, these would count as instances of recollection for Plato. The theory of recollection is a theory of association between ideas or concepts. The two conditions explained above work as follows: if I perceive a thing and am reminded of a second thing, I can be said to be recollecting that second thing. This also implies that I have somehow already encountered that second thing.

At this point we should pause and ask a question: recollection as I have been describing it so far seems quite unremarkable—it is simply a theory whereby we associate ideas, concepts, or thoughts. If so, why does Plato seem adamant to include the point that we have immortal souls and go through cycles of reincarnation? Plato certainly wants to give recollection a deeper meaning, but why? And more importantly, why should we think that anything he says on this point is worth considering at all? Is it just an interesting story? To answer these questions, I have to take a slight detour and give a brief sketch of Plato's Theory of Forms.[14]

To do this, I begin with the example that Plato uses in the *Phaedo*.[15] If we imagine that we have three sticks with the first two being approximately the same length, upon observing the pair of similarly sized sticks, we will say that they appear equal in length. We will also say that each is more equal to the other than to the third stick. At this point, Plato asks us to consider where we gained the ability to make these comparisons. What this ability presupposes, according to him, is that we are comparing the equality of the pairs of sticks to some independent standard, a paradigm of equality that is different from each of these sets. He calls this standard or paradigm the form of equality. We could describe it as the concept of equality.[16] It is a paradigm insofar as it provides a yardstick that we can "hold up" to every set of equal things, and it permits us to first declare whether members of a set are equal, and second to rank sets of equal things in terms of being less or more equal. The question that this raises for Plato is the following, considering that we can all appropriately rank sets in terms of equality: where did we learn about equality itself? We could not have perceived it since forms are not perceptible things. According to him, we must have known it even before we started perceiving, that is, before we were born. Furthermore, when we see equal things, we "not only know" those equal things, "but also think of" the form equality.[17] To sum up, what we recollect are things we knew before birth. This implies that our soul existed before we were born.

Let us look at an example we could glean from the show. If we want to say that "Agent Dale Cooper is a just man," we are claiming that the property "justice" belongs to him. The grounds on which we can make that claim is that we observe his actions and notice how they are just. In an interesting bit of insight, Plato is suggesting that the very reason why we are able to identify that "Cooper is just" is because we have prior knowledge of what justice is. In a sense, we already know what the form "justice" entails. This means that to perceive, and to be able to make comparisons through perception *presupposes* that we had prior knowledge. Furthermore, to perceive just things triggers our memories of the form justice.

For Plato, while we forgot these forms at birth, we can *relearn* them through recollection. Our subconscious memory is triggered, and we gather some insight from our perceptual experiences through our lives. This does not happen all at once. Slowly, we get a clearer and clearer picture of the form itself. In recollecting who he was before his metaphorical rebirth, Cooper as Dougie goes through a similar process. Through various experiences he comes to remember that he is FBI special agent Dale Cooper. Some of the things that do seem to resonate with him are his love of coffee, his love of cherry pie, and his being able to disarm hitman Ike "The Spike" Stadtler (3.7). Finally, the experience that seems to have been the turning point in "waking up" Cooper was seeing a clip from the 1950 film *Sunset Boulevard* on the television:

> DeMille: Good-bye, Norma. We'll see what they can do.
>
> Norma : I'm not worried. Everything will be fine. The old team together again. Nothing can stop us.
>
> DeMille: The old team. Yeah. Good-bye, dear.
>
> Norma: Good-bye, Mr. DeMille.
>
> William Holden: How'd it go?
>
> Gloria Swanson: It couldn't have gone better. It's practically set. Good. He has to finish this picture first. Mine will be his next.
>
> DeMille: Get Gordon Cole. Tell him to forget about our car. Tell him he can get another old car someplace— (3.15)

Here, we finally sense that Cooper is coming back to himself, and that he recognizes the name "Gordon Cole," the name of his superior at the FBI. The very fact that he recognizes the name Gordon Cole presupposes that he already knew it. But this encounter seems more important for him, he understands something more profound—namely that he must "wake up" and get Gordon Cole.

When he wakes up from his self-induced coma in the hospital room, he has fully recollected who he is. He also remembers all the things he learned in the Red Room and beyond. He knows how to defeat Mr. C and how to find Laura Palmer. Furthermore, he is the only one able to recognize Naido as Diane in the Twin Peaks Sheriff's Department (3.17). Using some of Plato's language, even though he was fumbling around as Dougie, Cooper retained all of his memories. He just could not recall them. Once he rediscovered who he was, triggered by his recollection of Gordon Cole, he was also able to recover all of these memories. These memories were *inside of him*, and rather than learning these things about himself and the Laura Palmer case, he remembered them—he *recollected* them. In *Twin Peaks*, Cooper recollects who he is. In the context of Plato's philosophy, the stakes are much higher.

FIND WHAT'S MISSING

To make these stakes clear, I must now turn to the second section of this chapter, about Meno's paradox. This paradox illustrates one of the difficulties associated with learning, inquiring, and discovering. It is first formulated by the character Meno in Plato's dialogue of the same name. To set the stage, we have Socrates asking Meno a number of questions to show him that neither of them know what virtue is. In the next passage, after Socrates urges Meno to start over and search for a definition of virtue with him, Meno famously responds with the following:

> And how are you going to inquire about it, Socrates, when you do not at all know what it is? For what sort of thing, from among the ones you do not know, will you take as the object of your inquiry? And even if you happen to bump right into it, how are you going to know that it is the thing you did not know?[18]

The point of Meno's challenge is the following: It seems futile to attempt to learn something I know absolutely nothing about. If, by sheer luck, I should find myself before that thing that I do not know at all, it seems that I will never be able to recognize it as that thing. Socrates begins by reframing the dilemma as follows: according to Meno's argument,

> it seems it is not possible for a person to inquire about what he knows, or about what he does not know. After all, he wouldn't inquire about what he knows—since he knows it, and there is no need to inquire about something like that—or about what he does not know—since he does not know what he is to inquire about.[19]

Meno's paradox is in two prongs, and each one leads to an absurdity. If it is correct, it is impossible to learn or discover, and pointless to inquire. According to the first prong, we cannot learn what we already know since we already know it. The second prong states that it is absurd to attempt to learn or discover what we do not know at all, since we have no way to recognize the thing we did not know *as that thing we did not know*. I will illustrate the difficulty as Meno presents it with two different examples. The first is not from *Twin Peaks*, but I think it is helpful. The second, however, comes directly from an exchange between Margaret Lanterman and Deputy Chief Hawk.

Imagine that on the moon there was a recorded message, on some unknown medium, left by an alien of some absolutely foreign level and kind of intelligence. Imagine also that the crew of Apollo 11 had come across this message. What would likely have happened? Chances are, they would not even have recognized the message as a message, since they had no way of doing so. Since they knew absolutely nothing about a message of any kind, they would have had no way of recognizing it as such.

Something similar happens when Margaret Lanterman calls Deputy Chief Hawk. Their conversation goes as follows:

> Hawk: Margaret, what can I do for you?
>
> Margaret: Hawk, my log has a message for you.
>
> Hawk: Ok.
>
> Margaret: Something is missing, and you have to find it. It has to do with Special Agent Dale Cooper.
>
> Hawk: Dale Cooper? What is it?
>
> Margaret: The way you will find it has something to do with your heritage. This is the message from the log.
>
> Hawk: Ok, Margaret. Thank you.
>
> Margaret: Good night, Hawk.
>
> Hawk: Good night, Margaret (3.1).

This exchange is enigmatic if it is taken by itself, and Hawk is rightly puzzled by it. He is told to find what is missing. But the problem is that a multitude of things are missing. If he comes across something, how will he know that it is missing, and that *it* is the missing thing that he has to find? Just like the alien message in the example above, if he does not know it, yet comes upon it, how will he know it was the thing he was looking for? After working it out, Hawk understands that he is caught in something of a paradox.

The next day, Lucy and Andy have retrieved the files from the Laura Palmer case. Hawk comes into the meeting room and the dialogue goes as follows:

> Andy: We laid everything out, Hawk, and we can't find anything that is missing.
>
> Hawk: If it's not here, then... how do you know it's missing?
>
> Lucy: But if it is here, then it isn't missing?
>
> Andy (gesturing at the case files): This... is here.
>
> Hawk: Let's sit down... Let, let me sit down. Let's start from the beginning.
>
> Andy: And...
>
> Hawk: Don't say a thing. I need to think out loud. Something is missing and I need to find it. And the way I'm gonna find it has something to do with my heritage.

Lucy: You're an Indian.

Hawk: Yes, Lucy. And apparently that's the way I'm gonna find what's missing.

Lucy (gasps): Ah!

Hawk: What is it?

Lucy: Aah!

Andy: Are you ok, Punky?

Lucy: I know what's missing!

Hawk: What's missing?

Lucy: The bunny! The bunny! I ate that bunny!

Andy: That's missing. That's missing. Do chocolate bunnies have anything to do with your heritage?

Hawk: No. It's not about the bunny.

Hawk: You ate the evidence, Lucy?

Lucy: I know! I never did it again. And I only ate one. And I never did it again. But I had a problem at that time with... And I don't like to say this in front of Andy. But I had a bubble of gas and I had read that sometimes chocolate, which I love, can be used as a remedy. Maybe by indigenous people? It that true, Hawk? Do you use chocolate as a remedy for gas?

Andy: Do you want another bunny, Punky? I can get you more bunnies.

Hawk: It's not about the bunny! Is it about the bunny? No. It's not about the bunny.

Lucy (sighs with relief) (3.3).

Here Hawk, despite the chatter from Andy and Lucy, comes to understand the difficulty. If what he is looking for is missing, it cannot be part of the stored files about the Laura Palmer case. It has to be somewhere else. Now there are surely a great number of things that are *relevant* to the case, but not stored with the files and the evidence. A great number of things are *missing*. How is he supposed to *know* if he does come across it? The only clues he has are that they are related to Cooper, and that "it has something to do with his heritage." The point of the difficulty is if something is *absolutely* unknown, there is no way to learn it. The point of Meno's paradox is that it is impossible to learn, inquire, or discover radically new knowledge. It also presupposes that all knowledge needs to be grounded in prior knowledge. And for Plato, some of this prior knowledge is recollected from the time before we are born.

LEARNING AND DISCOVERING

We finally get to the philosophical significance of this cluster of issues that are presented to us, both by Plato in the form of fanciful myths and in *Twin Peaks* in the form of a weird television show. What do these strange tales involving the immortality of the soul, reincarnation, and recollection have to do with philosophy? What can a show like *Twin Peaks* teach us about what it means to learn, to discover, to inquire, and ultimately, to know something?

Throughout the bulk of his texts, Plato is committed to the underlying principle that "all knowledge is based on knowledge."[20] To count as knowledge, whatever it is that we know has to be based on something already known. Intuitively, this seems correct. This could be as simple as me saying that I know there is a person in the next room because I can hear that person's voice. The knowledge that there is a person in the other room rests on the knowledge that this voice belongs to someone. However, the difficulty with such a principle is that we could, in theory, ask the following question: if this knowledge is based on prior knowledge, what knowledge is the prior knowledge itself based on? If all knowledge is based on prior knowledge and we proceed to ask that question, we will eventually be stuck in an infinite chain of questions about prior knowledge—we will be stuck in an infinite regress. We need a terminus, a point at which we get a non-inferential belief (i.e., a belief that is not based on any argument and that can be "justified" by itself). To avoid the infinite regress, we need knowledge that is grounded either in one or in a set of non-inferential beliefs that are self-justified or, according to some, self-evident.

And this is precisely the lesson that the *Meno* wants to teach us by invoking recollection—namely that there are self-evident beliefs and that the way we identify them *as self-evident* is because we *recollect them*. In other words, Plato's response to Meno's paradox is the following: Meno asks "how are you going to inquire about it ... when you do not at all know what it is?"[21] Plato responds that since we are born with knowledge that we learned in between our incarnations, it is not the case that we do not know *at all* what it is. According to the theory of recollection, we do know, in a way. We simply forgot these things at birth. Then, when we are reminded, we *recognize* that some inferences are true. Inquiring, discovering, and learning are really processes that involve *relearning*, and this is what permits us to know whether answers we are finding are correct. This is how we know that we have hit upon the truth. So since we have beliefs already inside of us, and we understand these to be true, we can be aware that we have found out a further truth.[22] The point is that basic, true beliefs are inside us.[23] After going through a fruitful process of inquiry, "these beliefs have been stirred up in [us] like a dream."[24] Recollection produces true beliefs, accompanied by an awareness that these beliefs are true.

At times, perhaps at first, when we are in the process of accessing this knowledge that is in us, we do not yet fully grasp what is happening, nor that we are coming to realize something important. There are a few cases of this in *Twin Peaks*. For instance, when Cooper as Dougie is encountering things that are very significant, he does not fully grasp them. He *fails* to completely recollect. There might be a glint of remembrance in his eyes, but not full awareness. These would only be examples of partial recollection. Again, it is only with the mention of Gordon Cole that he does something that will lead him to recollect completely.

A second lesson that is significant in *Twin Peaks: The Return* is how discovery is sometimes the result of pure chance. Hawk found the "missing something" when he dropped a buffalo nickel in the lady's room of the Sheriff's Department. He notices the damaged door of the stall. At the bottom of the door, he sees that it was made by "Nez Percé Manufacturing" (3.15). Both of these clues have something to do with his heritage: the nickel having an Indigenous head on it, and Hawk being a member of the Nez Percé tribe. It is through a series of chance events that Hawk makes the discovery. However, he would not have noticed the significance of these events without these hints from Margaret. He never would have realized that what is missing is a series of pages from Laura's diary. These hints make it so Hawk is aware he has found what was missing. This gives Hawk a way out of Meno's paradox: "And even if you happen to bump right into it, how are you going to know that it is the thing you did not know?"[25] Hawk does happen upon what is missing, and because he has further hints (i.e., because he has prior knowledge) he becomes puzzled and ready to learn or discover the pages.

What is perhaps most intriguing is not that we are able to learn, inquire, discover, or otherwise solve puzzles. Rather, what is intriguing is that we are aware when we have found correct answers. If we remove the mythology of reincarnation and the metaphysics of recollection, what remains is a theory whereby we have an ability to recognize the validity of certain claims.

CONCLUSION

To sum up, I have discussed how Cooper's process of rebirth as Dougie Jones, and his subsequent reawakening is reminiscent of Plato's theory of recollection. Cooper knows who he is but has forgotten. Through a series of associations, he finds a way to recover his memories about who he is. I have explored this parallel first by comparing Cooper's rebirth as Dougie Jones and Plato's theory of recollection. Second, I have discussed how recollection is Plato's response to Meno's paradox, a version of which is found in the enigmatic words of Margaret Lanterman. Finally, I offer a few ideas about how these stories, both in Plato's myths and in *Twin Peaks*, might offer us some philosophical insight.

NOTES

1. More specifically, we find these elements in Plato's so-called "metaphysical dialogues," where he discusses his famous theory of forms and theory of recollection.

2. Plato, *Phaedo* 64c. The Greek word for "soul" here is *psyche*. As Gallop points out, the soul is "often equivalent to 'intellect' or 'reason' a 'thinking faculty' or 'cognitive principle' by which the quest for wisdom is pursued." David Gallop, *Phaedo* (Oxford: Clarendon Press, 1975), 86. Unless otherwise noted, all translations are taken from the J.M. Cooper edition of Plato.

3. This is a popular Ancient Greek view on death. *Cf.* Plato, *Apology* 40c–d.

4. In the *Phaedo*, Plato develops his arguments for the immortality of the soul. In the course of his argument, he entertains the possibility that while the soul outlasts the body, it might not be immortal (86e–88b). Plato probably believes his arguments can counter that objection. I can neither discuss these arguments here, nor whether they are decisive. Readers interested in this issue should consult Bostock's excellent book (*Plato's Phaedo*), and Gallop's useful commentary (*Plato: Phaedo*).

5. Plato, *Meno* 81a–b (with slight modifications to the translation).

6. The versions of the myths of reincarnation that focus on the moral lesson are found at the end of the *Gorgias*, the *Phaedo*, and *Republic* X. For more details, *cf.* Julia Annas, "Plato's Myths of Judgement," *Phronesis* 27 (1982).

7. *Meno* 80e–81d (with slight modifications to the translation).

8. *Meno* 81c.

9. This is a common theme in Plato. Since sense perception is fraught with contradictions, it is an obstacle to gaining knowledge. Furthermore, the lesson of *Republic* V (474b–480a) is that perceptible things are not the kinds of things that can be known.

10. Gordon Cole's dream about Monica Bellucci is significant to the narrative. And of course, we should not forget Margaret Lanterman who gets privileged information from her log.

11. *Phaedo* 75e.

12. *Phaedo* 73a–b.

13. *Phaedo* 73c8–10 (with slight modifications to the translation). This second condition entails some difficulties for Plato's argument. For a discussion of these difficulties, see Ackrill, "*Anamnesis* in the *Phaedo*."

14. Plato's Theory of Forms is very complex, odd, and controversial. I cannot hope to do it any justice here. For more details about the theory, and some critical

remarks, see Terrence H. Irwin, "The Theory of Forms," Julia Annas, *An Introduction to Plato's Republic*, 217–241, and David Bostock, *Plato's Phaedo*, 194–213. This theory is prominent in the *Republic*, V–VII, as well as the *Phaedo*, the *Phaedrus*, and the *Symposium*.

15. *Phaedo* 74b–*ff*.
16. This would not be accurate for Plato, since forms exists independently from our minds.
17. *Phaedo* 73c.
18. *Meno* 80d.
19. *Meno* 80d–e.
20. I take this expression from Gail Fine, "Knowledge and Logos in the Theaetetus," *Philosophical Review* 88, no. 3 (1979): 367.
21. *Meno* 80d.
22. In the *Meno*, Plato uses a thought experiment to show how we recollect. He has Socrates ask an uneducated slave boy to solve a geometry problem, and with the proper questions, the boy is able not only to solve the problem, but also to be aware that he has given the right answer. This thought experiment runs from 82b–85d.
23. *Meno* 85c.
24. *Meno* 85c.
25. *Meno* 80d.

WORKS CITED

Ackrill, J.L. "*Anamnesis* in the *Phaedo*: Remarks on 73c-75c." In *Essays on Plato and Aristotle*, edited by J.L. Ackrill. Oxford: Oxford University Press: 13–22.

Annas, Julia. "Plato's Myths of Judgement." *Phronesis* 27 (1982): 119–143.

Bostock, David. *Plato's Phaedo*. Oxford: Oxford University Press, 1986.

Cooper, John M. *Plato: Complete Works*. Indianapolis: Hackett Publishing Company, 1997.

Fine, Gail. "Knowledge and Logos in the Theaetetus." *Philosophical Review* 88, no. 3 (1979): 366–397.

Gallop, David. *Plato. Phaedo*. Oxford: Clarendon Press, 1975.

Irwin, Terrence H. "The Theory of Forms." In *Plato 1: Metaphysics and Epistemology*, edited by Gail Fine. Oxford: Oxford University Press, 1999: 143–170.

Nine

Life in the Black Lodge

The Twin Challenge of Watching Twin Peaks

Shai Biderman, Ronen Gil, and Ido Lewit

The multigenerational experience of watching *Twin Peaks*—from the very first seasons in 1990–1991 to the last one in 2017—is both challenging and frustrating. Challenging, because if the purpose of watching a TV series is to derive pleasure from flexing our cognitive ability to understand and interpret it, and our emotional ability to identify with the characters and become carried away with the plot, then *Twin Peaks* does its best to deny us these satisfactions. It does so with its multiplicity of characters and the resulting difficulty of following each with an equal degree of emotional and cognitive investment; and of plotlines, twists, and details not all of which are equally relevant. Most critically, it burdens us with its ontological premises, its worldview, and the internal logic that guides its narrative. In all, it offers a continuous challenge that is well-nigh impossible to overcome.

This makes watching the series a frustrating experience, in two senses. First, while the very existence of the challenge is not new to the genre, the extreme length of this particular series makes for a frustrating viewing experience as you find yourself chronically unable to comprehend it in full. It twists and turns, it evolves and unfolds, tantalizingly evading cognitive captivity, so to speak, within that warm and satisfying glow of "now I got it!"

In the second sense, *Twin Peaks* viewers are frustrated by the violation of a promise implicit in the TV series format. For the viewers (in live broadcasts or reruns, streaming or binging), spectatorship represents an unwritten contract with the production. This contract guarantees an experience delimited to a given medium, involving certain viewing habits, and relying on a predetermined set of expectations and conventions. Thus, for example, the traditional TV medium has made us accustomed to series with a simple and coherent episodic structure. The episodes are grouped in seasons, which in turn make up the entire series. This structure habituates us to view the episodes one after the other as broadcast by the channel, expecting and being expected to understand the series as it unfolds episode by episode, season by season. In order to fulfill this promise and reinforce this habit, every episode commonly opens with brief review of the preceding ones (usually following a statement such as "previously on..."). This does not only remind us of the previous episodes (and broadcast times), but also, and mainly, provides us with a key for interpreting the episode we are about to view and understanding its role within the entire fabric of the series. It also validates the "serial" structure of the plot. Another instrument for providing meaning through the habit formed by the TV series format is the cliffhanger—the convention whereby a given episode ends with a moment of suspense, while at the same time making the promise, inherent to the very genre, that the suspense is bound to resolve at the beginning of the next episode.

These two frustrations are related to two aspects of the abovementioned challenge. The challenge of viewing *Twin Peaks* involves not only dealing with the contents and plot of the series itself but also, and perhaps mainly, with the series itself, the series *qua* series, the very concept of "TV series" as a distinct format, with all that it implies. Watching *Twin Peaks* is largely an ongoing variation on this dual challenge.

The viewer who chooses immersion in the fictional world of *Twin Peaks*—from its first iterations in the two "first seasons" in 1990–1991 to the recent return to the series' world in 2017—finds herself in a double bind. On the one hand, a frantic, almost erratic, rummaging through a variety of often contradictory interpretive tools lying around in the toolbox of TV spectatorship in a desperate attempt to make sense. Then there is the challenge posed by the format itself—is it at all a "TV series"? Apparently, this question makes no sense. *Twin Peaks* was produced and marketed as a "series"; it was broadcast, certainly in its 1990s version; divided (if only in retrospect) into seasons and packaged in distinct episodes with regular time slots, that constituted an ongoing narrative and diegesis—all as promised.

If we recall, however, that the individual most identified with the *Twin Peaks* phenomenon is no other than the esteemed and eccentric film director David Lynch, perhaps this question would make more sense. In fact, it is the filmmaker's eccentric reputation, carefully cultivated in classics such as *Eraserhead* (1977), *Blue Velvet* (1986), *Lost Highway* (1997), *Mulholland Drive* (2001) and *Inland Empire* (2006), that immediately casts suspicion over any seemingly conventional move he makes. In other words, having become famous as iconoclast of cinematic conventions, filmic expression and viewing habits—an avant-gardist bent on demolishing the conventional movie structure and replacing it with a completely novel experience. Lynch's cinema is above all an ongoing effort to challenge the coherence of viewer experience. Without detracting from the role of other contributors to the *Twin Peaks* phenomenon—above all, Mark Frost—we may assume that just as Lynch lynches cinema with his films, he lynches the model and very concept of the TV series with his series. In *Twin Peaks*, Lynch tampers not only with the content of filmic expression—narrative, plot, etc.—but primarily with its very tools, with the mechanisms and media patterns enabling that expression and constituting the habits of its consumption.

This suspicion, and the challenge it entails, is supported by Lynch's own words. In various interviews towards the launching of *Twin Peaks: The Return*, the filmmaker argued that although this was indeed a TV show or series, it had to be seen at the same time as made up of 18 parts, rather than episodes, whose broadcast times are irregular and whose broadcast schedule is not necessarily consistent with their serial number. Therefore, Lynch continued, *Twin Peaks* should be considered one long movie, which coincidentally (or not) found itself a guest in the medium, format, viewing habits and conceptual space associated with the TV world.[1] Thus, despite certain affinities with the traditional TV series model—a "seasonal" schedule (May–September 2017) and a channel/network identity that represents viewing habits and marks a target audience (ABC in 1990–1991 was replaced in 2017 by the Showtime cable network and production company)—then what we have here, as Lynch argues, is a series that is also a movie, a non-series series. By its very existence, this challenges the familiar TV format and calls upon the viewers to reorganize their orientation and conventions, if only to avoid the frustration attendant on the violated promise.

In what follows, we intend to present the double challenge and twofold frustration embodied in the experience of watching the *Twin Peaks* TV series. We argue that this challenge, and its attendant frustration, are not only deliberate, but constitute the series' message. Stated otherwise, the series is primarily designed to turn the experience of watching it—and the political and social meanings of spectatorship in general—into a challenging, sterile and therefore frustrating one. Desperate attempts to rise up to the challenge and overcome the frustration—whether in academic writings that struggle to decipher the series based on conventional narrative and generic theories or in the bustling textual cosmos of social media, filled to the brim with fan conspiracies, speculations, ruminations, discussions and support groups—inevitably frustrate the faithful.

Accordingly, we begin by presenting the overwhelming challenge of interpreting *Twin Peaks*. Next, we present the no less frustrating challenge involved in the TV series format. The twin challenge that leads to our conclusion: since the complexity defies deconstruction and the frustrating spectatorship experience defies attenuation, they must be comprehended as *positive* qualities of the series, and in fact as one of the defining objectives of the *Twin Peaks* phenomenon as a whole. As a reflection contemporary spectatorship per se, of the way we viewers experience, fathom, organize and give meaning to what we see. And the frustration due to failing to meet the challenge posed by that experience is immanent to its very nature. Accordingly, although on the surface it seems the series structures a story or perhaps a myth revolving around a murder in small-town America, under the surface, the series operates mainly to throw the viewer into a maelstrom of ongoing disorientation, and task her with the Sisyphean undertaking of cohering images and facts into a plot, and the latter into a set of meanings and conclusions. This undertaking is bound to fail as it contains the seeds of its own destruction.

"IT IS A RIDDLE, WRAPPED IN A MYSTERY, INSIDE AN ENIGMA": WHAT AM I WATCHING IN *TWIN PEAKS*?

To interpret the *Twin Peaks* plot, the viewers must first ask themselves: "What series am I watching?" Its generic assignment is conventionally the first key to the viewers' ability to derive insights and conclusions from the content broadcast to them. What, then, is *Twin Peaks*' genre? Do we have before us a drama series that demands emotional involvement and identification with the characters? Is it a whodunit, demanding cognitive concentration and nerve-cell mobilization to solve a crime? Is it a modern American tragedy bemoaning the predictable murder of a high-school beauty? Is it a soap opera, of the kind that places the crime and the other series events within an ironic or schmaltzy defusing context of an infinite melodrama? Or is it a symbolic and supernatural fantasy on the eternal struggle between the forces of good and the forces of evil? In short, what key do we need to use to trace the logic and structure of the series and give them meaning?

In the opening of the second episode of the first season of *Twin Peaks*, morning rises on the peaceful American town that is its namesake. FBI special agent Dale Cooper, called into town to solve the murder of all-American sweetheart Laura Palmer, rushes into the local police station, energetic but calm and composed as usual, and without further ado informs Sheriff Harry S. Truman[2] of new leads. Unfortunately, however, he finds Truman is preoccupied with a pastry and his mouth full of food remains, unable to take an active part in the conversation (1.2). While Cooper chats and Truman chews, we viewers wonder where our cogni-

Life in the Black Lodge

Figure 9.1. Episode 1.2 "Traces to Nowhere"
Twin Peaks

tive effort should be focused—on the soundtrack or the image. On the new and complex information brought by the special agent, or the sheriff's honest efforts to finish with his food?

Later in that episode, we meet Ben Horne, the owner of The Great Northern Hotel, who opens the door to his office by storm and stands threateningly behind his eavesdropping daughter Audrey. Dramatic music makes us believe that we are about to witness a dramatic father-daughter confrontation. But then we realized that it is in fact music Audrey is listening to on the gramophone—that is, the suspenseful music is actually diegetic. Our suspense turns out to be misleading, a kind of joke at our expense.

Five more minutes into the episode, we are party to a dinner at the Briggs'. Young rebel Bobby Briggs is smoking, while his father is lecturing him. The paternal preaching culminates in a powerful slap on the son's face, causing the cigarette to leap out of Bobby's mouth and land right into the flabbergasted mother's food. The melodramatic tone is immediately cut short, and the option to emotionally identify with the complex life of one of the protagonists is replaced by an inscrutable image, part symbolic and profound, and part slapstick gag.

The disorienting effect of these scenes illustrates the challenge posed by the series. How are the viewers to understand the plot unfolding before them? What should we attend to and what need we ignore? What is more and what is less important? Who is the main character and who are the secondary ones?

The series opens with the discovery of a body, without presenting the crime itself or identifying the murderer. In that, *Twin Peaks* defines itself as belonging to the whodunit genre. Apparently, this is a potential anchor for understanding the series. However, the series does its best, in myriad ways, to prevent the viewer from meeting the cognitive challenges inherent in the conventions of this genre. For example, the series repeatedly violates the demarcation principle so critical to the detective work—demarcation of the physical space of the plots that enables one to delimit the number of potential suspects. Take *Murder on the Orient Express*, for example. Whoever was on the train at the night of the murder is a potential suspect. Although this makes for a large number of suspects, it is still clear and finite. Conversely, although Twin Peaks is a small town, in terms of solving the mystery this is a huge and open-ended space. For the viewer, there are too many potential suspects to even begin guessing the identity of the murderer, let alone convicting one. To make matters worse, the suspect database only expands as the series continues, as new episodes introduce new characters and locations.

The demarcation is broken from another direction as well. Beyond the constant expansion of the demarcation line out of proportions with generic conventions, the contents of this expansion are significant. Throughout the series, Special Agent Cooper relies repeatedly on extrasensory sources of information. In doing so, he enriches the space of options where the plot unfolds on the one hand but denies us access to the sources that can validate this enrichment on the other. The problem does not lie in the very construction of a world that defies our daily logic, but in the fact that we viewers do not share with Cooper the ability to understand the alternative logic and the otherworldly world derived from it. We understand that he uses a given object as a clue. We understand that the Giant in his hallucinations knows something about the killer's identity; that the Red Room dwarf's enigmatic statements are valuable; that the owls are probably not what they seem. Usually, however, we have no way of using the data tantalizingly dangled in front of us, and all we can do is wait and see whether and how the FBI agent will manage to translate all that into effective information. This reliance on the supernatural in the series prevents us from solving the mystery ourselves—a fundamental violation of the unwritten contract between the crime story and its viewers.

Even if we did cross that hurdle, however, by solving the mystery despite the obscure and disharmonious demarcation of the reality of the series, we are in for another challenge. Similarly to its violation of demarcation, the series flagrantly violates another generic principle: the balance required in a crime story between plot drivers and fillers. The former includes all bits of information designed to help both the characters and the viewers to decipher the plot. Fillers are those items designed to enrich the characters' background. Information of the first kind is essential for promoting the plot, whereas the value of information of the second kind is mostly emotional and atmospheric. This is true in most movies and novels. In those belonging to the whodunit genre, however, the viewer/reader must decide at any given minute whether the piece of information now being received represents knowledge of the first or second kind. What contributes to solving the mystery and what is a distraction.[3]

Twin Peaks, however, poses a particular difficulty to the viewer struggling to distinguish between plot drivers and fillers, since their proportions are completely unreasonable. This imbalance makes the task of identifying the killer impossible, and consequently the very willingness to apply the genre's interpretive tools (to understand the series and decipher the murder mystery at its center) is lost.

Moreover, even if we have managed to perform the task against all odds, get through the first season and arrive at the midst of the second (assuming throughout that we are watching a whodunit), we run into an even higher obstacle. The mystery is solved and the killer—spoiler alert!—is revealed to be the victim's father Leland Palmer, who was possessed by a demon called BOB to murder his own daughter. Had this been a crime series, it would have ended here; there would have been no point in moving on. But the series continues, expands, twists and turns, shedding light on new details and ignoring details already known (without explaining how they relate to the plot), and finally stops—only to continue, twenty-five years later, in what seems to be a third season (a linear sequel of the first two, as well as to the sequel film *Twin Peaks: Fire Walk with Me* from 1992), and at the same time a standalone piece (which is both a series and a film, as well as a season).

The attempt to interpret the series in terms of the methodological tools and conventions of the genre is thus bound to fail. Have we gotten the genre all wrong? We have been led astray by the centrality of Laura Palmer's murder mystery, while we should have viewed the series as bound by the conventions of a different genre, such as soap opera or parapsychological fantasy. Even if we do try to proceed in this alternative route, we are bound to find out that it too ends in the same cul-de-sac. In terms of a soap opera, we can explain the plot's focus on relations and affairs between the characters—their conflicts, their betrayals and the almost parodic multiplicity of sentimental outbursts and interpersonal dramas. However, this will fail us in explaining the focus on the murder investigation. It will certainly fail us in explaining the supernatural or symbolic plot layer embodied in the Red Room/Black Lodge, the One-Armed Man, backward speech, etc. Conversely, if what we have here is a fantasy focused on a symbolic description of the cosmological struggle between good and evil, between our worlds and others, between Cooper and BOB, then all those details on the daily minutiae of the small-town characters are nothing but unnecessary distractions. Thus, whatever alternative genre we choose to adopt as an anchor, having been swept into the depth of the interpretive maelstrom by our reliance on the whodunit anchor, we will fail to bring the entire series together into the safe haven of coherence.[4] It therefore appears we must switch from looking *into* the series to looking *on* the series as a phenomenon—from the level of the genre as a potential organizer of meaning to the level of medium as a potential organizer of the feasibility of the viewing experience itself.

"THE MEDIUM IS THE MESSAGE": HOW AM I WATCHING *TWIN PEAKS*?

The second and major challenge *Twin Peaks* poses to its viewers is its subversion of the TV series format, the act of watching a series, and the very concept of spectatorship. This challenge is harmoniously and intimately interweaved in the diegesis of the series, particularly its twin focus on (1) the notion of the dream, the dreaming phenomenon and the dreamer's identity, and their allegorical use for understanding the TV series spectator's status; and (2) the gaze, the interactivity of spectating and the medium's double status and role as an object of the human gaze and an extension of the gazing subject.

"We live inside a dream"

Two sets of dreams are pivotal to *Twin Peaks*. In the 2017 season, the dreamer is Gordon Cole (Cooper's former supervisor and the present FBI deputy director, played by Lynch himself) and the dream is about a (casting) meeting in a Parisian café with actress Monica Bellucci, coupled with the reflection on the "dreaminess" of the encounter, which is present and actively constructive of the actual meeting (3.14). In the "first seasons," it is Cooper's dreams that reveal to us the Red Room/Black Lodge, the dancing dwarf, the generous giant, reverse speech, Laura Palmer exposing her killer—and mainly the key to the riddle: "break the code, solve the crime" (1.4).

Both sets of dreams are shaped with Lynchian aesthetics at its finest. And there lies the rub: Lynchian aesthetics is more than just style—it is a loyal representative and propagandist of Lynchian philosophy, which is all about persistent abuse (of the characters by the auteur, of one character by the other, and the viewer by all) of their very ability to distinguish between dream and reality. It appears that one of the covert and perhaps malicious goals of the Lynchian aesthetics is to fill us with doubt (let alone fear, let alone frustration) regarding our ability to identify that moment when the dream ends and reality begins, where reality ends and fantasy begins. For example, in *Eraserhead*, cinematic surrealism is mobilized as an aesthetic tool in service of the boundaries of the dream. Similarly, twenty years later, the camera—the black box itself—is mobilized in *Lost Highway* to speak for and constitute those same boundaries.

Charting the boundaries is just a pretext, however. It is the shallow surface of the Lynchian argument. The crux—the role played by the dreams in *Twin Peaks*—is exposing the illusoriness of the very concept of boundaries. In other words, the (aesthetical) surface of the Lynchian corpus raises constant doubt as to the unconscious trespassing of the boundary between dream and reality. The depth of the medium that serves as the ontological arena for this aesthetics challenges the conceptual reality of boundaries *ab initio*. It is not only our epistemic ability of identifying the boundary between dream and reality that collapses (into and thanks to the Lynchian aesthetics)—it is the conceptual framework that constitutes this boundary to begin with that collapses into oblivion. The question, "Is this a dream?" presupposes that conceptual distinction, and the question "Who's the dreamer?" presupposes a distinct, an autonomous identity to which, as such, one can assign the concept of dreaming.

To return to the aforementioned sentence that came in the flash of an apparent dream and guided the apparent dreamer in what appeared to be his reality: crack the code—solve the crime. Namely, the foundational assumption is that there is a code, and an additional assumption is that this fact is conceptually bound with the possibility of decoding. But why should we assume that? Why should we accept that as a binding conceptual framework? These assumptions, as primary and self-evident as they may seem, are nothing but illusory. And once we—erstwhile devoted spectators of "The Lynch Show"—reject those assumptions, our proverbial boat immediately hits the wall of the dome, only we do not meet our maker as in *The Truman Show*. For us, the Lynchian dream turns from an epistemic challenge to a radical metaphysical refutation of our conceptual framework with no alternative in sight.

The use of dreams in *Twin Peaks* is thus designed to confront the viewer with the challenge involved in the very existence of the (TV) medium and the experience of watching and decoding inherent to that interface. Recall that this experience presumes boundaries that in turn enable us to watch and decode. In the first section, we have seen how these assumptions—to the extent that they apply to the genre as the organizer of contents and interpretations—ill serve the viewer in decoding the plot.

Like the concept of genre, that of the dream also serves the spectator as a presupposition designed to organize contents and enable their interpretation. The dream is categorically differentiated from diegetic reality, and both are categorically differentiated from the viewer's reality. The Lynchian use of dreams undermines these assumptions. Cooper's dreams give him the key to solving the murder mystery (that exists in the diegetic reality); Cole's dream is about the meeting between Lynch (playing himself) and Bellucci (playing herself) in (extradiegetic) Paris (which is nevertheless not necessarily the City of Lights familiar to the TV viewer from her own reality). As they combine, on the face of it, in the diegesis of the series, both sets of dreams pose a major challenge to the very construction of the series as a distinct "series," that is, as the phenomenal product of a distinct medium. Are we inside a dream? Is this a real dream? Is this a (TV) reality which is itself a kind of dream (we dream)? But who is the dreamer?

"But who is the dreamer?"

As in most present-day TV series, every episode of *Twin Peaks: The Return* is preceded by a production company logo. At the center of the logo of Rancho Rosa Productions created especially for the last iteration of the TV-cinematic masterpiece by Lynch and Frost, a lightbulb flickers. A flash also ends each episode—in both the recent and the preceding seasons—these are the buzzing flashlights that light the logo Lynch/Frost Production, which appears after the end credits. Also in the para-text, a flicker accompanies the dance of the "man from another place" in the end credits of the third episode of the first season. But flashes or flickers in *Twin Peaks*—in all its TV and filmic iterations—appear not only in the margins of the text, but also in the diegetic contents themselves. This happens for example in one of the peak moments of the final episode of the second season, much of it occurs within that mysterious space called the Black Lodge.

The flicker effect is part and parcel of the cinematic experience from its emergence, since the screening technology involved a mechanism blocking the projector's lighting between every two frames. The flickering issue was resolved as early as in the 1910s, but the term "flick" has remained in use, and even found itself in the name of successful streaming company Netflix. The flicker effect is not unique to the cinematic medium—TV screens and computer monitors based on the cathode ray tube technology also flicker, as do TV screens and projectors based on newer technologies. Thus, across the moving image media, the flicker effect is a trace of the display technology, a reminder of the construction of the moving image illusion, of the basic fact underlying motion pictures from Eadweard

Muybridge's galloping horse in 1878 to contemporary YouTube flicks: these media only produce a technological construction of movement, which can only be effective when mediated by technology, no matter whether it changes across the generations, if at all.

Throughout his oeuvre, Lynch has taken an intensive interest in reality as experienced through media, as constructed by them. The flicker effect that frames and recurs in *Twin Peaks* is but a reminder, but an important one at that. In fact, Lynch has no trouble offering ridiculous excuses for his diegetic uses of the flicker effects. For example, in the pilot episode, when Special Agent Cooper and Sheriff Truman first inspect Laura Palmer's body under a flickering fluorescent bulb, the morgue attendant apologizes for the broken alternator. In *The Return*, Detective Macklay apologizes to his partner for his flickering flashlight as the two search a suspicious trunk (3.1). And in the movie *Twin Peaks: Fire Walk with Me*, the diner owner answers the FBI detectives' questions against a flickering background, later revealed to be the result of a flickering lightbulb another man tries to fix. Thus, Lynch keeps reminding us of the role of the medium in shaping the world revealed to us on the screen. More precisely, he keeps reminding us of the role of the *visual* medium in that regard. Meaning, to the extent we are dealing with media, we are also dealing with vision.

As early as its first iteration, *Twin Peaks* was preoccupied with vision, with emphasis on the eye: Dr. Jacoby's colorful glasses, Nadine's eyepatch, the lodge dwellers' glassy eyes, and the One-Eyed Jack's casino are a few examples out of great many references to the eye and the act of seeing. Unconventional modes of mediated seeing—or "visual media"—also appear in the series in the form of visions, dreams and mysterious maps. The preoccupation with vision, blindness, visual distortions, the reliability of vision or its lack and its technological mediation is also articulated by the multiplicity of TV screens, video recordings and surveillance cameras, in the movie as well as in the series—in scenes from the fictitious soap opera *Invitation to Love* and in other occasions. The combined preoccupation with screen and sight culminates in a scene where a videotape showing Laura Palmer several days before her murder is played, which unifies a flicker, a screen and an eye in a single moment (1.Pilot). Thanks to Cooper's freeze-frame on the recording and Lynch's close-up on the screen in that scene, we can notice Palmer's enlarged eye on the motorbike. This manipulation of the medium by Cooper and Lynch enables us to see at that moment that the eye is a medium as well. The hybridization of eye and camera produces an upgraded, bidirectional gaze, which reveals a field of vision hidden from the eye of the camera. In a symmetric reversal of the McLuhanite conceptualization of the technological medium as a prosthesis—the camera as the extension of the eye—here it is the organic that serves as the extension, the added feature or prosthesis of the technological medium.

Moreover, the hybrid moment of the organic and technological media is a reminder to the fact that vision itself is activated and shaped by the technological media through which it operates and by which it is surrounded. Obviously, visual media are constantly developing, primarily thanks to technological breakthroughs. According to media scholars such as Jonathan Crary[5] and Friedrich Kittler,[6] watching, observing, spectating, seeing and the sociopolitical implications of these concepts are constituted, shaped and activated within discursive frameworks that are in turn constructed and established by technologies as they are realized in media. According to Crary, the very nature of our visuality is subject to transformation. He reminds us that the main error we can make when studying optical media is to assume that the optical device and the subject "using" it are two separate entities, that the identity of the observer is independent of the instrument, of technology. Discursive transformations, Crary argues, cannot be separated from technological developments.[7]

These ideas indicate that the concepts of watching, observing, spectating, and seeing have no transcendent signified, but are historical concepts engaging in ongoing interrelations with social, political and technological practices, such that each period is characterized by different modes of seeing. In *The Railway Journey* (1986), Wolfgang Shivelbusch compares a landscape description taken from a carriage ride in 1797 with a landscape description taken from a train in 1837 and offers a fascinating example of the ways technological changes affect modes of seeing historically.[8] With the advent of much faster vehicles, the seeing subject learns to "swallow" the landscape as fast as the vehicle devours it and redefines the visible and invisible details. In a similar vein, the seeing subject of cinema is a historical subject. Cinema theoretician Jacques Aumont reminds us that the omnipotent, all-seeing subject designed by cinema is a temporary one, exclusively associated with modernity.[9] Moreover, it has long been replaced (or at least overshadowed) by other seeing subjects designed by subsequent technologies and visual media—the TV, the PC, and the all-eclipsing smartphone.

"I'll see you again in 25 years," says Laura Palmer to Agent Cooper—a promise kept in the summer of 2017. The transformations that have occurred in the meantime in the characterization of the seeing subject are nothing short of dramatic and constitute to a large extent the main theme of *Twin Peaks: The Return*. Whereas in its previous iterations, the flicker effect, multiple screens and eyes galore have alerted the spectator to the relation between vision and the TV medium, *Twin Peaks: The Return* seeks to rise to the heavens and circumspect this very discussion from a bird's (or rather owl's) eye view—expanding it beyond the particularities of this or that medium.

These intentions are even hinted by the opening sequence of *Twin Peaks: The Return*, with objects from the original sequence seen at a direct angle, at eye level, with others from a high vantage point. Even the familiar red curtain and zigzag floor pattern undergo a dizzying transformation that destabilizes the gaze and the very coordinates of vision. In other words, in its 2017 incarnation, *Twin Peaks* is largely a series about *Twin Peaks*, and does not seek to be a mere sequel to the first seasons. Much more than that, it seeks to inspect them, interrogate them, dissect them and reconstruct their themes—including or even mainly the relations between sight and media. *Twin Peaks* in 2017 thus offers us a gaze on the gaze.

CONCLUSION: THE OWLS ARE (EXACTLY) WHAT THEY SEEM

The gaze on the gaze—the medium looking at itself—is highly emphasized in two major foci in the series. The first is well articulated at the start of the first part of *Twin Peaks: The Return* through a glass box and the person whose job it is to gawk at the empty box and occasionally replace the memory cards in the myriad cameras that constantly monitor what does not happen within it. The gawker, student Sam Colby, tells Tracy, the girl he sneaks into the secure room where the box is located that he is supposed to "watch the box and see if anything appears inside" (3.1).

Sofa, box, viewer and gaze. The situation is familiar, from Archie Bunker through Homer Simpson to Al Bundy, this is the conventional paradigm of "watching TV" as presented in TV series. The Lynchian box is different, however: while nothing appears in it, the viewer is not bored—his look and facial expressions are similar to those of the engaged spectator. At the same time, the non-event, nothing of which is left except for the gaze itself, is itself being filmed—documented and monitored from every direction by a horde of cameras that stream the unending footage into an array of memory cards and hard disks.

Not only that, but the box itself is akin to a camera: with the large hole in the center, the uncanny feeling that it is looking at Sam just as he looks at it, with its flashlights, and with the accordion-like movement it makes an instant before the mysterious activity that takes place within it. Much like the Lumière cinematograph that could take, develop and project photos, Lynch's box both photographs and displays, it is both the generator of the visual spectacle and the spectacle itself—just like the "cinema of attractions" of the early days of film, where the apparatus and its remarkable capabilities were at least just as, well, attractive, as the content on display.[10]

Lynch's box is therefore the TV, stills camera, cinematograph and cinema of attractions all rolled into one. At the same time, it is also the ultimate reality TV show streaming dead-time, it is "a show about nothing," it is the social network that monitors the user's activity and itself. The function of the box as the medium itself enables Lynch to address the relations between technology, media and vision in the abstract-most. The box can be pure media only so long as it lacks any content. But at one moment, unsurprisingly the moment when Sam's gaze is distracted by Tracy (reminding us that the box is also a drive-in), a deus appears ex machina. A ghostlike image flickers as if conjured within the box, before it breaks free and viciously devours the viewers, consumes their eyes, their gaze, as if punishing them for having dared to turn it away. Thus, *Twin Peaks* exterminates the viewers' desperate attempt to give it meaning, and all that's left for us is to enjoy the experience—if we dare.

NOTES

1. See, for instance, Todd VanDerWerff, "Is Twin Peaks a movie or a TV show? The answer's more complicated than you'd think," *Vox*, last modified 08 December 2017, https://www.vox.com/culture/2017/12/8/16742798/twin-peaks-movie-or-tv-show.

2. The sheriff's name echoes, of course, the name of a well-known American president. President Truman goes down the lanes of history as the one who was forced to make (and then face) the decision to drop the atomic bomb on Hiroshima and Nagasaki, thus ending the Second World War (or so history tells us). Assigning this name for the sheriff's character is all but accidental. Following our argument in this chapter, we leave our readers to ponder the meaning of this directorial decision.

3. The distinction between plot drivers and plot fillers is based on Maya Arad's *Behind the Mountain* (Tel Aviv: Xargol, 2016), and also on David Bordwell's *Narration in the Fiction Film* (Madison, WI: University of Wisconsin Press, 1985). Using a different terminology (fabula and syuzhet), Bordwell deals with the way the detective film is playing with the viewer's knowledge of the story, thus by revealing and hiding alternately plot's information. According to Bordwell, the typical syuzhet (the narrative, or the order of events as shown on the screen) in a detective film is made up in a way that makes it hard for the viewer to put together the fabula (the chronological order of the events contained in the story).

4. Our argument here undermines the common opinion regarding the multiplicity (of plot's threads, TV genres, dramatic tones) embodied in the show. Multiplicity usually referred to as harmonic and coherent. See, for example, Kristin Thompson, *Storytelling in Film and Television* (Cambridge, MA: Harvard University Press, 2003), 124–134.

5. Jonathan Crary, *Techniques of the Observer: On Vision and Modernity in the Nineteenth Century* (Cambridge, MA: MIT Press, 1992).

6. Friedrich A. Kittler, *Discourse Networks 1800/1900* (Palo Alto, CA: Stanford University Press, 1992); Friedrich A. Kittler, *Gramophone, Film, Typewriter* (Palo Alto, CA: Stanford University Press, 1999).

7. Crary, *Techniques of the Observer*, 30–31.

8. Wolfgang Schivelbusch, *The Railway Journey: The Industrialization and Perception of Time and Space* (Berkeley, CA: University of California Press, 1986), 55.

9. Jacques Aumont, "The Variable Eye, or the Mobilization of the Gaze," in *The Image in Dispute: Art and Cinema in the Age of Photography*, ed. Dudley Andrew (Austin: University of Texas Press, 1997), 245.

10. Tom Gunning, "The Cinema of Attraction[s]: Early Film, Its Spectator and the Avant-Garde," in *The Cinema of Attractions Reloaded*, ed. Wanda Strauven. (Amsterdam: Amsterdam University Press, 2006), 381–388.

WORKS CITED

Aumont, Jacques. "The Variable Eye, or the Mobilization of the Gaze." In *The Image in Dispute: Art and Cinema in the Age of Photography*, edited by Dudley Andrew, 231–258. Austin: University of Texas Press, 1997.

Arad, Maya. *Behind the Mountain*. Tel Aviv: Xargol, 2016.

Bordwell, David. *Narration in the Fiction Film*. Madison, WI: University of Wisconsin Press, 1985.

Crary, Jonathan. *Techniques of the Observer: On Vision and Modernity in the Nineteenth Century*. Cambridge, MA: MIT Press, 1992.

Gunning, Tom. "The Cinema of Attraction[s]: Early Film, Its Spectator and the Avant-Garde." In *The Cinema of Attractions Reloaded*, edited by Wanda Strauven, 381–388. Amsterdam: Amsterdam University Press, 2006.

Kittler, Friedrich A. *Discourse Networks 1800/1900*. Stanford University Press, 1992.

———. *Gramophone, Film, Typewriter*. Palo Alta: Stanford University Press, 1999.

Schivelbusch, Wolfgang. *The Railway Journey: The Industrialization and Perception of Time and Space*. Berkeley, CA: University of California Press, 1986.

Thompson, Kristin. *Storytelling in film and television*. Cambridge, MA: Harvard University Press, 2003.

VanDerWerff, Todd. "Is Twin Peaks a movie or a TV show? The answer's more complicated than you'd think." *Vox*. 08 December 2017. https://www.vox.com/culture/2017/12/8/16742798/twin-peaks-movie-or-tv-show.

Index

America, 5, 19, 21–22, 25, 38, 46, 59–60, 62–64; 1950s in, 4, 5, 13–14, 16–17, 20, 23–25, 28, 35, 37–40, 98; American dream 63–64, 98; colonialism and slavery, 29, 38; 43; culture and politics of, 1, 3, 5, 13–14, 18, 36, 74, 98–99, 111; nostalgia and, 37–40, 42–43, 58; small-towns and, 1, 3, 6, 14, 20, 24, 35, 38–39, 45, 47, 55–61, 65, 126, 180, 182, 184; television and, 58, 102, 120, 122. *See also* mythology in America

Badalamenti, Angelo, 21, 35, 45, 129
Bellucci, Monica, 78, 174n10, 184
Black Lodge, 8, 15, 24–25, 40, 44, 46, 124, 130, 133, 148, 151–56, 159n19, 161, 163, 164, 177, 183–84, 186
Blue Velvet, 30n8, 39, 55, 58, 65, 166, 178
Bush, George H.W., 56, 58
Bush, George W., 63, 65

capitalism, 14, 18, 28, 30n4, 57, 72, 76–77, 79, 86, 98–99, 107, 127
Civil War, 42–43, 49n14
class, 6, 18–19, 30n4, 56–57, 59–64, 72–73, 98, 118. *See also* middle-class
Cold War, 3, 5, 13–14, 18–24, 28–29
comedy, 6, 69–72, 74–75, 78–83, 87–90, 92. *See also* Lynch and comedy
conservatism, 2, 17, 18–20, 25, 28–29, 37, 49n15, 56, 65, 95, 96, 98–99

consumerism, 18, 28, 62, 65, 83, 86, 97, 107–108

Dalai Lama, 145
Daoism, 7, 148–158
doppelgängers, 7, 21, 28, 35, 62–63, 124, 130, 148, 153–55
dreams, 21, 26, 39, 173; in *Twin Peaks*, 43, 45, 47, 78, 83, 98, 102, 145, 148, 150, 158n1, 165, 174n10, 184–187; in Lynch's films 55, 62, 65, 71–72

Eastern philosophy, 7, 146, 148
economic, 1, 6, 44, 56–59, 62–65, 72–73, 80, 84–86, 90n31, 98–99, 107, 127, 131, 135n16. *See also* socio-economic
Eraserhead, 14–15, 178, 185

family values, 96, 98–99
feminism, 7, 95–98, 101, 104–109, 111. *See also* violence against women
femininity, 3, 7, 80, 82, 96–97, 102, 104–111, 118–119, 122, 124,
Fire Walk with Me, 15, 21 47, 71, 152, 153, 157, 187
Foucault, Michel, 77–78, 121
Freud, Sigmund, 27, 72, 77, 81–82
Frost, Mark, 1–5, 7, 31–33, 35, 44, 46–48, 55, 57, 59, 60–61, 63, 65, 70, 158, 162, 179, 186

gender roles, 19, 64, 97, 122, 159n17
Great Northern Hotel, 40–41, 44, 57–58, 98, 165, 181

194 Index

heteronormativity, 125, 132

identity politics, 3–4, 7, 28, 36, 59
indigenous, 6, 43, 56, 85, 159, 171, 173

Johnson, Gary, 17

Karloff, Boris, 75
Kierkegaard, Søren, 71

liberalism, 20, 30n4, 37, 65, 90n31, 105. *See also* neoliberalism
Las Vegas, 6, 19, 21, 44, 62–64, 69, 70, 75, 154, 161–62, 165
literary trauma theory, 4–5, 14, 27
Lynch, David, 3, 4, 7, 13–14, 23, 27, 35, 45–47, 55, 60, 61–62, 120, 133–134, 166, 178, 186–87, 189–190; 1950s and, 4–5, 13, 19, 28, 37–39, 46–48; art and aesthetics of, 15, 17, 71, 117, 121–23, 125–26, 162, 179, 184–85; comedy and, 6, 69–71, 73–75, 77–78; nostalgia and, 13, 36, 48; politics of, 1–2, 5, 15–20, 25–26, 28–29, 56, 59, 63, 65, 72–73; suburban values and, 6, 39, 58, 63, 65

MacLachlan, Kyle, 75, 123
male gaze, 2, 19, 80, 97, 1110
masculinity, 7, 19, 77, 80–81, 99, 104–106, 110–11, 117–19, 122, 129, 133
middle-class, 63–64, 74, 79–80, 85–86, 98–99, 100–101, 106, 111
Mulholland Drive, 16, 30n8
murder, 61, 69, 72, 79, 84, 129, 149,182–83, 186; of Laura, 1–2, 39–41, 45, 47, 55, 62, 70, 98–100, 110, 118, 123, 145, 151, 156–57, 180, 182–83, 187; of Maddy, 41, 47, 95, 102
mythology, 1, 8, 58, 79, 82, 96, 102, 163, 172; in America, 79, 96, 98–99; in media, 105, 126; of reincarnation, 161–62, 164–65, 173; in Twin Peaks, 3, 13, 22, 62, 75, 174

neoliberalism, 14, 18, 20–21, 29, 70, 72–73, 76, 78–79, 80–81, 83, 86, 97, 107

Nine Inch Nails, 23
nostalgia, 5, 13–14, 17–18, 21, 23–24, 29, 35–48, 58, 87

Obama, Barack, 6, 65
One-Eyed Jack's, 2, 21, 41, 100-101, 109, 147, 187

parody, 74–75, 77, 80–83, 87, 90n31, 95, 122
Plato, 8, 161–69, 171–174
postmodernism, 3, 18, 20–21, 28–29, 71–73, 95, 97, 111, 125.

queer, 3, 7, 117–18, 122, 124–25, 127–34

Reagan, Ronald, 2, 6, 14, 17, 55–59, 61, 63, 65, 96, 98
Red Room, 8, 48, 133, 161, 163–165, 168, 182–4
Roosevelt, Franklin Delano, 49n15

Sanders, Bernie, 17
sexuality, 101, 105–106
Shakespeare, William, 41
socio-economic, 6, 38, 72, 81, 87. *See also* economic

trauma, 5, 13–14, 22, 25, 27–28, 39, 49n14, 81, 83, 154,
Trump, Donald, 6, 17, 20, 26, 37–38, 55–56, 59, 63–65, 73, 79, 83
tulpas, 7, 28, 148, 154–56, 159–60
Twin Peaks characters: Albert Rosenfield, 38, 58, 60, 62, 80, 129, 124, 147; Andy Brennan, 20–21, 38, 70, 105–106, 145, 170–71; Annie Blackburn, 147, 153, 155–156; the Arm, 19, 47–48, 123, 155, 165, 182, 184, 186; Audrey Horne, 2–3, 43–44, 61, 85, 90, 96, 98, 107–110, 147, 181; Benjamin Horne, 5, 40–44, 58, 60–61, 166, 181; Blackie O'Reilly, 100; BOB, 2–26, 40, 41, 47–48, 81, 83, 95, 98–102, 133, 152–53, 155–57, 159n19, 183–84; Bobby Briggs, 43, 45, 85, 100–101, 103, 132–33, 181; Bradley

Mitchum 76, 79–80, 88n12; Bushnell Mullins, 64, 76, 87; Candie, 19, 76, 80–82; Carrie Page, 47, 74, 157; Caroline Earle, 124, 155; Catherine Martell, 40–42, 58, 61; Chantal Hutchens, 79, 80, 88n12, 90n30; Charlie, 85; Chester Desmond, 15; Dale Cooper, 1–2, 7–8, 15, 19, 21, 35, 38–39, 44–48, 57–59, 60–63, 65, 74–78, 80–81, 103, 109, 122–24, 129, 131, 133–34, 145–48, 150–57, 161–71, 173, 180, 182, 184, 186–88; dancing dwarf. *See* the Arm; Denise Bryson, 39, 79, 89n24, 118, 122, 124; Diane Evans, 28, 90n30, 147, 156, 168; Dick Tremayne, 105–106; Doc Hayward, 110; Donna Hayward, 96, 99, 107–108, 110–11, 132; Dougie Jones, 8, 15, 19, 21, 45–46, 62, 64, 73–78, 80–81, 83–85, 88n16, 89n17, 133–34, 154–56, 160n22, 161–62, 165–66, 168, 173–74; Ed Hurley, 57, 86, 151; Emory Battis, 2, 109; Fireman, 23, 156, 162, 165; Frank Truman, 19, 156; Garland Briggs, Major, 132, 153, 165; Gary Hutchens (Hutch), 79–80; the Giant, 47, 123, 182, 184; Gordon Cole, 15, 78–80, 134, 156, 168, 173, 174n10, 184, 186; Hank Jennings, 106–107; Harold Smith, 47; Hawk, 6, 44, 85–86, 145, 14–48, 151, 163, 169, 170–71, 173; Harry Truman, Sheriff, 1, 39, 45 57, 103, 122, 129, 131, 133, 145, 150–51, 165, 180, 187; Ike (the Spike) Stadtler, 82, 168; Jacoby, Lawrence, 15, 42–44, 84, 187; Jacques Renault, 40–41, 61; James Hurley, 38, 47, 85, 100–101, 110, 132, 151; Janey-E Jones, 46, 64, 75, 77, 84–85, 90n30, 155, 160n22; Jean Renault, 122; Jerry Horne, 40, 44, 60, 78, 84; Johnny Horne, 82–83, 98; Josie Packard, 58, 98, 132, 151; Jouday, 25, 157, 159n19; Laura Palmer, 1–2, 7–8, 23–25, 35, 39–41, 45, 47–48, 57, 62, 70, 95–96, 98–102, 104, 109–110, 123, 129, 132–33, 145, 148, 150–51, 153, 155–157, 160–61, 165–66, 168, 170–71, 173, 180, 183–84, 187–88; Leland Palmer, 5, 39–41, 47, 61, 74, 87, 95, 99–102, 147, 155, 157, 185; Leo Johnson, 45, 102–103; Log Lady, 8, 44, 76, 124, 128, 148, 163, 169, 170, 174n10; Lucy Moran, 7, 20–21, 44, 76, 85–86, 96, 104–106, 124, 145, 170–71; Maddy Ferguson, 7, 41, 47, 9–96, 98, 101–102, 104, 110; Man From Another Place. *See* the Arm; Margaret Lanterman. *See* Log Lady; Mike, 47, 154–155, 160n22, 165, 183; Mike Nelson, 45, 80, 85, 104–105; Mr. C, 8, 19, 28, 44, 46, 154–57, 168; Nadine Hurley, 7, 45, 57, 84, 96, 104–105, 107, 187; Naido, 28, 156, 166, 168; Norma Jennings, 21, 45, 86, 96, 102, 104, 106–107, 151, 186; One-Armed Man. *See* Mike; the Packards, 58, 61; Phillip Jeffries, 78, 155–59, 165; Pete Martell, 47; Richard Horne, 19, 82; Rodney Mitchum, 19, 76, 79–81, 88n12; Ronette Pulaski, 1–2, 98, 102, 166; Sam Colby, 189; Sam Stanley, 15; Sarah Palmer, 24, 85, 101, 157; Shelly Johnson, 7, 19, 45, 96, 98, 102–104, 132; Sylvia Horne, 82–83; Tamara (Tammy) Preston, 25, 80, 89n24, 159n19; Windom Earle, 124, 153

Twin Peaks episodes: 1.1, *3*; 1.2, 103, 180–81; 1.3, 39–40, 58, 87, 14–46, 102, 150, 152, 165; 1.4, 40, 184; 1.5, 61, 102, 107; 1.6, 103, 109; 1.7, 103, 105; 2.1 41, 98, 110; 2.2, 2, 60; 2.3, 110, 129, *130*; 2.4, 61, 106; 2.7, 39–41, 47, 101–102, 2.9, 99, 106, 153; 2.10, 39, 82; 2.11, 39, 41, *42*; 2.12, 39; 2.13, 42, 122; 2.14, 42–43; 2.15, 43; 2.16, 107; 3.1, 23, 74, 86, 162, 165, 170, 187, 189; 3.2, 21, 74, 161; 3.3, 74–75, 154, 165–66, 171; 3.4, 21, 45, 74, 76, 79–80, 165; 3.5, *63*, 75, 77, 80, 84, 155, 165, 166; 3.6, 84–85; 3.7, 15, *16*, 155–56, 166, 168; 3.8, 5, 13–14, 21–26, 152, 74; 3.9, 78, 86; 3.10, 19, 77, 80, 148; 3.11, 74, 85; 3.12, 84–85; 3.13, 44, 69, *70*, 81, 85–86; 3.14, 24, 74, 78, 80, 156,

174, 184; 3.15, 19,21, 45, 74, 78, 80, 85, *163*, 168, 173; 3.16, 2, 46, 79, 81, 85, 88, 155–57 160; 3.17, 46–47, 81, 156, 168; 3.18, 29, 47, 74, 157

violence, 27, 30n8, 38, 69, 73–74, 80, 99, 125, 129; against women, 7, 19, 39, 41 96–98, 102–104, 111. *See also* feminism; America, colonialism and slavery

White Lodge, 47, 148, 151–53, 155
Wild at Heart, 16, 75, 122
working-class, 19, 30n4, 98, 101

Zhuangzi, 150, 159n14

About the Contributors

Shai Biderman (PhD, Philosophy; Boston University, 2012) teaches film and philosophy at Tel Aviv University and at Beit-Berl College, Israel. He is the co-editor of *The Philosophy of David Lynch* (UPK, 2011), *Mediamorphosis: Kafka and the Moving Image* (Walflower/Columbia, 2016) and *Plato and the Moving Image* (Brill, Forthcoming). He published numerous articles and book chapters in philosophy of film, film analysis, and film-philosophy, in journals such as *Film and Philosophy* and *Cinema: journal of philosophy and the moving image*, and in edited volumes such as *Inter-Art Journey* (Sussex Academic Press, 2015), *The Philosophy of the Western* (UPK, 2010), *The Philosophy of Science Fiction Film* (UPK, 2008), *Lost and Philosophy* (Blackwell, 2008) and *Movies and the Meaning of Life* (Open Court, 2005).

Amanda DiPaolo is an associate professor of human rights at St. Thomas University in Fredericton, New Brunswick. Her current research examines human rights issues as depicted in popular culture. Recently, she has published on issues of race and equality in *Mad Men* and has a forthcoming article on consciousness and dignity in HBO's *Westworld*. She is also the author of *Zones of Twilight: Judicial Decision Making in Times of War* (Lexington Books, 2010).

Darci Doll has a little secret. Once a day, every day, she gives herself a present and you should too. Don't plan it, don't wait for it. Just let it happen. She writes things down sometimes—letters, words—hoping they will serve us and those with whom we wish to communicate. Letters and words, calling out for understanding. She does this at Delta College where she teaches philosophy. There is a story behind that. It is a story of many, but begins with one—and she knew the one leading to the many. Darci is a PhD candidate at Michigan State University. She has appeared in volumes such as *Orphan Black and Philosophy*, *The Princess Bride and Philosophy*, and *Mr. Robot and Philosophy*.

About the Contributors

Martin Fradley teaches film and screen studies at the University of Brighton, UK. He is co-editor of *Shane Meadows: Critical Essays* (Edinburgh U.P., 2013), and has also written for *Film Quarterly, Screen, Journal of British Cinema and Television*, and *Canadian Journal of Film Studies*. His recent work appears in *Directory of World Cinema: American Independent 3* (Intellect, 2016), *Tainted Love: Screening Sexual Perversion* (I.B. Tauris, 2017) and *Make America Hate Again: Trump-Era Horror and the Politics of Fear* (Routledge, 2019).

Ronen Gil is a PhD candidate at the Tel Aviv University's Steve Tisch School of Film and Television. He has an MA (summa cum laude) from that school. His dissertation focuses on TV fiction series. Using cognitive research perspective, mainly David Bordwell's theory, Gil offers a new understanding of TV series narration. His article "Adapting Masculinities: Israeli and American Genres Redefining Mizrahi Masculinity in the TV Series Haborer" was published in *Jewish Film & New Media* (2016).

Jamie Gillies is associate professor of communications and public policy at St. Thomas University in Fredericton, New Brunswick. A political scientist by training, his academic work is focused on political communications and public policy, in particular American presidents and Anglo-American executive leadership, the personalization of political leadership, and media studies. He is the editor of the recent book *Political Marketing in the 2016 U.S. Presidential Election* (Palgrave Pivot, 2017).

Ashlee Joyce is an instructor in the Department of Humanities and Languages, University of New Brunswick, Saint John. She is currently developing a scholarly monograph entitled *The Resurgence of the Gothic in Recent British Trauma Fiction*.

Ido Lewit is a PhD candidate in the Department of Germanic Languages and Literatures and the Program in Film and Media Studies at Yale University. His fields of concentration include media-theory, Franz Kafka, narratology, film-philosophy, film adaptation, and temporality in film and literature. Ido is the co-editor of *Mediamorphosis: Kafka and the Moving Image* (Walflower/Columbia, 2016) and is the author of a number of articles on Kafka and cinema, philosophy in film, the cinema of the Coen Brothers, and time and space in film and literature.

Ben Kruger-Robbins is a PhD candidate in visual studies at the University of California, Irvine. He earned a BS and an MA in radio-television-film from the University of Texas at Austin, and his research interests include marginalized television reception, TV network branding, and

LGBTQ media histories. His doctoral dissertation, *Queering and Qualifying the Wasteland: Network Television, Awards Discourse, and Gay Legitimation in Primetime from 1971–1997*, explores industrial connections and political corollaries between quality TV production and gay representation during mass broadcasting's multi-decade decline. He has previously published in *Flow*.

Jean-Philippe Ranger is associate professor in the Department of Philosophy at St. Thomas University in Fredericton, NB, Canada. His research deals with issues in ancient epistemology. He works on Plato and recollection and on Epicurus' empiricism. Previously, he has published on the foundational values in Plato, Aristotle, and Epicurus.

John A. Riley is assistant professor of English at Woosong University, South Korea. He has published articles and book chapters about Andrei Tarkovsky, Georgian documentary film, and *Twin Peaks*. He is currently working on a project about the film *Stalker*.

Stacy Rusnak is associate professor of film at Georgia Gwinnett College. She received her PhD in communications/moving image studies from Georgia State University and holds an MA in Spanish language and literatures. Her publications include chapters on Giorgio Agamben's concept of the state of exception in *Children of Men*, the role of MTV and the music video during the 1980s satanic panic, and the intertwining of cannibalism and Mexican urban identity in *Somos lo que hay*. She is currently working on a book project on feminism, popular culture and the final girl.

www.ingramcontent.com/pod-product-compliance
Lightning Source LLC
Chambersburg PA
CBHW070830300426
44111CB00014B/2514